access to history

The Early Tudors: Henry VII to Mary I 1485–1558

ROGER TURVEY

SECOND EDITION

HODDER
EDUCATION
AN HACHETTE UK COMPANY

The Publishers would like to thank Robin Bunce, Nicholas Fellows, David Ferriby and Sarah Ward for their contribution to the Study Guide.

The Publishers would like to thank the following for permission to reproduce copyright material:

Photo credits: p8 Apic/Getty Images; **p30** TopFoto; **p62** National Portrait Gallery, London; **p66** World History Archive/ TopFoto; **p74** TopFoto; **p90** Wellcome Library, London, Copyrighted work available under Creative Commons Attribution only licence CC BY 4.0 http://creativecommons.org/licenses/by/4.0/(detail of Cromwell); **p91** World History Archive/ TopFoto; **p96** http://commons.wikimedia.org/wiki/File:Thomas-Cranmer.jpg?uselang=en-gb; **p97** Titlepage, The Seventh Book, from 'Acts and Monuments' by John Foxe, ninth edition, pub. 1684 (litho), English School, (17th century)/ Private Collection/The Stapleton Collection/Bridgeman Images; **p112** Portrait of Sir Thomas More (1478–1535) (oil on panel), Holbein the Younger, Hans (1497/8–1543) (after)/National Portrait Gallery, London, UK/Bridgeman Images; **p113** Wellcome Library, London, Copyrighted work available under Creative Commons Attribution only licence CC BY 4.0 http://creativecommons.org/licenses/by/4.0/(detail of More); **p131** King Edward VI (1537–53) and the Pope, c.1570 (oil on panel), English School, (16th century)/National Portrait Gallery, London, UK/Bridgeman Images; **p164** Portrait of Mary I or Mary Tudor (1516–58), daughter of Henry VIII, at the Age of 28, 1544 (panel), Master John (fl.1544)/National Portrait Gallery, London, UK/Bridgeman Images; **p172** Wellcome Library, London, Copyrighted work available under Creative Commons Attribution only licence CC BY 4.0 http://creativecommons.org/licenses/by/4.0/(detail of Gardiner).

Acknowledgements: are listed on page 204.

Every effort has been made to trace all copyright holders, but if any have been inadvertently overlooked the Publishers will be pleased to make the necessary arrangements at the first opportunity.

Although every effort has been made to ensure that website addresses are correct at time of going to press, Hodder Education cannot be held responsible for the content of any website mentioned in this book. It is sometimes possible to find a relocated web page by typing in the address of the home page for a website in the URL window of your browser.

Hachette UK's policy is to use papers that are natural, renewable and recyclable products and made from wood grown in sustainable forests. The logging and manufacturing processes are expected to conform to the environmental regulations of the country of origin.

Orders: please contact Bookpoint Ltd, 130 Milton Park, Abingdon, Oxon OX14 4SB. Telephone: +44 (0)1235 827720. Fax: +44 (0)1235 400454. Lines are open 9.00a.m.–5.00p.m., Monday to Saturday, with a 24-hour message answering service. Visit our website at www.hoddereducation.co.uk

© Roger Turvey
Second edition © Roger Turvey 2015

First published in 2008 by
Hodder Education
An Hachette UK Company
Carmelite House, 50 Victoria Embankment
London EC4Y 0DZ

This second edition published 2015

Impression number   10 9 8 7 6 5 4 3 2
Year   2019 2018 2017 2016 2015

Cover photo: Henry VIII (1491–1547), c.1600 (panel), English School, (17th century)/Private Collection/ Photo © Philip Mould Ltd, London/Bridgeman Images
Produced, illustrated and typeset in Palatino LT Std by Gray Publishing, Tunbridge Wells
Printed and bound by CPI Group (UK) Ltd, Croydon CR0 4YY

A catalogue record for this title is available from the British Library

ISBN 978 1471838859

Contents

Dedication

Keith Randell (1943–2002)

The *Access to History* series was conceived and developed by Keith, who created a series to 'cater for students as they are, not as we might wish them to be'. He leaves a living legacy of a series that for over 20 years has provided a trusted, stimulating and well-loved accompaniment to post-16 study. Our aim with these new editions is to continue to offer students the best possible support for their studies.

CHAPTER 1

Henry VII: establishing the dynasty 1485–1503

A nation's government, security and well-being depend on the character and strength of its ruler. This was particularly true during the Middle Ages when kings had the power to pass laws, raise revenue and make war. The nature, powers and limits of medieval and early modern monarchy have long fascinated historians. Richard III's illegal seizure of the throne encouraged claimants like Henry Tudor to challenge him for the crown. Following Henry's victory at the Battle of Bosworth he sought to establish and consolidate his dynasty. These issues are examined through the following four themes:

★ Introduction: the nature, powers and limits of monarchy

★ Claim, aim and character of the new king

★ Securing the throne: pretenders, protests and threats

★ Crown and nobility

Key dates

1485		Henry crowned as King Henry VII	1489		Rebellion in Yorkshire
1486		Marriage of Henry and Elizabeth of York. Birth of a son and heir, Arthur	1495		Council Learned in the Law established
1487		First law passed against illegal retaining	1497		Rebellion in Cornwall
	June	Battle of Stoke	1499		Warbeck and the Earl of Warwick executed
1489		Thomas Howard, Earl of Surrey, released from prison	1502		Death of Prince Arthur
			1503		Death of Queen Elizabeth

1 Introduction: the nature, power and limits of monarchy

▶ *How powerful were Tudor monarchs? What areas have been identified by historians as being worthy of debate?*

During the last century or two, three strands of enquiry from the years 1485–1558 have been identified as being worthy of historical debate. The first strand concerns the 'restoration of the monarchy', the second 'the reformation in religion' and the third 'the revolution in government'.

- The first strand has two features: establishing a new royal dynasty and restoring the power and authority of the Crown. The key debate here revolves around the question of whether the advent of the Tudors led to the establishment of a 'New Monarchy'.
- The second strand has three features: a discussion of the role of the monarchy and its government in carrying through religious change; an explanation on how the relationship between Church and State altered; and an assessment of how the State and people were affected by the political and religious developments of the period.
- The third strand has two features. First, a long-running debate on the personality and character of the monarch, including a consideration of the part he or she played in the politics and government of their time; and secondly, an assessment of the significance of the monarchy, and its chief ministers, in the long-term political development of the country which may, for the sake of convenience, be described as England.

The key themes that run through these strands concern the personality, power and influence of the monarch. Thus, to appreciate fully the way in which religion and government changed in this period, it is important to gain an understanding of the nature of and the authority wielded by the monarchy. Equally important is an understanding of how personal, political, diplomatic, religious and financial factors affected both the growth and the practical limits of royal power in late fifteenth- and early sixteenth-century England.

🔑 **KEY TERM**

Dei gratia By the will of God.

The powerful element in Tudor monarchy

English monarchs claimed to rule ***dei gratia***. This belief in divine right, that, as a person apart, the monarch was regarded as God's instrument on earth, was supported by the Church. Parish priests would regularly remind their parishioners of the terrible torments of hell that awaited those who dared rebel against the Crown. In practical terms this meant that any rebellion against the monarch was regarded as being the same as a rebellion against God.

This is why the charge of treason, to betray one's king (or queen) and country, was regarded as a serious crime. It can be argued that the only armed rebellion to succeed in the sixteenth century was that involving Mary Tudor, who claimed that her rightful place as monarch in legitimate succession to her brother, Edward VI, had been usurped by traitors. Her success in seizing the throne in 1553 was due not only to the legality of her position, as she was the legal heir to the throne according to the Act of Succession of 1544, but also to her actions being represented as a triumph of the divine will.

This belief in the divine will was a powerful element in the faith systems of the period. It served as the basis for legitimising Henry VII's seizure of the throne in 1485 and underlined the power of God's will in delivering victory in battle at Bosworth. Henry was no traitor and he had committed no treason because he had removed a usurper. Nevertheless, Henry was well aware that his position as monarch needed to be rooted in law to strengthen and consolidate his authority as king.

Rex est Lex and *Lex est Rex*

For a monarch like Mary who had once been declared illegitimate, in 1533 (she was later legitimised in 1537), her succession was a triumph. This shows the importance of the law and the legal structure that had evolved in tandem with the development of the monarchy. The monarch was expected to act as the protector and enforcer of the laws of the kingdom. The old Latin maxim *Rex est Lex* and *Lex est Rex* ('the king is the law' and 'the law is the king') demonstrates the extent to which English monarchs had come to identify with the processes of law making. Although they came to hold a highly privileged position within the legal structure of the kingdom, they could not ignore or break the law but were expected to set a good example by acting within the accepted structure. Thus, no monarch could afford to behave as if he or she was above the law and nor could they make the mistake of emphasising too strongly the power of the divine will over the rule of law.

The powers of monarchy

This does not mean that English monarchs were weak or had little power; on the contrary, their powers were extensive. For example, the monarch alone could raise troops, wage war and conclude peace, conduct foreign affairs, summon and dissolve Parliament, pardon offenders, manage the coinage and arrange the marriages of members of the royal family. These political, military and economic powers constituted what became known as the **royal prerogative**.

The limits of monarchy

On the other hand, there were limits to their authority. For example, the monarch could not levy taxes, or make laws at will, set aside the rights of the subject or behave as a tyrant, especially as the Church had long taught that it was lawful to kill a tyrant. However, it should be noted that this issue was disputed. In short, the monarch had a duty to respect the notion that all who lived within the kingdom, from the lowliest peasant to the mightiest king, were bound by the common 'weal' or good.

Even a king as powerful as Henry VIII recognised the need to give legal basis to his break from Rome by seeking the support of his people, via Parliament, and by framing the **schism** in English statute law. The fact that he may have bullied and harried his subjects into consenting to the break with Rome does not alter the fact that he had to be seen to be seeking their backing. This balance of rights and duties between monarch and subject allowed for co-operation, compromise and even partnership.

KEY TERMS

Royal prerogative Certain rights and privileges enjoyed by the monarch such as making war, negotiating peace treaties, and calling and closing Parliament.

Schism Literally meaning 'break', but used by historians to describe England's break with the Pope in Rome.

The personal element in Tudor monarchy

The Tudor monarchy was one in which the ruler was directly responsible for policy and closely involved in the business of government. An agenda for the monarch's attention, drawn up by his chancellor or senior royal councillor, might be such as to require his or her signature on state papers several times a day. Because monarchy was personal, everything depended on the monarch's willingness to devote himself or herself to business.

Henry VII had been a model in this respect. Henry VIII, however, frequently behaved as though he wanted government to take care of itself. Henry did almost all his work by word of mouth so that state papers had to be either read to him or summarised for him. Nor was Henry willing to delegate his authority on a consistent basis. He always reserved for himself the freedom to intervene as and when he wanted.

In contrast, his daughter Mary found the business of government a burden she had not desired and a task for which she had had little training or preparation. Nevertheless, from the beginning of her reign she indicated she would take an active part in governance. This she did throughout her short reign, working long hours in trying to solve problems that would have tested the limits of her father's abilities. Since Mary was the first woman to rule England in her own right, issues of gender complicated the early days of her reign (see Chapter 6).

Henry VIII's and Mary's particular brands of personal monarchy explain why the dispute over their respective personalities has been running since the early seventeenth century and why it shows no sign of ending. For most of this time writers have tended to take up extreme positions.

Henry VII

Henry has been overshadowed somewhat by the more colourful personalities of his son and granddaughter Elizabeth, which, perhaps, is why he is less well known than any of his Tudor descendants. Historians have been more concerned with Henry's aims and achievements than his character but this, too, has attracted notice. Polydore Vergil, one of the first writers to pass judgement on the king (in 1513), was impressed by the 'slender, but well built' Henry whom he described as 'brave and resolute', 'shrewd and prudent' but also 'gracious and kind'. The historian John Guy (writing in 1988) offered a more balanced verdict: 'he could be ruthless and severe, but was neither bloodthirsty nor egotistical'. Some historians consider Henry to be the most able and, arguably, the most successful of all the Tudors.

Henry VIII

Henry has been regarded either as a wicked tyrant or as an able and charming renaissance prince. Sir Walter Raleigh, one of the earliest authors (writing in 1614) to pass general comment in print, was in no doubt where he stood: 'Now for King Henry the eight: if all the pictures and patterns of a merciless prince were lost in the world, they might be again painted to the life out of the story of this king.'

On the other hand, one of Henry's modern biographers, J.J. Scarisbrick (writing in 1968), is perhaps more objective: 'He was a formidable, captivating man who wore regality with splendid conviction. But easily and predictably his great charm could turn into anger and shouting.'

That Henry has the power to divide opinion is evidenced by the assessment of another modern historian, John Guy, who stated that: 'Henry's character was fascinating, threatening, and sometimes morbid. His egoism, self-righteousness, and capacity to brood sprang from the fusion of an able but second-rate mind with what looks suspiciously like an inferiority complex.'

Edward VI

Edward VI alone has escaped the kind of critical analysis reserved for his predecessors, mainly on account of his youth and lack of involvement in policy making. Consequently, it is not Edward who concerns historians so much as the men who governed in his stead, namely, Edward Seymour, the Duke of Somerset, and John Dudley, the Duke of Northumberland. Traditionally, Somerset has been viewed as the 'good Duke', an idealist, friend of the common man and an opponent of religious persecution. However, this opinion of Somerset has been challenged by revisionist historians who see him as arrogant, self-seeking and prone to making mistakes when pressured. Similarly, Northumberland's image has been transformed from that of a cynical schemer devoid of principle to that of a talented minister who led, in Geoffrey Elton's opinion (writing in 1988), 'a genuine reform administration'.

Mary

'Bloody' Mary too has suffered criticism. John Strype in the seventeenth century and James Froude in the nineteenth perpetuated the 'black legend' of persecution, corruption, mismanagement and national betrayal ascribed to Mary by propagandists writing during the reign of Elizabeth. Source A is one such example.

SOURCE A

John Foxe, one of the earliest writers to criticise Mary in print in his *Book of Martyrs*, 1563.

We shall never find in any reign of any Prince in this land or any other, which did ever show in it so many great arguments of God's wrath and displeasure as were to be seen in this reign of this queen Mary … whether we behold the shortness of her time, or the unfortunate event of all her purposes. From the first beginning of queen Mary's reign, wherein so many men, women, and children were burnt, many imprisoned, and in prison starved, many exiled, some despoiled of goods and possessions, a great number driven from house and home, so many weeping eyes, so many sobbing hearts, … and in conclusion never a good man in all the realm but suffered something during all the time of this bloody persecution.

Study Source A. What does the title of Foxe's book reveal about his religious beliefs and why might it explain why he was critical of Mary?

Mary has also divided modern opinion, for whereas Elton regarded her life as being 'one of almost unrelieved tragedy' for which she deserves no pity on account of the 'obstinate wrong-headedness of her rule', fellow historian C. Erickson (writing in 1998) believed she had ruled England 'capably and with courage'.

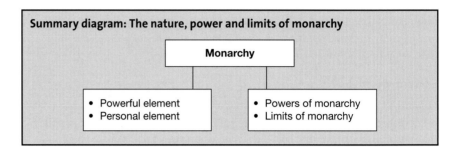

Summary diagram: The nature, power and limits of monarchy

Monarchy

- Powerful element
- Personal element

- Powers of monarchy
- Limits of monarchy

② Claim, aim and character of the new king

▶ *What was the basis of Henry VII's claim to the throne?*

Henry VII's claim to the throne

'Henry VII was by right and just title of inheritance, and by divine providence, crowned and proclaimed king.' Writing in 1542 in his chronicle, *The Union of the Two Noble and Illustre Families of Lancastre and Yorke*, Edward Hall was convinced that there was no problem with Henry's claim to the throne. However, the legitimacy of Henry's right to the kingship of England was not always so clear or so certain. To the majority of Henry's contemporaries the Battle of Bosworth on 22 August 1485 was just one more battle in the long dynastic struggle for the Crown that dominated the second half of the fifteenth century. On this occasion the victor happened to be the obscure Lancastrian claimant, the 28-year-old Henry, Earl of Richmond. It was only victory in battle that had brought Henry to power, as his claim to the throne by inheritance was rather weak.

Maternal claim to the throne

Henry's claim came through his mother, Margaret Beaufort, who was a direct descendant of Edward III by the marriage of his third son, John of Gaunt, Duke of Lancaster, to Katherine Swynford (see family tree on page 7). Their children had been born prior to the marriage, when Katherine was Gaunt's mistress, so that there was some uncertainty about their legal standing. For example, although an Act of Parliament in Richard II's reign had legitimised them, a further Act in Henry IV's reign had excluded them from the line of succession.

Lancastrians, Yorkists and Tudors

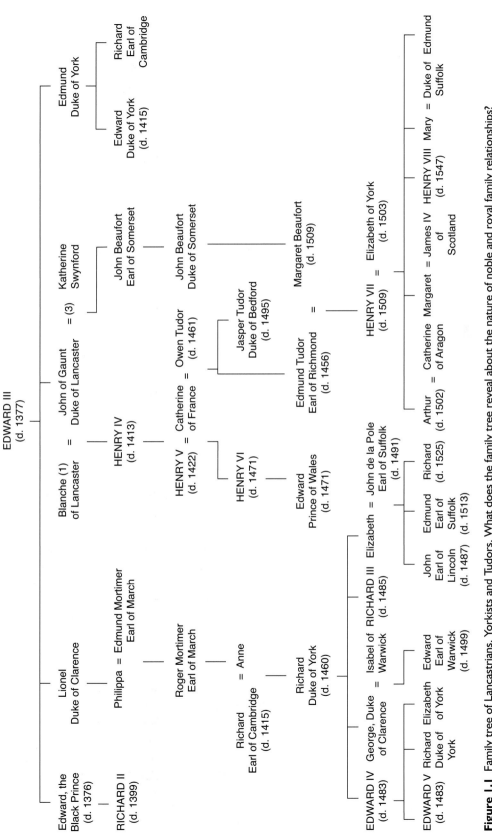

Figure 1.1 Family tree of Lancastrians, Yorkists and Tudors. What does the family tree reveal about the nature of noble and royal family relationships?

Paternal claim to the throne

Henry VII also inherited royal blood, although not a claim to the throne, from his father Edmund Tudor. This was because Edmund's mother, Catherine, was a French princess who had been married to Henry V of England before she became the wife of Edmund's Welsh father, Owen Tudor. After the death of her husband, Henry V, Queen Catherine had no claim to the throne. By virtue of this marriage, Edmund and his brother Jasper were the half-brothers of the king, Henry VI. In 1452 Henry VI raised his half-brothers to the peerage by creating Edmund Earl of Richmond and Jasper Earl of Pembroke. Therefore, Henry VII was the half-nephew of the king of England and a member of the extended royal family.

Acutely aware of the weakness of his claim to the throne, Henry determined to enhance and magnify his royal credentials by pursuing a ruthless policy of propaganda. By combining the red rose of Lancaster and the white rose of York, Henry was symbolically uniting the two noble houses. In addition, he traded on his Beaufort descent and familial link to Edward III. At the same time, Henry portrayed Richard III as an illegitimate usurper. The policy was so thorough and successful that by the time Hall wrote his chronicle few would have questioned (or dared to question) the legitimacy of the Tudors. Hall was one in a long line of writers and chroniclers who embraced, and willingly spread, Tudor propaganda.

SOURCE B

? Why might Henry VII have approved of the painting in Source B?

Portrait of Henry VII painted in 1505 by an unknown artist.

Henry VII's aims

Henry VII had one essential aim: to remain king and establish his dynasty by handing on an unchallenged succession to his descendants. His policies at home and abroad were shaped and dictated by this aim. He knew that if he were to prove himself a strong king and retain full control of his realm he would have to establish effective government, maintain law and order, control the nobility and secure the Crown's finances. He would also need good advice, friends abroad and a considerable amount of luck.

Character and personality of the new king

The character and personality of Henry VII remain shadowy and elusive today, just as they did to his own subjects in 1485. There is less evidence about him than about any other of the Tudors. This uncertainty about the personality of the first Tudor monarch is a good example of how limited evidence can lead to widely differing opinions. Historians tend to disagree about Henry's character, mainly because kings rarely recorded their own thoughts, with the result that historians have had to draw their own conclusions from his actions and policies.

Some of the views of his contemporaries, however, have survived. Among the more interesting, if not necessarily the most useful, is the portrait of Henry VII attributed to Michael Sittow, a talented artist of the northern Renaissance in Flanders. It is thought to have been painted from life in 1505. The following description is by Polydore Vergil, a brilliant Italian scholar who arrived at the English court in 1501. Henry was so impressed by his understanding of history that he urged him to write a history of England.

SOURCE C

Henry VII is described by Polydore Vergil in his book *Anglica Historia*, published in 1513.

His appearance was remarkably attractive and his face was cheerful, especially when speaking; his eyes were small and blue, his teeth few, poor and blackish; his hair was thin and white; his complexion sallow.

In government he was shrewd and prudent so that no-one dared get the better of him through deceit and guile … He well knew how to maintain his royal majesty …

> Study Source C. Why might Vergil's description and opinion of the king be a truthful reflection of what Henry VII was really like?

Bacon's *History of the Reign of King Henry the Seventh*

Francis Bacon's *History of the Reign of King Henry the Seventh*, published in 1622, remained the major work on the reign until the twentieth century. He described Henry as 'one of the best sort of wonders: a wonder for wise men', but 'for his pleasures, there is no news of them'. This implies that Henry was admired for his intellectual ability but that his lifestyle was rather colourless. Bacon wanted his contemporaries and future generations to learn from his *History*, which is why he was prepared to pass judgement on those who came under his scrutiny.

Henry VII devoted so much of his time to replenishing the Crown's empty coffers that historians have accused him of being a miser. In fact, Henry's account books make fascinating reading, for we catch a glimpse of Henry the man, as well as Henry the king. From them we discover his weakness for dicing and playing cards, and the way he indulged his own and his younger daughter's love of music. This 'miserly' king was rash enough on occasions to pay £30 'for a little maiden that danceth' and around £13 on a leopard for the Tower menagerie!

A European visitor commented on Henry's sumptuous table for 600 guests. The king was a keen sportsman, playing tennis and chess regularly, but his great passion was the hunt and he kept an impressive stable of horses. Henry is portrayed as rather a cold man but his warmer, more human side was revealed on the death of his eldest son, Prince Arthur, when he rushed to comfort his wife. When Elizabeth herself died, Bacon explains that 'he privily departed to a solitary place and would no man should resort unto him'.

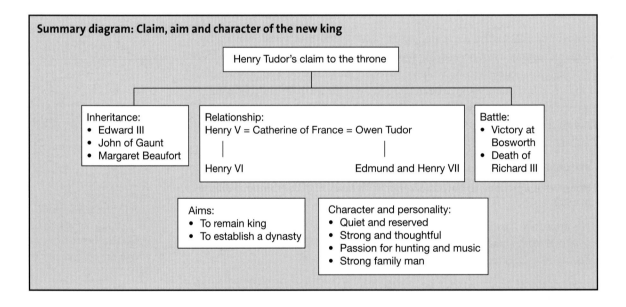

Summary diagram: Claim, aim and character of the new king

Henry Tudor's claim to the throne

Inheritance:
- Edward III
- John of Gaunt
- Margaret Beaufort

Relationship:
Henry V = Catherine of France = Owen Tudor

Henry VI   Edmund and Henry VII

Battle:
- Victory at Bosworth
- Death of Richard III

Aims:
- To remain king
- To establish a dynasty

Character and personality:
- Quiet and reserved
- Strong and thoughtful
- Passion for hunting and music
- Strong family man

3 Securing the throne: pretenders, protests and threats

▶ *How was Henry able to secure the throne in the face of serious threats and opposition?*

First steps to securing the throne

Henry's first actions revealed his concern about the succession and his desire to stress the legitimacy of his position, regardless of defeating Richard or his marriage to Elizabeth of York. For example:

- He dated the official beginning of his reign from the day before Bosworth. Therefore, Richard and his supporters could be declared traitors. This was doubly shrewd because it meant that their estates became the property of the Crown by act of attainder.
- He deliberately arranged his coronation for 30 October, before the first meeting of Parliament on 7 November. Thus, it could never be said that Parliament made Henry VII king.
- He applied for a **papal dispensation** to marry Elizabeth of York. This was necessary because they were distant cousins. Henry and Elizabeth were married on 18 January 1486, finally uniting the Houses of Lancaster and York.

After Bosworth, Henry's most immediate and perhaps greatest problem was ensuring that he kept the crown. Although many potential candidates had been eliminated from the succession during the Wars of the Roses and their aftermath, it was not until 1506 that Henry could feel really secure on his throne. By that time, the most dangerous claimants to the crown were either dead or safely locked away.

> **KEY TERM**
>
> **Papal dispensation** When the Pope exempted a person from a certain punitive clause in law.

Rival claims to the throne

In 1485 there were still a number of important Yorkists alive (see Figure 1.1 on page 7) with a strong claim to the throne. The most direct male representative of the family was Richard III's ten-year-old nephew, Edward, Earl of Warwick (son of his brother Clarence). Henry successfully disposed of him, at least temporarily, by sending him to the Tower. Although it was a royal stronghold, the Tower was also a royal residence, so Warwick lived in relative comfort, although without the freedom to come and go as he pleased. Richard had named another nephew, John de la Pole, the Earl of Lincoln, as his heir. However, both he and his father, the Duke of Suffolk, professed their loyalty to Henry and the king accepted this. Lincoln was invited to join the government and became a member of the King's Council.

The surviving Yorkist nobility

Although Richard's supporters at Bosworth were naturally treated with suspicion, Henry was prepared to give them a second chance as long as he could be persuaded of their loyalty to him. The Earl of Surrey had fought on the Yorkist side with his father, the Duke of Norfolk, who died at Bosworth, and Henry kept him in prison until 1489, by which time he was convinced of his good intentions. However, another of Richard's allies, the Earl of Northumberland, was released even sooner, at the end of 1485, and was given the opportunity to prove his loyalty by resuming his old position in control of the north of England. Ex-Yorkists were therefore not automatically excluded from the Tudor court: loyalty was the new king's only requirement for them to regain royal favour.

Minor risings and protests 1485–6

When Henry came to power he was a largely unknown and untried nobleman with royal credentials. Few of his subjects believed that the civil wars were over or that he would remain king for long. The uncertainty of his rule, the continuing political instability and the economic dislocation caused by war affected nobleman and commoner alike. Therefore, Henry had to deal with the disgruntled – protestors against such things as high taxes – alongside the dangerous – pretenders or rival claimants to the throne. Henry could not afford to ignore or treat lightly any protest or rebellion but it was clear that the main threat to his position came from the pretenders Lambert Simnel and Perkin Warbeck.

In spite of his precautions, Henry faced minor risings before the first anniversary of his accession. Although, with hindsight, they appear rather insignificant, they still proved alarming for Henry.

Lovel and Stafford rising

Trouble broke out while the king was on royal progress to his northern capital of York. This was a public relations exercise in an unruly area, whereby the king showed himself to his people in an attempt to secure their support. Since Bosworth, Francis, Lord Lovel and the Stafford brothers, Thomas and Humphrey, faithful adherents of Richard, had been in **sanctuary** at Colchester. The Church offered protection from the law for up to 40 days but, by the fifteenth century, sanctuaries were becoming a source of dispute with the Crown.

As Henry travelled north in April 1486, the three lords broke sanctuary. Lovel headed north and planned to ambush the king, while the Staffords travelled to Worcester to stir up rebellion in the west. Henry heard of this while he was at Lincoln. Nevertheless, he continued with his progress, but sent an armed force to offer the rebels the choice of pardon and reconciliation or, if they fought and lost, excommunication and death. The rebels dispersed, but Lovel evaded capture and fled to Flanders. The Staffords sought sanctuary once again and

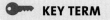

KEY TERM

Sanctuary A place of safety within a church or monastery guaranteed by the authority of the Church.

were granted it by the Church. However, Henry felt that it was unreasonable for declared traitors to be allowed sanctuary a second time, so the Staffords were forcibly removed, arrested and sent to the Tower. Humphrey was executed but Thomas was pardoned and remained loyal thereafter.

Henry's policy of 'calculated mercy' – severity towards the major ringleaders and clemency to the rank and file – proved successful. The royal progress to the disaffected areas produced the required reaction of loyalty and obedience, and Henry was seen as the upholder of justice and order. As if to put the seal on this success, the queen gave birth to a healthy son at Winchester, England's ancient capital. Evoking memories of the country's great past, the baby was christened Arthur. These events helped towards securing the dynasty by giving it an air of permanence.

Rebellions in Yorkshire (1489) and Cornwall (1497)

These rebellions stemmed not from dynastic causes but from the king's demands for money. However, they did influence the way in which Henry responded to dynastic challenges and showed how delicate the balance was between public order and lawlessness.

Yorkshire

Henry planned to go to the aid of Brittany and the Parliament of 1489 granted him a **subsidy** of £100,000 to pay for it. The tax caused widespread resentment because it was raised in a new way, as a sort of income tax. The king appears to have received only £27,000 of the total granted. The demand was particularly badly received in Yorkshire, which was suffering the after-effects of a bad harvest the previous summer. The people also resented the fact that the counties to the north of them were exempted from the tax because they were expected to defend the country from the Scots. Henry Percy, Earl of Northumberland, put their case to the king, but Henry refused to negotiate. When the Earl returned north with the news he was murdered by the rebels.

The Earl of Surrey defeated the rebels outside York. The king travelled north to issue a pardon to most of the prisoners as a gesture of conciliation, but he failed to collect any more of this tax. Henry appointed the Earl of Surrey as his Lieutenant in this area. Surrey had no vested interest in the north and his loyalty was guaranteed because the restoration of his own estates in East Anglia rested on his success here.

Cornwall

It was another request for money that ignited a rebellion in Cornwall. In January 1497 Parliament voted for a heavy tax to finance an expedition north to resist the expected invasion by the Scottish king, James IV, and the pretender Perkin Warbeck. The Cornish, who were traditionally independently minded, refused to contribute to the defence of the northern part of the kingdom. In May the rebels set out from Bodmin and marched through the western counties,

---

🔑 **KEY TERM**

Subsidy A grant of money made by Parliament to the king, usually for a specific purpose.

acquiring their only leader of any significance, the impoverished Lord Audley, at Wells. On 16 June, about 15,000 strong, they reached the outskirts of London and encamped on Blackheath. The Cornishmen were confronted by a royal army under the command of Lord Daubeney and Sir Rhys ap Thomas.

Historians estimate that about 1000 rebels were killed in the battle and that the rest swiftly fled. Only Audley and the two original local leaders were subsequently executed. Despite the fact that the rising had been defeated, it was worrying that the rebels had been able to march as far as London before facing any opposition. Henry had been directing his attention towards Scotland and Warbeck and, as the Cornish rising was an independent rebellion, unconnected with any Yorkist conspiracy, he had not responded to it early on. The rebellion hardly endangered his throne, but it had shown that he could not afford a serious campaign against Scotland. Henry now attempted to come to terms with James.

The pretenders: Lambert Simnel and Perkin Warbeck

Henry was king because he had defeated Richard III in battle. The nature of the usurpation meant that a rising from Richard's Yorkist followers was almost inevitable. The careers of the two pretenders, Lambert Simnel and Perkin Warbeck, were of great significance to Henry VII. They presented such a dangerous challenge to his hold on the Crown both because of their entanglement with other European states, particularly Burgundy, and because they continued for such a long time.

Lambert Simnel's conspiracy and rebellion 1486–7

Trouble began in the winter of 1486 when conflicting rumours circulated about the fate of the Earl of Warwick. Many concluded that he must be dead, as he had not been seen for some time. In this unsettled climate, a priest from Oxford, Richard Symonds, seized his opportunity. Symonds passed Simnel off as the younger boy, Richard of York. However, in the light of fresh rumours about the Earl of Warwick, he seems to have changed his mind and to have decided that Simnel, the ten-year-old the son of an organ maker, would now impersonate Warwick.

Symonds took Simnel to Ireland, a centre of Yorkist support, where the Lord Lieutenant, the Earl of Kildare, and other Irish leaders, readily proclaimed Simnel king in Dublin. The pretender was also supported by Edward IV's sister, Margaret, Dowager Duchess of Burgundy, who was always ready to seize any opportunity to strike at Henry. She sent money and a force of 2000 German mercenaries to Ireland, commanded by the capable mercenary captain Martin Schwartz. This formidable support led the Irish to go as far as to crown Simnel as King Edward VI in Dublin in May 1487.

Although the conspiracy had begun in the autumn of 1486, Henry himself does not appear to have been aware of it until New Year 1487. The real Earl of Warwick was exhibited in London to expose the imposter. However, the sudden flight of the Earl of Lincoln to join Lord Lovel in Flanders at the court of his aunt, Margaret of Burgundy, made clear the gravity of the situation. Lincoln then accompanied Lovel and Schwartz to Ireland in May 1487. It is probable that the earl had been involved from an early stage. Lincoln knew that Simnel was an imposter, but possibly planned to put forward his own claim to the throne when he judged the time to be right.

The Battle of Stoke 1487

On 4 June 1487 Lincoln and his army landed in Lancashire, marched across the Pennines and then turned south. He received less support than he expected because people were weary of civil strife. The king was prepared and the two armies met just outside Newark, at East Stoke, on 16 June 1487. Lincoln's 8000 men faced a royal army of some 12,000 strong.

The Yorkist forces were decisively defeated. Lincoln, Schwartz and Kildare's younger brother, Thomas, all perished, along with nearly half their army. It is likely that Lovel, too, was killed. Lambert Simnel and Richard Symonds were both captured. Symonds was sentenced to life imprisonment in a bishop's prison. Recognising that Simnel had been merely a pawn in the hands of ambitious men, Henry made him a turnspit in the royal kitchen. He was later promoted to be the king's falconer as a reward for his good service.

Henry's calculated mercy was apparent yet again. He could afford to be generous to Simnel because Symonds was now in prison and the real ringleaders were dead. As a deterrent to others in the future, those nobles who had fought at Stoke were dealt with swiftly in Henry's second Parliament, which met from November to December 1487. Twenty-eight of them were **attainted** and their lands were confiscated.

> **KEY TERM**
>
> **Attainted** Accused and declared guilty of treason by a vote in Parliament.

Some historians view Stoke as the final battle of the Wars of the Roses. Certainly, Henry never again faced an army composed of his own subjects on English soil, although further rebellions did follow. Indeed, Stoke could have been a second Bosworth, with Henry this time in the role of Richard III. What was most important was that Henry was victorious. However, the fact that such a ridiculous scheme almost succeeded indicates that the country was still unsettled and shows how fragile Henry's grasp was on the Crown. It was no coincidence that on 25 November his wife, Elizabeth, and mother of his heir, was finally crowned queen. This was designed to do the following:

- unite the nation
- secure the goodwill of the people
- satisfy disaffected Yorkists.

Perkin Warbeck 1491–9

Further troubles arose for Henry in the autumn of 1491 when Perkin Warbeck, a seventeen-year-old from Tournai in France, arrived in Cork, Ireland, on the ship of his master, a Breton merchant. He seems to have deeply impressed the townsfolk, who assumed that he might be the Earl of Warwick. Warbeck denied this, claiming instead to be Richard, Duke of York, whose murder in the Tower was assumed but had never been proved. The known figures behind Warbeck were men of humble origin. However, S.B. Chrimes (writing in 1972) believes that Warbeck's appearance in Ireland was 'no accident but was the first overt action in the unfolding of a definite plan'. He thinks that Charles VIII of France, and probably Margaret of Burgundy, wanted to use Warbeck to put pressure on Henry.

Warbeck and France

The conspiracy achieved international recognition from the predictable trouble spots of Ireland, Scotland and France. Charles VIII welcomed Warbeck at the French court and by the summer of 1492 approximately 100 English Yorkists had joined him in Paris. However, the Treaty of Etaples, which Henry VII had negotiated with the French, meant that he had to find a new refuge, so he fled to Flanders where he was accepted by Margaret of Burgundy as her nephew.

Warbeck and Burgundy

It is unlikely that Margaret believed Warbeck's claim of identity but, in the absence of any genuine Yorkist claimant at liberty, supporting him would have been her best opportunity to dislodge Henry. Margaret calculated that faithful Yorkists would be prepared to back anyone in order to gain their revenge on Henry VII. Margaret's support of Warbeck worried Henry to the extent that in 1493 he temporarily broke off all trade with Flanders even though this jeopardised the cloth trade that was so important to the English economy.

Warbeck and the Holy Roman Empire

Not content with Margaret's support alone, Warbeck found an even more influential patron when Maximilian, the newly elected Holy Roman Emperor, recognised him as Richard IV in 1494. However, Maximilian did not have the resources available to finance an invasion of England.

The conspiracy and executions of Stanley and Lord Fitzwalter

In the meantime, Henry's intelligence network had informed him who was implicated in plotting treason, both at home and abroad, and in the Parliament of 1495 a number of acts of attainder were passed. The most important victim was Sir William Stanley, Henry's step-uncle and the man who had changed the course of the Battle of Bosworth. As chamberlain of the king's household, he was one of Henry's most trusted officials. Henry must have been disappointed and frightened by his betrayal. His execution showed that Henry would spare no one, no matter how eminent. Lord Fitzwalter, his steward, was also executed. It appears that a supposed conspirator, Sir Robert Clifford, revealed vital names to the king. It is probable that Clifford was in Henry's service from the beginning, for he received a pardon and rewards for breaking the conspiracy.

Warbeck and Scotland

The efficient work of Henry's agents and the king's swift reaction meant that Warbeck's attempted landing at Deal in Kent in July 1495 was a fiasco. He failed to gather sufficient local support and he set sail for Ireland, ruthlessly abandoning those of his men who had already gone ashore. He laid siege to the town of Waterford for eleven days without success. Warbeck then departed for Scotland, where he met with more encouragement when James IV gave him refuge and support. It is difficult to be certain how far James was convinced by Warbeck, if at all, but he did go so far as to give him his cousin in marriage together with an annual pension of £1200.

These actions were enough to challenge Henry's government and to threaten the marriage alliance with Spain, between Catherine of Aragon and Arthur, Prince of Wales. King Ferdinand and Queen Isabella would not contemplate sending their daughter to marry the heir to a contested crown. Fortunately for Henry, the Scottish invasion of England was a disaster. Warbeck received no support south of the border and retreated, horrified at the manner in which the Scots raided and pillaged the countryside. James did not take advantage of the rebellion in Cornwall to attack again. Disillusioned with Warbeck, he thought that Henry's conciliatory offer of his eldest daughter, Margaret, in marriage was more to Scotland's long-term advantage. In September 1497 a seven-year truce was agreed at Ayton which was formalised in 1502: the first full peace treaty with Scotland since 1328.

Warbeck's failure

Warbeck himself eased the situation by returning to Ireland in July 1497, hoping for more success there. However, he found that even Kildare was temporarily loyal to Henry, so he set sail for the south-west of England hoping, as a last resort, to find support from this traditionally rebellious area. Again he was to be bitterly disappointed; having landed in Devon, he was driven out of Exeter and Taunton by local militia and only a few thousand people joined him. Within a fortnight it was all over, and Warbeck once again abandoned his followers. This time he fled to the sanctuary of Beaulieu Abbey in Hampshire. In August 1497 he was persuaded to give himself up and to make a full confession.

As a foreigner it would have been difficult at this stage to accuse him of treason under English law. Henry allowed him to remain at court with his young Scottish bride, but Warbeck was not content with this and foolishly escaped in 1498. He was recaptured, publicly humiliated by being forced to sit in the stocks twice, and was then imprisoned in the Tower. As for his wife, she remained at court and became a lady-in-waiting to the queen.

The plot and execution of Warbeck and Warwick

Historians have long argued over the truth of whether Warbeck and Warwick entered into a plot to escape the Tower and murder the king. Some suggest that the prisoners were the victims of a cynical attempt by the king's agents to manipulate them into conceiving a plot. Others believe that Warwick, weary of imprisonment, was persuaded by Warbeck to enter into a conspiracy. All that can be said with certainty is that Henry's patience with Warbeck had been exhausted. The pretender, and his powerful foreign backers, had succeeded in causing Henry eight years of considerable anxiety and expense that the king could well have done without. Consequently, in 1499, Warbeck was charged with trying to escape yet again and this time he was hanged.

The Earl of Warwick was found guilty of treason and was executed a week later. Although Warwick himself might not have been dangerous, he was always there for others to manipulate and weave plots around. Very probably pressure from Spain forced Henry to act in this way. Ferdinand and Isabella wanted to ensure that their daughter was coming to a secure inheritance.

De la Pole

On the death of Warwick, the chief Yorkist claimant to the throne was Edmund de la Pole, Earl of Suffolk, brother of the rebellious Earl of Lincoln who had died at Stoke. Suffolk appeared reconciled to Henry's rule, but there was underlying tension because the king refused to allow him to inherit his father's dukedom. Suddenly, in July 1499, Suffolk took flight to Guîsnes, near Calais. Henry, fearing a further foreign-backed invasion by a rival claimant to his throne, persuaded him to return and he remained on amicable terms with the king until 1501. In that year he fled with his brother, Richard, to the court of Maximilian (see page 49).

What remained of the old Yorkist support gathered once more in Flanders. That Henry now acted more ruthlessly than ever before reveals how insecure he must have felt. Suffolk's relations who remained in England were imprisoned and, in the Parliament that met in January 1504, 51 men either retained by or connected with the earl were attainted. This was the largest number condemned by any Parliament during his reign. The most famous victim was Sir James Tyrell, once constable of the Tower, and latterly Governor of Guîsnes where Suffolk had sought shelter. Before his execution, Tyrell conveniently confessed to murdering the two young princes, the sons of Edward IV, thus discouraging any further imposters.

The end of Yorkist threats 1499–1506

Henry was determined to pursue and destroy Suffolk, but so long as the latter remained on the Continent protected by foreign princes there was little he could do. However, Henry's luck changed in 1506 when a storm caused Philip of Burgundy and his wife to take refuge in England. Henry persuaded Philip to surrender Suffolk. Philip agreed to do so on condition that the earl's life would be spared. Henry kept his promise; Suffolk remained in the Tower until his execution by Henry VIII in 1513. Meanwhile, his brother, Richard de la Pole, remained at large in Europe trying in vain to muster support for his claim to the English throne. However, few Yorkists now remained and Henry was proving a strong and just monarch to those who were loyal. The Yorkist threat died with Richard when he was killed in 1525.

Henry secure?

It was not until 1506 that the persistent threat of Yorkist claimants was, for the most part, eliminated. Even then, the security of the dynasty rested on the heartbeat of his only son, Prince Henry. Queen Elizabeth had died in February 1503, and Henry's fear for the future of his dynasty was evident in the way he searched the courts of Europe for a second wife. Nevertheless, it is a credit to Henry's clear, decisive judgement and diplomatic skill that he managed to hand on his throne intact to his son, when the previous three kings of England had failed to do so.

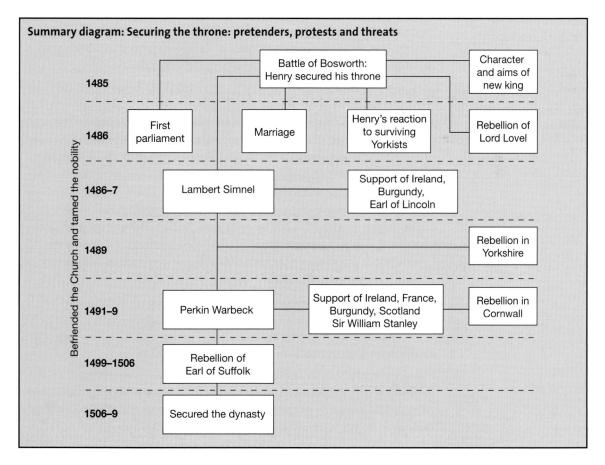

Summary diagram: Securing the throne: pretenders, protests and threats

4 Crown and nobility

▶ *What was the nature of Henry's relationship with his nobility?*

The 'problem' of the nobility

The stability and security of the realm rested on the nature of the relationship between the king and his nobility, and their ability to co-operate. According to the teachings of the Church, the nobility had a duty to serve their social superior, the king, who was held to be God's deputy on earth. By the same token, the king, too, was obliged to protect them, to reward them for their loyalty and service and, above all, to rule wisely and fairly. This theory of obligation, known as the **Great Chain of Being**, was the natural order of society. However, this theory did not always work well in reality.

The Wars of the Roses had temporarily upset this natural order of society, with the crown being fought over by rival factions. This damaged and reduced the status of the monarchy. The nobility had profited most from this, seizing the opportunity to take the law into their own hands. Although they had always tried to control their localities, they now took this a step further, using their servants and retainers as private armies to settle their petty quarrels and to make or unmake kings on the battlefields of the recent civil wars.

Asserting control over the nobility

In 1485 it was this class over whom Henry had to assert his authority if he was to restore the dignity and authority of the monarchy. His problem, according to one historian, S.T. Bindoff (writing in 1969), was 'how to suppress the **magnates**' abuse of their power while preserving the power itself'. A great nobleman had the power to provoke disorder and even revolt, but he could also quell rebellion and act as a mediator between the people and central government. Henry hoped that by imposing his will by ruthless impartiality the nobles might learn to accept that their position was one of obedience, loyalty and service to the Crown. If this was achieved the rest of his subjects would follow suit because the nobility were the natural leaders of society.

In this context it can be argued that Henry's reign marks the end of an independent **feudal** nobility and the beginning of a service nobility.

Promotion and demotion: the size of the nobility

In order to make his task of bringing the nobility to heel easier, Henry deliberately kept the peerage small by limiting the number of new lords that he created. This was unusual and in direct contrast to the policies of Edward IV and Henry VIII, in whose reigns the nobility grew significantly in size.

KEY TERMS

Great Chain of Being Belief in the divine order of things extending from God down through the angels, humans, animals, vegetables and minerals. It was used by the Church to justify the hierarchy of life from the king down through the nobility, gentry and peasantry.

Magnate A powerful nobleman.

Feudal The medieval social and political system.

Henry VII deliberately refrained from making new creations for three reasons:

- A limited noble class was easier to control.
- He so rarely elevated anyone to the upper levels of society that it was regarded as a particularly prized honour and distinction when it did happen.
- The grant of a title might involve the king in expenditure on quite a large scale. A title often brought with it large estates and, as these were usually granted from Crown lands, the creation of new peers resulted in a loss of income for the king. If titles were handed out on a large scale, it could mean quite a considerable drop in the rents that the Crown received.

Whereas Edward IV created nine new Earls, Henry created only three:

- his stepfather, Thomas, Lord Stanley, who became Earl of Derby
- Philibert de Chandee who, in recognition of his military skill as captain of his mercenary troops at Bosworth, became Earl of Bath
- Sir Edward Courtenay, who became Earl of Devon.

Shrinking nobility

Even after Bosworth, Sir William Stanley and Sir Rhys ap Thomas, to whom Henry owed so much for his victory, were not made peers. However, his uncle, **Jasper Tudor**, who had acted as his guardian and mentor through childhood and exile, was elevated from Earl of Pembroke (restored to him in 1485) to Duke of Bedford. Other than that, he created only one marquis (briefly), one viscount and eight barons during the remainder of his reign, as compared with Edward's two viscounts and thirteen barons. Of Henry's creations only three were genuinely new peerages which needed to be accompanied by grants of land. The peerage consequently shrank from around 62 in 1485 to about 42 in 1509 as new creations failed to keep pace with the number of noble families that died out through natural, and in some cases, unnatural causes. According to historian T.B. Pugh (writing in 1974), 'Royal intervention was far more effective than the failure of male heirs in diminishing the group of great magnate families.'

The Order of the Garter

Henry found a useful alternative to the bestowal of a peerage on his loyal subjects namely, the award of **Order of the Garter**. Dating back to the reign of Edward III (1327–77), this was an old-established honour which was in the gift of the Crown but which involved it in no financial obligations. Some 37 of Henry's closest followers (including peers) received this privilege during his reign. Among those honoured were Sir William Stanley and Sir Rhys ap Thomas but, whereas the latter embraced the award with enthusiasm, Stanley considered it scant reward for his loyal service.

Overmighty subjects

Henry was fortunate that he faced fewer of the overmighty nobles who had so troubled Edward IV. One reason for this was his lack of close male relatives.

 **KEY FIGURE**

Jasper Tudor (1437–95)
Second son of Owen Tudor and Queen Catherine. In 1452 he was ennobled as Earl of Pembroke by his half-brother, Henry VI. He was a dedicated Lancastrian and supported Henry VI in the Wars of the Roses. Jasper became his teenage nephew's guardian and mentor and took him to safety in France when Edward IV secured the crown for a second time in 1471. Following fourteen years in exile, Jasper returned with his nephew to secure victory in the Battle of Bosworth in 1485. Jasper was rewarded with the title of Duke of Bedford.

 **KEY TERM**

Order of the Garter
Founded in 1348, this honour was bestowed on the most important knights who then attained the senior rank of knighthood.

Whereas Edward had had to cope with two powerful brothers, the Dukes of Clarence and Gloucester, Henry, apart from his stepbrothers who never received a dukedom, had none. The other was the king's cautious policy in rewarding his followers. The lands that came to the Crown from extinct peerage families were not given away again. They were mostly retained by the Crown, particularly the great estates that were acquired from the extinct Yorkist families of Warwick, Clarence and Gloucester.

Henry also controlled the marriages of his nobles, carefully ensuring that leading magnates did not link themselves to great heiresses in order to create dangerous power blocs. He was able to do this because, as their feudal lord, his permission was necessary for them to marry. For example, when Katherine Woodville married her third husband, Sir Richard Wingfield, without royal licence, a fine of £2000 was imposed. That she was the queen's aunt and had once been the wife of Henry's uncle, Jasper Tudor, was never allowed to come between the king and his duty.

Some of these overmighty subjects, such as the Percy Earls of Northumberland and the Stafford Dukes of Buckingham, still remained, but such families were kept under surveillance. Even closely related families with the potential to become overmighty, like the Stanley Earls of Derby to whom Henry owed much for his throne, were kept firmly in check. Fearful of the family's growing wealth and power, the core of which had been given to them by Henry, in 1506 the king took the opportunity to fine Bishop Stanley, his stepbrother, the huge sum of £245,680 (equivalent to £119 million today) for illegally **retaining**. So, partly through good fortune and partly through a carefully thought-out policy, the greater magnates posed less of a threat to Henry than they had in previous reigns.

KEY TERM

Retaining Employing and maintaining servants.

Henry's attitude towards the nobility

On the other hand, one of the main reasons why Henry kept some of the nobility close to him at court was so that he could keep an eye on them. According to one of his most notorious agents, Edmund Dudley, 'he was much sett to have the persons in his danger at his pleasure'. It is clear also that the nobility involved themselves in the political dynamics of Henry's court. Court faction and political infighting, so much a feature of the reigns of Henry VI and Edward IV, took on a more significant and sinister role in Henry's final years. Two notable victims of court politics are thought to have been Thomas Grey, second Marquis of Dorset, suspicion of whom had been 'stirred in Henry' by others, and George Neville, Baron Bergavenny, who was the only nobleman to suffer the public disgrace of being tried, fined and imprisoned for illegal retaining. It seems that, whereas Henry mistrusted many of his nobility, he did favour a few. This imbalance may have contributed to feuding at court.

Like his predecessors, he recognised the nobles' importance to him in controlling the provinces in the absence of a standing army. He never attempted to interfere with their authority in the localities and they continued to dominate local government. Moreover, Henry continued the medieval practice of granting the overlordship of the outlying areas of his kingdom to the greater magnates as a gesture of goodwill. Thus, the Yorkist Henry Percy, Earl of Northumberland, was released from captivity only a few weeks after Bosworth and was regranted the wardenship of the north of England.

Henry and patronage

One aspect of Henry's treatment of the nobility that was new was his attitude towards **patronage**. Unlike his predecessors, he did not try to buy the loyalty of the nobility through the use of patronage. He was as careful in this as he was over the distribution of titles. The criterion he used in selecting those to receive royal favour was good and loyal service to the Crown. This meant that it was not necessarily the nobility who fell into this category. The beneficiaries of Henry's generosity were quite simply valuable servants of the Tudor government. Some were peers, such as Jasper Tudor, the Duke of Bedford, the Earl of Oxford and George Talbot, Earl of Shrewsbury, but many were not. Edmund Dudley, the Sussex lawyer, who rose to become one of Henry's most trusted advisers, was not made a peer, but as one contemporary put it, he 'used his title of King's Councillor as proudly as any peerage'. Henry believed that patronage was not an automatic privilege of the upper class; it had to be earned.

Thomas Howard, Earl of Surrey

The career of **Thomas Howard**, Earl of Surrey, illustrates clearly how Henry was prepared to forget past mistakes if their perpetrators subsequently performed loyally for him. The earl's father had enjoyed the title of Duke of Norfolk, an honour bestowed on him by Richard III, and he had died fighting for his king at Bosworth. After Henry's accession, the earl was imprisoned in the Tower and both he and his father were attainted. However, he was released in 1489 and put in charge of maintaining law and order in the north, probably because he had impressed the king by turning down the chance to escape from the Tower during the Simnel plot. The attainder was revoked and his title was restored, but Henry only returned some of his lands.

After his success in suppressing the Yorkshire rebellion, Surrey was given back more but not all of the Howard estates. The ducal title was also denied him and Henry kept this final prize to ensure his loyalty to the end. It was not until 1513 that Henry VIII finally rewarded Surrey with the dukedom for his leading role in defeating the Scots in battle.

Henry frequently used acts of attainder in this 'cat and mouse' way to punish disobedient magnates. After a period of time he would often arrange for Parliament to revoke them, but he would only gradually restore the confiscated lands as rewards for actions of particular loyalty and support.

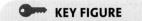

KEY TERM

Patronage The award and distribution of royal favours.

KEY FIGURE

Thomas Howard (1443–1524)

Former Yorkist who governed the north of England on behalf of Henry VII. He was the richest and most powerful nobleman in England after the death of Jasper Tudor in 1495.

Financial penalties

Henry also used financial threats to strengthen royal authority and curb the power of the nobility, particularly where he was suspicious of an individual but could not prove treason. In such cases he manipulated the existing system of bonds and recognisances for good behaviour to his advantage. These were written agreements in which a person who offended the king in a particular way was forced either to pay up front or to promise to pay a certain sum of money as security for their future good behaviour. This technique, sometimes with conditions attached, such as the carrying out of a certain duty, was used with all the elite classes as a method of ensuring their loyalty. Henry used the system not only to act as a financial threat against potentially disloyal magnates but also to raise much needed revenue for the Crown. The sums stipulated in these agreements ranged from £400 for a relatively insignificant person to £10,000 for a peer.

As with his policy over acts of attainder, the greater the magnate, the more likely Henry was to bring him under this type of financial pressure. Typical was the case of Lord Dacre, in 1506, who was forced to enter into a bond of £2000 as proof of his loyalty. Even the senior clergy were not spared the king's ruthless treatment. For example, the Bishop of Worcester had to promise to pay £2000 if his loyalty was ever in question, as well as agreeing not to leave the country. But the most important noble to suffer in this way was Edward IV's stepson, the Marquis of Dorset. The king had believed him to be implicated in the Simnel plot and, after further treachery in 1491, his friends signed bonds totalling £10,000 as a promise of his good behaviour. When Henry was planning the invasion of France in 1492 he even went so far as to take the Marquis's son as hostage in case he seized this opportunity to rebel again.

Livery and maintenance

Henry VII openly condemned retaining at the beginning of his reign and two laws were passed against it in 1487 and 1504. Henry knew that retainers could be armed and trained to provide their noble masters with an army. The practice of retaining had helped to perpetuate the Wars of the Roses, which explains why Henry was keen to stop it. In 1487 Henry forced the members of both Houses of Parliament to swear that they would not retain illegally. Only licensed retainers were permitted by the Act of 1487. Strict limits were placed on the numbers of retainers each nobleman could legitimately employ. The size of a nobleman's retinue was determined by his status: a duke could retain around 120 servants while an earl could employ 80. The legislation of 1504 laid down much stricter methods of enforcement. It introduced a novel system of licensing whereby men could employ retainers for the king's service alone. To do this a lord had to have a special licence endorsed with the privy seal, and the entire retinue had to be listed for royal approval.

SOURCE D

Sir Francis Bacon, *The History of the Reign of King Henry the Seventh*, 1622. Bacon was Lord Chancellor of England during the reign of King James I (1613–25)

The king was entertained by the earl of Oxford at his castle of Heningham. The king called the earl of Oxford to him and said 'My Lord, are these gentlemen which I see on both sides of me your servants?' The earl smiled and said, 'it may please your Grace that most of them are my retainers'. The king was surprised and said, 'I thank you for my entertainment but I cannot have my laws [against retaining] broken in my sight. My attorney must speak with you'. And for this offence the earl of Oxford had to pay a fine of 15,000 marks [£10,000].

> Study Source D. Why did Henry consider it important that he punish his friend and royal councillor?

Curbing the practice of retaining

Evidence of Henry's success in this matter is seen in the reduction of the numbers of retainers that magnates maintained. Those they employed appear to have been limited to the legitimate categories of servants, officials and lawyers. However, studies of individual nobles, such as the Duke of Buckingham and the Earl of Northumberland, show that they might have got round official policy by employing more estate officers than were necessary.

If nobles did retain without royal permission while Henry was on the throne, they were careful not to leave any evidence. Those magnates who did break the law and were found out were made examples of. In 1506 Lord Bergavenny was fined the statutory £5 per month per retainer, which amounted to the enormous sum of £70,550. Although Henry suspended this in favour of a recognisance, the culprit had learned his lesson and was a warning to other would-be offenders. This was a particularly extreme case, complicated because Bergavenny had also been implicated in the Cornish rebellion.

The biggest difference in attitude between Edward IV and Henry over retaining is seen in their reaction to their friends. Whereas Edward turned a blind eye towards the misdemeanours of those close to him, Henry treated everyone alike. Among those **indicted** for illegal retaining in 1504 was the Duke of Buckingham, the Earls of Derby, Essex, Northumberland, Oxford and Shrewsbury, and even the king's mother, Lady Margaret, Countess of Richmond and Derby!

Retaining continued well into the reign of Elizabeth I, so Henry certainly did not eliminate the practice, but he controlled it to a far greater extent than his predecessors and prevented it from being a significant problem.

 **KEY TERM**

Indicted Legal term used to describe those charged with a crime.

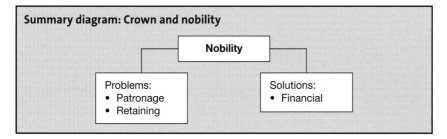

Summary diagram: Crown and nobility

Nobility

Problems:
- Patronage
- Retaining

Solutions:
- Financial

Chapter summary

The chaos of the Wars of the Roses enabled Richard III to seize the throne from Edward V. This encouraged noble claimants like Henry Tudor, Earl of Richmond, to challenge Richard for the throne. Following his victory at the Battle of Bosworth Henry VII's primary aim was to establish and consolidate his dynasty. Given his weak claim to the throne, Henry VII faced many difficulties but his strength of character and talent in appointing men of ability helped him in seeking to secure his kingship. His marriage to Elizabeth of York followed by the birth of a son and heir, Arthur, contributed to the security of his throne. Nevertheless, he had to deal with pretenders such as Lambert Simnel and Perkin Warbeck, who challenged his kingship. Backed by disaffected Yorkists and funded by foreign rulers such as Margaret of Burgundy, the threat posed by the pretenders was real and dangerous. Foreign intrigue allied to domestic troubles such as the tax rebellions in Yorkshire and Cornwall made Henry's task of securing the dynasty all the harder. He was careful to cultivate the support of the nobility but was prepared to punish those who showed any signs of disloyalty.

Refresher questions

Use these questions to remind yourself of the key material covered in this chapter.

1 What was Henry Tudor like?

2 How did Henry VII secure the throne?

3 Who was responsible for the risings of 1485–6 and how were they suppressed?

4 Why did the people of Yorkshire and Cornwall rebel?

5 How serious a challenge to Henry's kingship was Lambert Simnel's rebellion?

6 How significant a danger to Henry VII were Perkin Warbeck and his supporters?

7 How serious a threat to Henry VII were the later Yorkist challenges?

8 Did Henry deliberately try to limit the power of the nobility?

9 What was Henry's attitude towards patronage?

10 What was Henry's attitude towards punishing the nobility?

11 Why did Henry threaten the nobility with financial ruin?

12 What was livery and maintenance?

13 What was Henry's attitude towards retaining and how did he deal with it?

14 When did Henry feel secure on the throne?

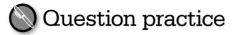 Question practice

ESSAY QUESTIONS

1 'Henry VII was able to defeat the threats to his throne because of the weakness of his enemies.' Explain why you agree or disagree with this view.

2 'Henry's success in establishing the dynasty was due almost entirely to the fact that he was a ruthless and brutal tyrant.' Assess the validity of this view.

3 How successful was Henry VII in controlling the nobility?

4 How significant was the challenge posed by Lambert Simnel's rebellion in 1487 to the government of Henry VII?

CHAPTER 2

Henry VII: governing the kingdom 1485–1509

Henry VII was determined to re-establish 'good governance' after the turmoil of the Wars of the Roses. In the hope that financial security would help him to consolidate his power, he sought to make the Crown solvent. Henry pursued an energetic foreign policy but this was marked more by diplomacy than by war. The means by which Henry governed the kingdom, restored the nation's finances and pursued an effective foreign policy are examined as three themes:

★ Government and administration

★ Financial policy

★ Foreign policy

The key debate on *page 46* of this chapter asks the question: What was the 'New Monarchy' theory and why did it lead to so much debate among historians?

Key dates

1485	Meeting of Henry's first Parliament	**1496**	Trade agreement known as *Magnus Intercursus* signed
1487	First law passed against illegal retaining		
	Battle of Stoke	**1497**	Truce of Ayton signed
1489	Treaties of Redon and of Medina del Campo	**1501**	Marriage of Arthur and Catherine of Aragon
		1502	Treaty of Ayton
1492	Treaty of Étaples		Death of Prince Arthur
1493	Council in Wales and the Marches re-established	**1504**	Second law passed against illegal retaining
			Sir Richard Empson appointed head of the Council Learned in the Law
1494	Sir Edward Poynings appointed Lord Deputy of Ireland	**1509**	Death of Henry VII

1 Government and administration

▶ *How effective and successful was Henry's government of the kingdom?*

Central government: the King's Council

The centre of medieval English government was the king himself and the men he chose to sit on his council. The functions of the council were to advise the king over matters of state, to administer law and order, and to act in a judicial capacity. During Henry's reign there was a total of 227 councillors, but there were not more than 150 at any one time, most of whom rarely attended meetings. When all the active members were present the council totalled about 40.

The difficulty in controlling this led Henry to rely on a small, core group of councillors who met with the king regularly. This elite group included the chief officers of state, the Lord Chancellor, **John Morton**, the Lord Privy Seal, Richard Fox, the Lord Treasurer, John, Lord Dynham and a handful of others. These men gave stability to the new regime because Henry kept them in power for so long. For example, Morton served as Lord Chancellor for fourteen years until his death in 1500, while Fox served as Lord Privy Seal for 22 years until the king's death in 1509.

In order to improve the efficiency of central government, Henry decided to use smaller committees formed from within the council, as his Yorkist predecessors had done. For example, Henry revived Richard III's Court of Requests, which was nicknamed the 'Court for Poor Men's Causes'. One of the first committees to be set up by Henry, in 1487, undertook responsibility for the implementation of the act of livery and maintenance. Another was the Court of General Surveyors, which audited the revenues coming in from the Crown lands.

SOURCE A

Extract from Polydore Vergil, *Anglica Historia* (*The History of England*), 1513. Vergil was an Italian priest and humanist scholar who lived much of his life in England.

Henry VII established a Council in his household by whose opinion all things should be justly and rightly governed and causes brought to it to be decided without the bitterness of lawsuits. And for this Council, he chose men renowned for their shrewdness, loyalty and reliability, John, Earl of Oxford; Jasper, Duke of Bedford; Thomas Stanley, Earl of Derby; John Morton, Bishop of Ely; Richard Fox, Edward Poynings. And he chose other wise men to council for specific business among whom were Rhys ap Thomas, a Welshman; Thomas Grey, Marquis of Dorset, a good and prudent man; George Talbot, Earl of Shrewsbury, wise and moderate in all things; Thomas, Earl of Ormond, an Irishman; William Say, a prominent knight; Thomas, Earl of Surrey, a man of great wisdom, reliability and loyalty.

The Council Learned in the Law

The Council Learned in the Law (normally referred to simply as the Council Learned) was a small and very professional body. Its name derived from the fact that most of its members had some sort of legal training or experience. This council came into being in 1495 to defend the king's position as a feudal landlord. It was responsible for keeping up to date with the wardship, marriage

---

🔑 KEY FIGURE

John Morton (1420–1500)

Archbishop of Canterbury and Lord Chancellor of England, he was especially trusted by Henry VII and was able to exert considerable influence over the king. Morton's control of the Church ensured that it remained loyal to the Crown and his methods of government gave rise to the term 'Morton's Fork'. According to Morton's logic, wealthy subjects of the Crown obviously had money enough to pay their taxes, and poor subjects were clearly sitting on savings. Rich and poor alike found themselves at the points of 'Morton's Fork' – paying high taxes.

Study Source A. Why did Henry think it was important to rely on such a small group of councillors?

and relief of all the king's tenants, and the collection of the feudal dues that were owed to him. Contemporaries criticised it because it operated without a jury, but this was true of all the conciliar committees. In fact, it was done deliberately because of the frequent charges of bribery brought against juries. The Council Learned was particularly hated because of its connection with bonds and recognisances (see pages 44–5) as it supervised the collection of these financial agreements. By the end of the reign it had become the most detested but the most important of all Henry's institutions of government.

The Council Learned became increasingly feared after the promotion of Sir Richard Empson to the Chancellorship of the Duchy and the Presidency of the Council Learned in 1504. Under the joint leadership of Empson and his colleague, Edmund Dudley, royal rights were scrupulously enforced. Henry's disciplinary use of financial penalties, such as bonds and recognisances, was certainly an effective way of keeping the peace, but under the management of these two councillors the practice seems to have become much more widespread. As Henry was by this time more secure than ever before, the harsh enforcement of such penalties by Empson and Dudley, through this court, was bitterly resented. So hated had the pair become that on Henry's death they were arrested for fraud, tried and executed.

SOURCE B

Study Source B. What impression of Henry VII is the artist attempting to convey through this painting?

Henry VII in conference with Sir Richard Empson (left) and Edmund Dudley (right), a contemporary painting by an unknown artist.

The personnel of government: clerics, nobles and the 'New Men'

The membership of Henry's council differed very little from that of the Yorkists. The majority of its members came from the Church and the nobility. It has been argued that the most important members of Henry's council came not from the Church or from the nobility but from a third group, the gentry. Some historians have referred to this group as being 'middle class' because they were lower in degree than the nobility and higher than the masses. Other historians, such as Steven Gunn, have dubbed them the 'new men' serving a 'new monarchy'.

Clerics

The largest social grouping on the council was the clerics, who accounted for about half of the total membership between 1485 and 1509. Among the most favoured of them were John Morton, whom Henry VII appointed his chancellor or chief minister in 1487 and Richard Fox, who became the king's principal secretary. Morton was a doctor of civil law and he had practised in the Church courts, while Fox had a degree in theology and had studied in Paris. This sort of education and legal expertise proved ideal for administrators.

Nobles

There were also a substantial number of nobles, which seems to weaken the case of those commentators who have claimed that Henry sought to oust them from government. What was different about Henry's council was that he demanded real service from those who sat on it, so that what counted was not noble blood but how loyal and useful a councillor proved to be. Those nobles who served him well were amply rewarded. Among these was **John de Vere**, the Earl of Oxford, who had supported Henry since his days in exile; he was given the offices of Great Chamberlain and Lord Admiral. Jasper Tudor received the dukedom of Bedford and the control of Wales. Henry wisely did not wish to alienate the former Yorkists permanently, so, once they had paid in some way for their 'treachery', they were given opportunities to prove their loyalty to the new regime. The Earl of Lincoln was a member of the council until he joined the Simnel rebellion, while Thomas, Earl of Surrey, became a councillor after his release from the Tower and was appointed Lord Treasurer of England in 1501.

'New men'

Henry did not rely on a particular nobleman or family as Edward IV and Richard III had done. Instead, Henry's chief advisers and servants were drawn from the ranks of the lesser landowners or gentry, and from the professional classes (especially lawyers) – men like Sir Reginald Bray (see page 40), Edmund Dudley and Sir Edward Poynings. This has led some historians to label them the 'new men' because they were not noble and they did not come from families with a tradition of royal service. Although Henry made less use of the nobility in

> **🔑 KEY FIGURE**
>
> **John de Vere (1442–1513)**
>
> Earl of Oxford and a staunch Lancastrian. He was arrested and imprisoned by Edward IV but escaped to join Jasper and Henry Tudor in exile in France and Brittany. He was a talented military commander who commanded Henry's army at Bosworth. He became one of Henry VII's most trusted royal councillors.

central government than his predecessors, there was nothing particularly 'new' about his reliance on the gentry rather than on the aristocracy. For example, Richard III had employed lawyers from landowning gentry families. The ancestors of these 'new men' had generations of experience in local government, justice and landowning. As Henry was exploiting his lands through more efficient methods of estate management, he needed servants who understood auditing and property laws and had administrative skills. Real ability in these areas was what mattered to Henry, not social class.

Regional government

When Henry VII became king he faced the problem of restraining the individual nobles in the provinces. He saw the strengths in Edward's policy and followed it in principle, but, wherever possible, he stopped individuals building up too much power and he always insisted on their absolute loyalty to the Tudor dynasty.

Two of Henry's strongest supporters were rewarded with estates which brought with them a considerable amount of local control:

- Jasper Tudor, Duke of Bedford, became the most influential nobleman in Wales.
- John de Vere, Earl of Oxford, became the most influential nobleman in East Anglia.

Supporters of Richard III found it virtually impossible to regain the positions that they had enjoyed under the Yorkists. Although Henry Percy, Earl of Northumberland, was allowed to continue in his former role of Lord Lieutenant of the north, his powers were greatly restricted and, on his death in 1489, Henry used the fact that the Percy heir was a minor to replace the Earl with Thomas Howard, Earl of Surrey, who had neither land nor influence in the northern counties. As Surrey was hoping to win back the lands and title lost by his father after Bosworth, Henry could expect good service from him. In 1501 the northern families were once again overlooked when Surrey was replaced by a council under the Archbishop of York, Thomas Savage. Savage's uncle was Thomas Stanley, Earl of Derby.

The same pattern emerged in Wales after the deaths of Jasper Tudor and the Prince of Wales (in 1502). Control was in the hands of a council under the presidency of William Smyth, Bishop of Coventry and Lichfield, who had no power base in the principality. So, by the end of his reign Henry was moving away from the idea of appointing a local magnate to control a particular region. This prevented the growth of magnate power and overmighty subjects in the provinces and in doing so forged far stronger links between central and regional government.

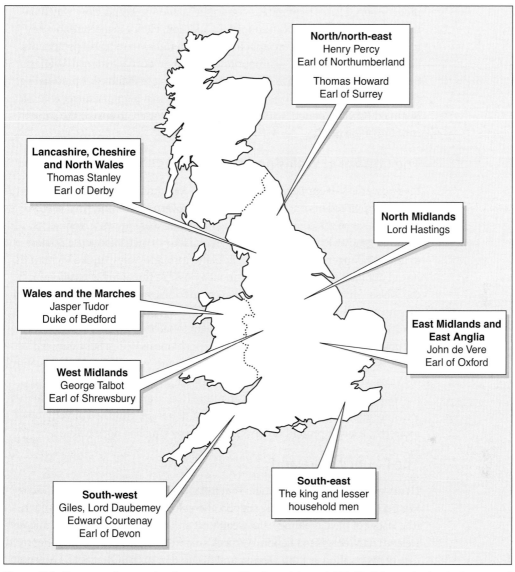

Figure 2.1 Divisions of power: localities governed by the nobility, c.1485–95. Why might the deployment of nobles to the localities indicated in the map help Henry VII to govern the kingdom?

The Council of the North

The Council of the North differed from the conciliar committees in having a clearly defined function dating from the time of Richard of Gloucester as governor. Yet it was closely linked to the main council, enjoying similar administrative and judicial power to enable the law to be enforced swiftly and efficiently, and, of course, it was ultimately subordinate to the king. Unlike his predecessors, Henry required his council in London to keep a close watch on the activities of his provincial council. In addition, Henry made sure that key members of the council were appointed by him rather than by his lieutenants. For example, one of the most important officials on Surrey's council, William Sever, Bishop of Carlisle, was appointed by the king to enforce his prerogative rights in the north. Sever was also required to keep in regular contact with Sir Reginald Bray in London, with whom he worked closely to ensure the smooth running of the north.

The Council in Wales and the Marches

Like Edward IV, Henry appreciated the need for administrative order. This is why he appointed his uncle, Jasper Tudor, to govern Wales, and why, later in 1493, he revived the council appointing his seven-year old son Arthur as its nominal head as Prince of Wales. Although Henry's own experience pointed out to him the danger of an invasion of England through Wales, unlike Richard III, he did not have to worry too much about a possible threat to his position from the Welsh. His family links and Welsh connections, highlighted and celebrated by native poets and writers, ensured for him the support of the people. He rewarded their faith in him by trusting them to see to their own affairs, hence his policy of appointing Welshmen to key positions in Wales. For example, Sir Rhys ap Thomas was appointed to govern south-west Wales. Henry's control of Wales was helped by the fact that, by 1495, due in part to inheritance and purchase, and on account of death and forfeiture, scarcely half a dozen Marcher lordships remained in private hands. Henry, therefore, governed directly, and indirectly, a larger proportion of Wales than any king had done before.

The Council of Ireland

Henry quickly learned the danger that Ireland could pose when Simnel and Warbeck received considerable support there. In 1492, after the Earl of Kildare (the leader of the Geraldines, the wealthiest and most powerful noble family in Ireland) had recognised Perkin Warbeck's claim to the throne, the king deprived him of his position as Lord Deputy and his brother of the Great Seal. Only after they had sought the king's pardon in person was Henry willing to restore their titles.

In 1494 Henry set about reorganising Irish government. He made his infant son, Prince Henry, Lord Lieutenant, so as to echo the nominal headship exercised by his elder son in Wales, and appointed Sir Edward Poynings, one of his most trusted advisers, as deputy. Poynings' main task was to bring the most rebellious areas under the king's control and to impose a constitution on Ireland that would ensure its future obedience to the English Crown.

Poynings succeeded in establishing a constitution at the Parliament which met at Drogheda in 1494; Poynings' Law, as it became known, decreed that an Irish Parliament could be summoned and pass laws only with the king's prior approval. No future legislation was to be discussed unless it had first been agreed by the king and his council. In addition, any law made in England would automatically apply to Ireland. This gave the king far greater control over Ireland by destroying the independent legislative power of the Irish Parliament.

In the short term, he hoped to prevent the calling of an unauthorised Irish Parliament, which might recognise another pretender. In the long term, it proved to be largely a theoretical victory. The expense of attempting to rule Ireland directly soon proved to be unsustainably high, and the experiment was abandoned. Henry returned to his earlier policy of ruling through the Irish chieftains. Kildare was reinstated as Lord Deputy and, for much of the rest of the reign, Ireland ceased to be a problem for Henry.

Local government

Supervision from the centre was the key feature of the exercise of law and government in the localities. This did not mean that Henry made royal progresses around the kingdom as Edward IV had done. Instead, Henry was the central figure directing all operations from London and making his commands felt in three ways:

- through the exploitation of Crown lands
- by encouraging more frequent use of the royal council and its offshoots for the settlement of local lawsuits
- by increasing the powers of the **justices of the peace (JPs)**.

Henry's more efficient management and exploitation of the Crown lands had extended the authority of the monarch to all parts of the country, as well as increasing the income that he received in rents. In developing the role of the royal council and JPs – who owed their offices to the king – Henry was also exerting his control more effectively over the localities. This arrangement worked relatively well under a strong king, who could ensure that his instructions were obeyed and that the local nobility did not develop too much power, or seize the opportunity to pursue their private feuds. Although the problem of keeping the peace had not been completely solved, Henry had gone a long way to extending his control of the situation by centralising the system of local government.

The sheriffs and justices of the peace

The **sheriff** and the justice of the peace continued to be the two most important royal officials in each county. As the power of the JP increased that of the sheriff continued to decline. Nevertheless, sheriffs were given a new lease of life in the Tudor period as far as they:

- became the Crown's representative in every county throughout England (in effect, they became the 'eyes and ears' of the monarch)
- took on greater responsibility for the conduct and management of parliamentary elections.

> **🔑 KEY TERMS**
>
> **Justices of the peace (JPs)** Chief magistrates in quarter sessions and responsible for general administration in a county.
>
> **Sheriff** Chief law enforcement officer in a county.

Unlike the JPs, who were appointed to the commission of the peace for life, the sheriff was selected annually so that the Crown could exert greater control over these local officials.

After 1485 JPs, like sheriffs, continued to be selected from the landowning county elite. They met and dispensed justice in local courts known as Quarter Sessions (meeting four times a year). For more serious offences, the JPs sent criminals to the senior courts or Courts of Assize, which were staffed by judges appointed by the Crown. The highest criminal court was the Court of the King's Bench, which could override decisions made at the Quarter Sessions and the Courts of Assize. After 1485 JPs were commanded to read out a proclamation at the beginning of each session stating that grievances against justices could be taken to either an assize judge or the king.

Hundred and parish

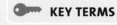

KEY TERMS

Hundred An administrative subdivision in a county.

Petty constable Assistant law enforcement officer serving under the high constable.

Just as the king was dependent on JPs for the maintenance of law and order in the counties, so the JPs were dependent on lesser officials in the countryside to bring offenders to them. By law every **hundred** (a subdivision of a county) had to provide itself with a high constable and every parish with a **petty constable**.

Weakness of local government

The weakness in this type of local government was that the king was dependent on the goodwill of his officials. Henry had to rely on the justices' own self-interest as leaders of society for the upholding of law and order. Virtually his only control over them was the threat of removal from the commission of the peace if they acted improperly, which would be regarded by most JPs as a considerable social disgrace. What Henry wished to avoid was the fate that befell the Crown on the sudden usurpation of Richard III when some nobles seized their opportunity to take authority into their own hands and deliberately chose to ignore royal commands. A system of paid servants, as existed in France, would have been more efficient but, given the financial constraints on the English Crown, the system adopted by Henry VII worked relatively well.

Parliament

In the 24 years of Henry VII's reign, Parliament was summoned on only seven occasions, and five of those were in his first decade as king when he was relatively insecure in his possession of the throne. Several reasons have been advanced to explain why Henry so rarely summoned Parliament:

- He did not need to ask for war taxes very often because his foreign policy was based on avoiding expensive campaigns abroad.
- He did not wish to strain the loyalty of his subjects by too many requests for grants of money, so he found other ways of filling his treasury.
- He did not feel the need to initiate legislation on a large scale. The government bills most frequently passed were acts of attainder designed to subdue the more troublesome of his political opponents.

The king might not have summoned Parliament frequently but, by the way he used it, he continued its traditional role as an institution where the most important business of the kingdom was transacted. This is clear not only in the number of attainders against individual nobles that he requested Parliament to pass, but in the way he used it to ratify his claim to the throne in 1486.

Legislation was also used to carry out his policies against riots and retaining, and ten per cent of all statutes dealt with the responsibilities of the JPs and the control of the provinces. Further Acts dealt with social discipline, such as that of 1495 which laid down rules on wages and hours of work. Henry's use of Parliament emphasised the fact that all power derived from the Crown. So, although Parliament did not meet on a regular basis during Henry's reign, there was no threat of its ceasing to exist as a political institution. The king used it as and when circumstances demanded, just as his predecessors had done.

Table 2.1 List of parliamentary meetings under Henry VII. What does the list of meetings reveal about Henry VII's use of Parliament?

Year	Date of session	Approximate length of session
1485–6	07/11/85–04/03/86	3 months
1487	09/11/87–10/12/87	1 month
1489	13/01/89–23/02/90	1.5 months
1491	17/10/91–04/11/91	0.5 month
1495	14/10/95–22/12/95	2 months
1497	16/01/97–13/03/97	2 months
1504	25/01/04–01/04/04	2.5 months

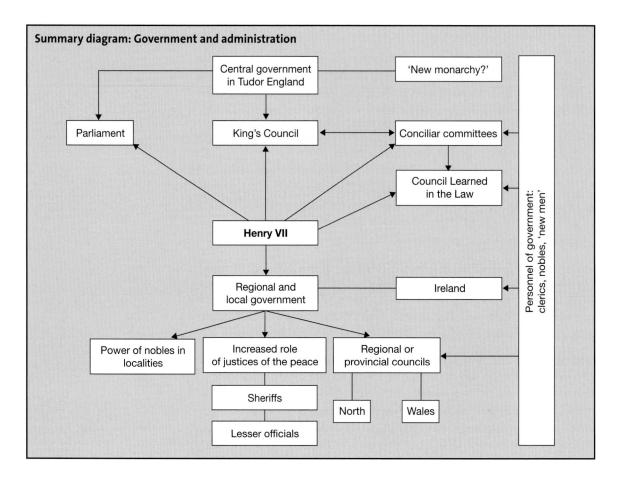

Summary diagram: Government and administration

2 Financial policy

▶ *In what ways did Henry consider finance to be important?*

Henry's financial aims

Henry VII's financial aims were quite simple: to achieve solvency by increasing royal income, decreasing expenditure and thereby restoring the Crown's financial strength.

Henry VII has been described as 'the best businessman ever to sit upon the English throne', and on his death he was credited with being the 'richest lord that is now known in the world'. However, the truth is Henry lacked experience in government and was untried and untested in the rigours of financial administration and diplomacy. Nevertheless, in spite of his shortcomings, he was acutely aware of the importance of strong finances if he was to remain safely on his throne. His usurpation of the Crown meant there was always the possibility of others putting forward their own claim. The availability of revenue together with financial stability was essential if he was to be able to raise an army to defeat them.

Henry did not feel secure unless he was rich: he could use his wealth to reward loyal service, bribe potential opponents and fund armies if necessary. It helped him to consolidate the dynasty because if the succession was still challenged at the time of his death, a full treasury would provide his heir with the resources to fight to retain the throne. This is why Henry was so keen to reorganise the financial administration, because he believed that a wealthy king was better able to finance his way out of trouble. However, Henry was well aware that his determination to make the collection of revenue more efficient would encounter opposition from those who would be expected to pay.

Financial administration

In the first two years of his reign, Henry VII had neither the experience nor the time to continue the Yorkist practice of using the Chamber to deal with the kingdom's finances. The Chamber was an office within the royal household that was responsible for the king's private income but the Yorkists had enlarged its powers to take over the functions of the Exchequer. Under Henry, the Exchequer resumed its control of the nation's finances. However, as early as 1487 Henry admitted that in focusing so intensely on his own security, he had neglected to take adequate care of his estates and that they had 'greatly fallen into decay'. The accounts bear witness to this. In Richard III's reign they had earned £25,000 per annum, but by 1486 this had declined to £12,000.

From 1487 Henry gradually began to restore the Chamber system to its former position as the most important institution of financial administration in the kingdom. By the late 1490s it was once again the centre of royal finance, handling an annual turnover well in excess of £100,000. It dealt with the transfer of all revenue from:

- Crown lands
- profits of justice
- feudal dues
- French pension.

In fact, it dealt with all sources of income except custom duties and the accounts of the sheriffs (the officials responsible for the maintenance of law and order in the shires). These remained under the control of the Exchequer because their collection involved detailed information and a complex organisation of officers and records not available to the **Treasurer of the Chamber**.

The Privy Chamber

The development of the Chamber into the national treasury from 1487 led to further reorganisation within the royal household, from where the Chamber had originated. The department that increased most in importance was the

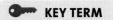

KEY TERM

Treasurer of the Chamber Chief financial official responsible for the king's money.

Sir Reginald Bray

1465	Appointed steward of the Stafford household
1485	Knighted by Henry VII and appointed chancellor of the Duchy of Lancaster
1492	Appointed to serve on the King's Council as chief financial adviser
1494	Appointed high-steward of Oxford University
1497	Participated in the defeat and dispersal of the Cornish rebels at Blackheath, London
1499	Presided over the Council Learned in the Law
1501	Elected a knight of the garter
1503	Died

Reginald was born in St John Bedwardine, Worcestershire, in 1440, the second son of Sir Richard Bray, and educated at the Royal Grammar School Worcester. Bray's royal contacts may have been as a result of his father, who is reported to have been a physician to Henry VI. Bray first found employment in the household of Sir Henry Stafford, second husband of Margaret, mother of Henry VII.

His successful stewardship earned him promotion to the Chancellorship of the Duchy of Lancaster. His skill and expertise in estate management and financial administration impressed Henry VII, who appointed him a royal councillor.

Bray was one of the most powerful of Henry VII's councillors. His importance for the history of the reign of Henry VII lies in his long and loyal service to the king, whom he served as chief financial adviser. His close relationship with the king was such that he alone (with the possible exception of Jasper Tudor) had the freedom to rebuke as well as to influence Henry. As chancellor of the Duchy of Lancaster he presided over the novel institution of the Council Learned to direct a penal system of bonds, and the enforcement of the prerogative rights of the king.

Bray is credited with restructuring the revenue system and restoring the financial health of the Crown. His financial management enhanced the financial power of the Crown, ensuring it became solvent by the end of Henry's reign.

king's 'Privy [private] Chamber', made up of his personal household servants. This now took over the administration of the household as well as taking care of Henry's private expenditure, formerly a responsibility of the Chamber. The transformation of the Privy Chamber is important because it continued to play a vital role in Tudor government throughout the sixteenth century, and many Tudor ministers rose from its ranks.

The head of the financial system, on paper at least, was the Treasurer of England, but he had long been merely a figurehead and the office was traditionally given to an important noble as an honorary position. The only holders of the office during Henry's reign were Lord Dinham (1485–1501) and the Earl of Surrey (1501–22). In practice, the Treasurer of the Chamber had become the chief financial officer of the Crown. Under Henry VII, this position was held by two of the king's most loyal and efficient servants, Sir Thomas Lovell (1485–92) and Sir John Heron (1492–1521). The main advantage of the Chamber system was that it gave the king much closer control over his finances.

The financial resources of the Crown

Ordinary revenue

Ordinary revenue was the regular income on which the Crown could rely to finance the costs of monarchy.

Crown lands

Henry inherited all the lands which had belonged to the houses of York and Lancaster, including the Earldoms of Richmond, March and Warwick, the Duchy of Lancaster and the principality of Wales. On the death of his uncle and his wife, their lands reverted to him as well. He also further enriched the Crown through **escheats** and attainders.

Henry was fortunate in having few relatives who expected to benefit from his territorial acquisitions. He had no brothers; his uncle, Jasper Tudor, died in 1495, and his elder son, Arthur, in 1502. This left only Prince Henry requiring provision. Henry had no obvious favourites, nor was he inclined to shower honours on his supporters. Therefore, on his death, the Crown lands were more extensive than they had ever been. Efficient management, a thrifty nature and good fortune meant that the annual income from Crown lands had increased from £29,000 in 1485 to £42,000 in 1509.

In Henry's first Parliament of 1486 an Act of Resumption was passed in which the Crown recovered all properties granted away since 1455. However, having stated his claim, he did not take back all the estates involved because he did not wish to antagonise the majority of noble families affected by the Act. Henry knew that if he was to consolidate the dynasty he must try to gain the support of the nobility by showing them he was prepared to compromise.

The most valuable of Henry's Crown lands was the Duchy of Lancaster. It had its own organisation, centred on its chancellor, and had adopted new methods of estate management. At the beginning of Henry's reign it brought in £650 a year to the Chamber, but by 1509 this had increased tenfold (to nearly £7000) under the skilful management of Sir Reginald Bray (see opposite).

Customs duties

By 1509 the revenue derived from customs duties had been overtaken by the revenue from Crown lands. However, customs duties were still providing a third of the Crown's ordinary revenue. Henry tried to block many of the loopholes in the custom system. For example, from 1487 merchants involved in coastal trading, shipping merchandise from one English port to another, were required to produce a certificate from the first port specifying the duties paid. In 1496 he tried to reduce some of the privileges enjoyed by foreign merchants, for example, immunity from English taxation. Twice during his reign he updated the **Book of Rates** of customs duties to be paid in London.

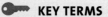

KEY TERMS

Escheat When a landholder died without heirs, his lands passed by right to the king.

Book of Rates An account book recording the rates of tax paid by foreign merchants on goods imported and sold in England.

Despite Henry's efforts income from customs did not greatly increase. The average annual receipts were about £33,000 for the first ten years of the reign and about £40,000 thereafter. Smuggling seems to have continued, in spite of stricter control, and even Henry could not manipulate international trade, which was dependent on the fragile and changing relationships between all the European powers.

Feudal dues

Henry was determined to enforce these traditional rights to the full and to extract the maximum income possible from them. Initially, the proceeds from wardship and marriage were small, amounting to only £350 in 1487, but after 1503 a new officer (the Master of the King's Wards) was appointed to supervise them, and by 1507 the annual income had risen to £6000.

Profits of justice

Legal fines made a significant contribution to Henry's income because he ensured that most criminal acts, including treason, were punished by fines rather than by imprisonment or execution. This brought him much more profit, as happened with his treatment of the rebels after the insurrection in Cornwall in 1497. Another type of fine that the king used as punishment against opponents was that of attainder. Sir William Stanley paid the Crown £9000 in cash (in income from his lands) and £1000 per annum in this way after his treason in 1495. There was only one Parliament during the reign which omitted to pass any attainders and the highest number in any session was 51.

Table 2.2 Attainders passed during the reigns of Edward IV, Richard III and Henry VII. Which king can be charged with the excessive use of attainders?

Attainders	Number
Passed by Edward IV	140
Reversed	42
Passed by Richard III	100
Reversed	1
Reversed by Henry VII directly after Bosworth	99
Passed by Henry VII	138
Reversed	46

Extraordinary revenue

Extraordinary revenue was money which came to the Crown on particular occasions and, therefore, with no regularity.

Parliamentary grants

Henry was cautious in his demands from Parliament. However, he did request financial assistance in 1487 to pay for the Battle of Stoke, in 1489 to go to war against the French, and in 1496 to defend the throne against attack from the

Scots and Perkin Warbeck. Historians have accused Henry of cheating his subjects by raising money for wars that never actually took place, as in 1496. However, it could be argued that the money was still needed in the event of a Scottish attack some time in the future. In the event, there was no further trouble from Scotland, but some of the money was used to suppress the Cornish rebellion.

Loans and benevolences

In 1496 Henry was desperate for extra cash to defeat Warbeck and the Scots. He appealed to his landholding subjects for financial support. Such requests were virtually impossible to decline, even though they were traditionally in the form of 'agreements'. Henry seems to have asked for only modest sums, around £10,000, and there is no evidence of any resentment, probably as most of the loans appear to have been repaid. In truth, Henry had little choice but to repay them because those subjects who were owed money by the king were more likely to support a rival claimant to the throne.

In 1491 Henry raised a forced loan when he intended to take his army across the Channel to protect Brittany from French aggression; this produced £48,500, a considerable amount when compared with the sums yielded by direct taxation. Royal Commissioners were stringent in its collection.

SOURCE C

Adapted from an extract of a letter sent by the king to Sir Henry Vernon requesting a loan, 1492. Vernon of Haddon Hall was one of the most wealthy and powerful landowners in Derbyshire.

Letting you know that from our spies we understand that our enemies of France prepare themselves to do all the hurt and annoyance that they can. For the defence of our realm and subjects we desire and heartily pray you that you will lend unto us the sum of £100 and to send it to our Treasurer of England by some trusty servants of yours.

> Study Source C. How does the king justify his request for a loan?

Clerical taxes

Henry received quite substantial sums from the Church. On several occasions, usually when Parliament made a grant, the **Convocations** followed suit with their own contributions. In 1489 they voted £25,000 towards the cost of the French war.

Henry also made money from **simony**, charging £300 for the Archdeaconry of Buckingham on one occasion. Like many of his predecessors, the king kept bishoprics vacant for many months before making new appointments so that he could pocket the revenue in the meantime. Owing to a rash of deaths among the bishops in the final years of his reign, Henry received over £6000 a year in this way. However, he did not exploit this method as much as some of his contemporaries: Henry rarely left a diocese without a bishop for more than twelve months.

🔑 KEY TERMS

Convocation Church equivalent of Parliament where clerics meet in two houses – upper house of senior clerics and lower house representing parish priests – to discuss and transact Church affairs.

Simony The selling of Church appointments and offices.

Feudal obligations

Another type of extraordinary revenue was connected with feudal obligations. As the chief feudal lord, the king had the right to demand feudal aid on special occasions, such as the knighting of his eldest son, the marriage of his eldest daughter, and his own ransom if he were ever captured in war, a fate which Henry avoided. He was also able to levy distraint of knighthood, the medieval practice of forcing those with an annual income of £40 or more to become a mounted knight to fight for the king in time of war.

The French pension

As part of the Treaty of Étaples in 1492 Henry negotiated a pension from the king of France. The pension was a bribe offered by the French king so that the English armies would be removed from French soil. Henry was promised £159,000 to compensate him for the cost of the war, a sum to be paid in annual amounts of about £5000.

Bonds and recognisances

In general terms, bonds and recognisances meant the practice of subjects paying a sum of money to the Crown as a guarantee of their future good behaviour. However, there was a subtle difference between the two:

- Bonds were written obligations in which people promised to perform some specific action on pain of paying money if they failed to carry out their promise. Bonds had long been used as a condition for the appointment of officials, particularly customs staff, but in the later fifteenth century their use was extended to private individuals as a way of keeping the peace and ensuring loyalty to the government.
- Recognisances were formal acknowledgements of actual debts or other obligations that already existed. Under Henry, recognisances became the normal way of ensuring payment of legal debts owed to the Crown. Such was Henry's personal interest in these matters that none was issued without his explicit agreement. Almost immediately after Bosworth, he demanded a recognisance of £10,000 from Viscount Beaumont of Powicke and a similar sum from the Earl of Westmorland as guarantees of their loyalty in the future.

Most of these commitments entered into with the king were for routine transactions, such as those with merchants who postponed payment of customs duties. Others were somewhat dubious, for example, recognisances to cover the release of criminals from prison or for the pardon of murderers. At its best, and certainly in those early insecure years of his reign, this financial screw was an effective way of restoring law and order and the evidence shows that, in most cases, it brought in the revenue Henry wanted.

Henry's use of bonds and recognisances

In the first decade of the kingship 191 bonds were collected, rising to well over 200 in the later years of his reign. This is reflected by the fact that the receipts from bonds rose from £3000 in 1493 to £35,000 in 1505. Those who fell behind in these payments were hounded by the king's officials, particularly those from the Council Learned in the Law, which was made responsible for bonds and recognisances. The Council became greatly feared because of the efficiency of two of its officials, Richard Empson and Edmund Dudley, in pursuing defaulters. Indeed, after Dudley's arrival, the records of the council trebled.

It has been calculated that out of 62 noble families in existence during Henry's reign, 46 were at one time or another financially at his mercy: seven were under attainder, 36 were bound by recognisances or obligations, and three by other means. It is such evidence that has earned for Henry a reputation for cynicism and greed.

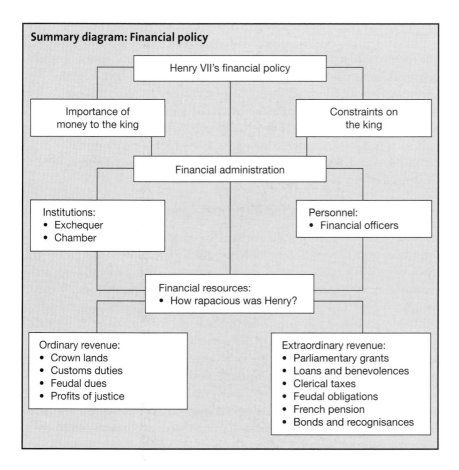

Summary diagram: Financial policy

- Henry VII's financial policy
  - Importance of money to the king
  - Constraints on the king
- Financial administration
  - Institutions:
    - Exchequer
    - Chamber
  - Personnel:
    - Financial officers
- Financial resources:
  - How rapacious was Henry?
  - Ordinary revenue:
    - Crown lands
    - Customs duties
    - Feudal dues
    - Profits of justice
  - Extraordinary revenue:
    - Parliamentary grants
    - Loans and benevolences
    - Clerical taxes
    - Feudal obligations
    - French pension
    - Bonds and recognisances

③ Key debate

▶ *What was the 'New Monarchy' theory and why did it lead to so much debate among historians?*

The nature of the restored monarchy after the Wars of the Roses was once hotly debated. The debate began with the publication, in 1874, of J.R. Green's *Short History of England,* in which he first outlined his theory of a 'New Monarchy'. The core of his thesis is that the period between 1471 and 1509 witnessed the creation of a new kind of monarchical authority. In Green's opinion, Edward IV and Henry VII (Richard III is largely overlooked owing to the brevity of his reign) were responsible for the restoration and centralisation of monarchical power, which was so thorough that it developed into despotism. In Green's view, the autocratic nature of this 'New Monarchy' was necessary because the image, status and authority of kingship had been tarnished during 30 years of civil and dynastic strife. In short, the dignity and power of monarchy required urgent restoration.

The controversial nature of his theory naturally attracted the attention of other historians, some of whom were especially critical. Two years later, in 1876, J.S. Brewer wrote a critical article in which he dismissed Green's thesis as 'leftist, revolutionary, and highly dangerous reading for younger people'. Not all historians were as critical of Green, although even those who supported him, such as A.F. Pollard, did so by seeking to modify his theory. As the debate developed, Pollard's modifications to the 'New Monarchy' theory were challenged by revisionist historians.

Pollard's 'New Monarchy' interpretation

Inspired by Green's theory, Pollard refined the interpretation by shifting his focus away from Edward IV towards Henry VII. Pollard believed that Henry VII innovated a whole new concept of monarchy that sought to establish peace and security after the disastrous Wars of the Roses. In basic terms the 'new dynasty' brought with it a 'new monarchy' and this new style of organised, centralised and tightly controlled government saw the promotion of 'new men'. These 'new men' were drawn from the ranks of the gentry and the professional classes (especially lawyers) who became the king's chief advisers and filled the offices of central government. By employing these 'new men' the king was seeking to rely less on the nobility, if not to deliberately undermine their power. By working alongside these men Henry succeeded in doing what his Yorkist predecessors had apparently failed to do, namely, deal with the serious problems arising out of the dynastic civil wars that had raged since 1455: widespread lawlessness and disorder, aristocratic oppression and 'livery and maintenance'. To support their arguments, the 'New Monarchy' theorists pointed out how peaceful, solvent and well governed the country was after 1485 compared to what had gone before.

EXTRACT 1

From A.F. Pollard, *The History of England: A Study in Political Evolution*, Williams & Norgate, 1912, pp. 88–9.

National states were forming; the state which could best adapt itself to these changed and changing conditions would outdistance its rivals; and its capacity to adapt itself to them would largely depend on the strength and flexibility of its national organization. It was the achievement of the New Monarchy to fashion this organization, and to rescue the country from an anarchy which had already given other powers the start in the race and promised little success for England. Henry VII had to begin in a quiet, unostentatious way with very scanty materials. With a bad title and many pretenders, with an evil heritage of social disorder, he must have been sorely tempted to indulge in the heroics of Henry V. He followed a sounder business policy, and his reign is dull, because he gave peace and prosperity at home without fighting a battle abroad. He left to his son, Henry VIII, a stable throne and a united kingdom.

The revisionist interpretation

The case put forward by Green and refined by Pollard was compelling and influential until challenged in the 1950s. It was inevitable that a new generation of historians would seek to challenge and revise the 'New Monarchy' theory. Among the first to challenge the 'New Monarchy' theory was G.R. Elton, who rejected the use of the term 'New Monarchy' but not the theory. He simply moved the idea of a restoration of monarchical power forward to the reign of Henry VIII, which he claimed witnessed an altogether more thorough reform of government. This was his 'revolution in government' theory, which was even more controversial than Green and Pollard's 'New Monarchy'. Elton did, at least, concede that the revolution in government undertaken by Henry VIII and his chief minister, Thomas Cromwell, owed something to the work of Henry VII, who restored the power of the Crown and stabilised the kingdom (see pages 11–19).

EXTRACT 2

From G.R. Elton, *The Tudor Revolution in Government*, Cambridge University Press, 1953, p. 424.

The true driving force of government continued to be with the king in person and the men who immediately surrounded him. The restoration of good government by the Yorkists, Henry VII and Wolsey, employing as they did the old methods of elastic household system proved that point. But the reforms of the 1530's did more than improve details of old practice. They cast off the central principle of centuries and introduced a new one. When an administration relying on the household was replaced by one based exclusively on bureaucratic departments and officers of state, a revolution took place in government.

Post-revisionist interpretation

Critics of Elton rejected the notion of a 'revolution' in government and upheld the idea of a 'New Monarchy' but the debate continued as to what this meant. In 1964 S.B. Chrimes stated that 'The foundations of what has commonly been called the "New Monarchy" were laid not by Henry VII but by Edward IV.' Thus, the term still had currency, as evidenced by the publication of Anthony Goodman's book in the late 1980s, *The New Monarchy: England 1471–1534*. In the mid-1990s A.J. Pollard, too, explored the theme of the 'New Monarchy' in which he described the period 1471–1509 as one in which 'royal authority recovered and normal politics were restored'. J.A.F. Thompson has further refined the post-revisionist interpretation.

EXTRACT 3

From J.A.F. Thompson, *The Transformation of Medieval England 1370–1529*, Routledge, 1983, p. 230.

Recent writing has played down the importance traditionally assigned to 1485 as a turning point in English history, and it has been shown that many of the methods of government employed in the early Tudor period had been foreshadowed under Edward IV. Indeed, it is fair to say that Henry VII's approach to government was strongly traditional. The search of historians for a 'New Monarchy' or a 'more modern' form of kingship, whether of the Yorkists or the Tudors, is in that sense the pursuit of a myth. In political terms, however, there is some justification in regarding Henry VII's accession as the start of a new epoch, because the dynastic change brought with it in the long run a more securely based royal authority than had previously existed.

? In what sense, if any, according to Extracts 1–3, did Henry VII found a 'New Monarchy' in England?

4 Foreign policy

▶ *What were Henry's aims in foreign policy and how successful was he in achieving them?*

Henry's aims

Polydore Vergil wrote that Henry was 'more inclined to peace than to war'. Henry's vulnerable position in dynastic and financial terms made non-intervention on the Continent the logical approach. Henry's foreign policy was very obviously subordinated to his domestic policies of enriching the monarchy and ensuring the obedience of his subjects. Dynastic threats dominated his dealings with foreign rulers, which is why the issue of security lay at the heart of the treaties he concluded with France, Spain, Scotland and Brittany.

Consequently, Henry's aim in foreign policy was defensive because of the nature of his succession. As we have seen, there were several claimants to his throne who successfully sought aid from foreign powers, and Henry had to be constantly on his guard against possible invasion. The most vulnerable border was the northern one with Scotland; as Pope Sixtus V remarked, England was 'only half an island'. Scotland was traditionally the back door into England, and one with which the French were particularly familiar. However, Henry could not afford to ignore Wales, through which his own armed invasion had come, or Ireland, which was volatile and prone to challenging the authority of the English Crown.

Consolidating support

In the first three years of his reign (1485–8) Henry's actions in foreign affairs were deliberately designed to give him time to consolidate support. He had to ensure he had at least nominal support abroad if he was to secure his throne at home. As France had helped to finance the expedition which had led directly to Bosworth, he seized the opportunity to maintain good relations with England's traditional enemy. He immediately negotiated a one-year truce with France which was subsequently extended to January 1489. The Scots were inclined to be more favourably disposed towards Henry's regime than those of his predecessors. In July 1486 he succeeded in persuading James III to agree to a three-year truce. The assassination of James III in 1488 and the accession of the fifteen-year-old James IV meant that, for a short while at least, Henry had little to fear from across the border. However, Henry was wise enough to keep his contacts at the Scottish Court in case of future aggression.

In spite of the truce with France, in July 1486 Henry negotiated a commercial treaty with Brittany, the other country to offer him hospitality during the long years in exile. Finally, in January 1487 he concluded a treaty with Maximilian, king of the Romans, the heir to the Holy Roman Emperor, for one year. So Henry had done his best to ensure that he would not suffer invasion from his principal foreign rivals while he was securing his throne at home. For the time being at least, he was fairly confident that they would not offer assistance to the other claimants to the throne. Perhaps most importantly for Henry, these treaties revealed that he was accepted as king of England by his European counterparts and that they expected him to remain so.

Problems caused by the Simnel rising

It was the pretender, Lambert Simnel, who led Henry to play a more active role in foreign affairs than he had originally intended. Simnel caused various diplomatic problems because he received support from Ireland and Burgundy. Whereas Irish antagonism was not unusual, that of Burgundy was. Throughout the Hundred Years' War against France, Burgundy had been England's main ally. It was also the main outlet for the sale of English cloth. However, Margaret, the Dowager Duchess of Burgundy, the sister of Edward IV, had supported the Yorkists in the recent civil war and was only too willing to provide 2000 mercenaries for Simnel's cause. Fortunately for Henry, other support for Simnel

officially part of France. It seemed that Henry had to choose between attempting to liberate Brittany by conquering France, as Henry V had tried, or leaving Brittany to its fate while obtaining the best terms he could for himself.

France and the Treaty of Étaples 1492

With the loss of Brittany seemingly imminent in 1491, Henry announced his intention to assert his claim to the French Crown and sent commissioners to collect a forced loan. In October he summoned a Parliament which made a formal grant of two subsidies. Having spent the year preparing for the invasion of France, the English army, an imposing force of 26,000 men, crossed the Channel in October 1492 and laid siege to Boulogne.

Fortunately, Charles was eager to be rid of his English aggressor because greater glory was to be won in Italy; so nine days after Henry had set foot on French soil Charles offered peace and on 3 November the Treaty of Étaples was concluded. Charles's only concerns were to keep Brittany and to get rid of Henry. Therefore, he promised to give no further aid to English rebels, particularly Warbeck, and to pay most of Henry's costs of intervening in Brittany. This totalled 745,000 gold crowns, payable at the rate of 50,000 crowns a year. In contemporary English currency this equalled about £5000, approximately five per cent of the king's annual income.

Henry had not won a glorious victory, for the independence of Brittany was gone forever and the whole of the southern side of the Channel, apart from Calais, was now in French hands. However, the outcome had not been a complete failure. He had prevented Charles VIII from helping Perkin Warbeck and he had secured a sizeable annual pension from the French. While contending with French aggression he had made a valuable alliance with Spain and had also shown that England under a Tudor king could not be completely overlooked in Continental affairs. Perhaps it would be unreasonable to expect Henry to have achieved more, given the situation in which he found himself.

Spain and the Treaty of Medina del Campo 1489

The most significant achievement of Henry VII's foreign policy was the alliance negotiated with Spain in the Treaty of Medina del Campo, signed in March 1489. Spain had emerged as a major power in the late fifteenth century after the unification of the country in 1479. Initially, England and Spain were commercial rivals, but both were willing to sink their differences in a common animosity towards France.

Early in 1488 Henry suggested a marriage between his eldest son, Prince Arthur, and Ferdinand and Isabella's youngest daughter, Catherine of Aragon, when they reached marriageable age. Catherine, then aged three, was six months older than her intended husband! The negotiations were laborious as both fathers wanted to secure the best possible terms. Finally, Ferdinand agreed to Henry's demands about the size of Catherine's **dowry** and promised not to help any English rebels.

The fact that the Tudor dynasty had been recognised as an equal by one of the leading royal families of Europe was of major importance to a usurper who was desperately keen to secure international recognition of the legitimacy of his position as king.

The Holy League and *Magnus Intercursus* 1496

This marked the beginning of Henry's most successful period (1496–1502) in diplomatic affairs. Initially this was a result of Charles VIII's successes in Italy. The other European rulers feared that France was becoming too powerful and in 1495 the Pope, Ferdinand, Maximilian, Venice and Milan formed the **League of Venice** with the aim of driving Charles out of Italy. England was not included because the theatre of conflict was outside the country's usual sphere of interest, but by 1496 Ferdinand had realised that it might be dangerous to exclude England. Perhaps he suspected that Henry wished to preserve good relations with France and was fearful of losing England's goodwill to the French. Certainly Charles appeared to be ingratiating himself with Henry by offering assistance against Warbeck.

In October 1496 Ferdinand and Henry concluded a further agreement for the marriage of Catherine and Arthur. Also in the same year Ferdinand secured England's entry into the revamped League of Venice, now called the Holy League. However, Henry showed that he was no one's puppet by joining the League only on condition that England was not bound to go to war against France. To Henry's credit he also managed to make a commercial treaty with France while maintaining good relations with his allies in the League. So 1496 was a successful year for Henry, particularly as he also concluded the *Magnus Intercursus* (Great Treaty), the basis on which good trading relations were resumed between England and Burgundy.

Problems caused by the Warbeck rising

The significance of Warbeck's career to Henry in the field of foreign affairs was that he involved other rulers in England's dynastic problem. Warbeck received support at different times from Ireland, France, Burgundy and Scotland. This greatly complicated Henry's foreign policy. This was particularly evident over the treaty with Spain as Ferdinand and Isabella did not wish their daughter to marry the heir to an insecure crown. A further example was in 1493 when Henry went as far as disrupting England's cloth trade by placing a temporary **embargo** on commercial dealings with the Netherlands because Philip and Margaret were offering Warbeck aid. It also highlighted the long-term problem of possible invasion of England via Scotland. It came as something of a relief to Henry when, in 1497, Warbeck was finally captured and peace was made with Scotland.

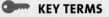

KEY TERMS

Dowry Money or property paid by the bride's father to the groom's family on his daughter's marriage.

League of Venice Diplomatic and military organisation formed by the Italian states to resist the French conquest of Italy.

Embargo The prohibition of commerce and trade with a particular country.

Scotland and the Truce of Ayton 1497

Relations between Scotland and England were always tense, with the Scots taking any opportunity to cross the border and cause problems for their overlord, the king of England. The kings of Scotland traditionally owed allegiance to the English kings, although they resented this and were always looking for ways to avoid it. James IV of Scotland was no exception to the rule and, despite a truce made with Henry when he came to the throne in 1488, he took Perkin Warbeck into his favour when he arrived in Scotland in 1495. He even went as far as to give Warbeck his cousin in marriage, which appeared extremely threatening to Henry. However, Warbeck's invasion of England with Scottish help came to nothing; he gained no support south of the border and, when the Scots heard that Henry was sending an army to oppose them, they took flight.

For Henry the situation was made worse by the simultaneous outbreak of a rebellion in Cornwall. The people resented having to pay for an invasion which was unlikely to affect them. Fortunately for Henry, James IV was losing faith in Warbeck and did not take advantage of this rebellion to launch another attack of his own. Henry was now able to offer terms on which a treaty with Scotland could be based. The Truce of Ayton was concluded in 1497, but it was not until Warbeck had been executed that it became a full treaty of peace. The treaty was sealed by the marriage of James to Margaret, Henry's eldest daughter, in August 1503. However, Scotland did not abandon her ancient pact with France; this meant that the peace depended on the continuation of good relations between England and France, but while Henry lived this did not pose a problem.

Marriage of Prince Arthur and Catherine of Aragon 1501

Another of Henry's diplomatic marriage alliances was also achieved in this period. In October 1501 Catherine of Aragon arrived in England with 100,000 crowns of her dowry. On 14 November she and Arthur were married in St Paul's Cathedral in London. This alliance was now of even greater significance than when it had originally been mooted. Not only did Henry hope that England would play a part in the growing Spanish empire in the New World, but the marriage of Catherine's sister, Joanna, to Philip of Burgundy united the two states and provided the possibility of another ally for Henry if he were to need one. The two marriage alliances were the pinnacle of Henry's success in his foreign policy.

The deaths of Prince Arthur, Queen Elizabeth and Isabella of Spain

This final period of Henry's foreign policy was marred by dynastic upsets and changes in Europe that acted against England's interests.

Death of Prince Arthur

The major blow to Henry's policy was the sudden death of Prince Arthur at Ludlow in April 1502, only five months after his wedding. It seemed that Henry's dynastic hopes had been shattered, but within five weeks of Arthur's death Ferdinand and Isabella were instructing their ambassador to conclude a marriage with Prince Henry, the new heir to the throne, and to settle the terms of the dowry. A formal treaty was confirmed in September 1502, but it recognised that a dispensation would be needed from the Pope because Catherine was considered to be too closely related to Henry (see page 7) because of her marriage to Arthur. The required papal document arrived in 1504.

Death of Queen Elizabeth

In February 1503 Henry suffered another personal loss when Queen Elizabeth died shortly after giving birth to a daughter. This provoked new dynastic worries. Two of Henry's three sons were already dead, and with the death of his wife he had no hope of more children to come. As if to emphasise Henry's vulnerable position, Edmund de la Pole chose this time to flee abroad. Henry began to consider the possibility of taking a second wife who might be able to bear him more heirs; he seems to have sought the hand of Joanna of Naples, Margaret of Savoy and Joanna of Castile and Burgundy in turn. The once-popular idea that he intended to marry his daughter-in-law, Catherine of Aragon, can be dismissed as it is not based on any firm evidence. His first choice in 1504 seems to have been the young widow, Queen Joanna of Naples, the niece of Ferdinand of Aragon. This match was encouraged by Spain because Ferdinand was keen to strengthen his links with England as his relations with France were worsening. However, this possibility came to nothing because of a third significant death, that of Isabella of Castile, later in 1504.

SOURCE D

Queen Isabella writing in a letter to Duke de Estrada, the Spanish ambassador in England, 1502, quoted in *Calendar of State Papers, Spain*, Volume 1, 1485–1509. Originally published by Her Majesty's Stationery Office, 1862, pp. 274–6.

It is vital that there should be no delay in making an agreement for the marriage of the Princess of Wales, our daughter, to the new Prince of Wales. This is now even more urgent since we hear that the King of France is trying to stop the marriage.

After the marriage, our anxiety will cease and we will be able to get England's help in our war against France. Let King Henry know that the King of France is sending a force against us. Henry knows that, under the terms of the treaty signed between us, England and Spain agree to defend each other's possessions. So try to get King Henry to take part in our war with France. Tell him that we will never have such a good chance again of recovering his territories in France.

Study Source D. Why was Queen Isabella so keen on the marriage of her daughter Catherine to Henry VII's son Arthur?

Death of Queen Isabella

Queen Isabella's death did not just mean that Henry and Ferdinand were now rivals in the matrimonial stakes, it also threw into question the continued unity of Spain because of the position of Castile. Joanna was her mother's heir to the kingdom, so the unity of Spain could only be preserved if she allowed her father to act as regent on her behalf. However, Joanna's husband, Philip of Burgundy, dazzled by the prospect of a crown to add to his other titles, forced her to take up her inheritance immediately. It therefore appeared to Henry that his major ally might be reduced in status from king of the whole of Spain to that of Aragon only. In addition, his two allies, Spain and Burgundy, on whom he depended in case of enmity from France, were now rivals. Henry had to struggle hard to ensure that he lost the support of neither. This explains why in the last few years of his life his foreign policy was subject to sudden changes of direction in a way that it had never been before.

Relations with Burgundy

In 1505 Henry attempted to establish more amicable relations with Philip in case of a possible break with France. He also wanted to ensure better trading links with Antwerp and to persuade Philip to surrender the Earl of Suffolk (see page 18). Friendship with Philip at this time automatically made relations with Ferdinand more difficult, particularly after Henry had lent Philip money to finance his expedition to claim the throne of Castile. Henry also considered marrying Margaret of Savoy but she rejected his proposal. As the daughter of Maximilian and sister of Philip, Henry's marriage with Margaret would have jeopardised the prospective marriage of Prince Henry and Catherine of Aragon. Henry further antagonised Ferdinand by keeping the Princess's dowry, despite her father's requests to complete the marriage settlement or return the bride and her dowry to Spain. The young prince was even persuaded to formally protest that a marriage with the widow of his brother was against his conscience.

Henry now began to seek a French or a Burgundian (see the map on page 51) bride for his son. In 1506 Philip was forced to take shelter at the English court because of storms and Henry seized this opportunity to negotiate a treaty with him. This stated that Suffolk should be handed over to the English and that Henry would marry Philip's sister. Isolated, Ferdinand sought an agreement with France, as Louis XII was glad to see the union between Spain and the Netherlands shattered. This was cemented in October 1505 when Ferdinand married Germaine de Foix, Louis' niece.

The diplomatic scene was completely altered in September 1506 when Philip of Burgundy died. Henry's diplomacy had to alter direction rapidly to keep pace with these changes. Fearing that France would seize on the weakness of the Netherlands to take lands there, Henry repaired his relationship with Ferdinand and strengthened relations with Maximilian. By 1508 Henry had achieved a measure of stability in his foreign relations and his position on the throne was now secure from foreign intervention.

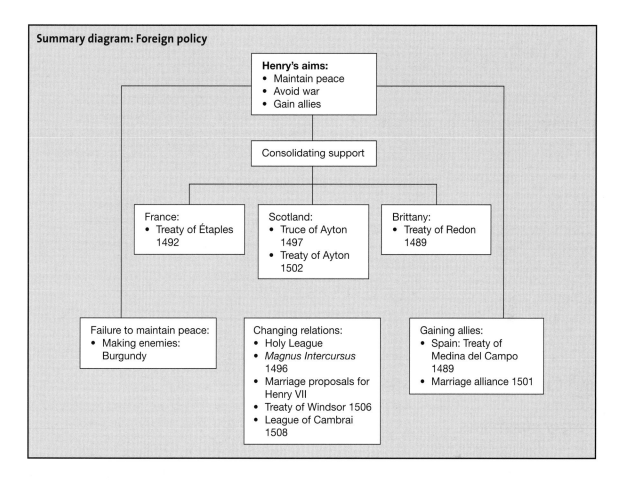

Summary diagram: Foreign policy

Henry's aims:
- Maintain peace
- Avoid war
- Gain allies

Consolidating support

France:
- Treaty of Étaples 1492

Scotland:
- Truce of Ayton 1497
- Treaty of Ayton 1502

Brittany:
- Treaty of Redon 1489

Failure to maintain peace:
- Making enemies: Burgundy

Changing relations:
- Holy League
- *Magnus Intercursus* 1496
- Marriage proposals for Henry VII
- Treaty of Windsor 1506
- League of Cambrai 1508

Gaining allies:
- Spain: Treaty of Medina del Campo 1489
- Marriage alliance 1501

Chapter summary

In order to secure his position on the throne Henry VII pursued a policy of 'good governance'. To achieve this he sought to overhaul the government's administration by increasing its efficiency. He used Parliament sparingly but effectively, ensuring that it did his bidding in passing attainders against rebels, granting subsidies and passing laws such as those against retaining. Henry was especially determined to make the Crown solvent in the hope that financial security would help him to consolidate his power. He was helped in his quest to improve the government by the men of talent he promoted to positions of power such as Sir Reginald Bray, Sir Richard Empson and Sir Edward Poynings. The Crown ensured that its power was felt in the furthest corners of the kingdom including Wales and Ireland. Henry's foreign policy was designed to support his kingship and secure his dynasty, which is why he pursued a policy marked more by diplomacy than by war. Apart from one limited Continental campaign, Henry spent most of his time at the negotiating table agreeing the terms of several important treaties with nations such as France, Spain, Brittany and the Holy Roman Empire.

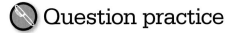

Refresher questions

Use these questions to remind yourself of the key material covered in this chapter.

1 What was the King's Council and how effective was it?

2 Who were the key men in Henry's government?

3 What was the Council Learned in the Law?

4 How effective was Henry's government of Wales and Ireland?

5 Why did Henry feel it was important to extend the power of the Crown into the localities?

6 How far did Henry allow magnates to build up power in the localities?

7 Why did Henry call so few Parliaments?

8 Why did Henry consider it so important to improve the Crown's financial position?

9 What were the main financial institutions?

10 How successfully did Henry exploit the different forms of revenue available to him?

11 Did Henry cynically exploit bonds and recognisances?

12 What were Henry's aims in foreign policy?

13 Why did Henry conclude a treaty with Brittany?

14 Why was the Treaty of Medina del Campo so significant?

15 How successful was Henry's diplomacy during this period?

Question practice

ESSAY QUESTIONS

1 'Henry VII considered it highly important to improve the Kingdom's finances so that he could secure his claim to the throne.' Explain why you agree or disagree with this view.

2 'Henry's greatest success as king was in establishing a "New Monarchy".' Assess the validity of this view.

3 How far can Henry VII be credited with the successful government and administration of England?

4 To what extent had Henry VII succeeded in securing the dynasty by 1509?

CHAPTER 3

Henry VIII: Wolsey, government and the king's 'great matter' 1509–30

This chapter is intended to help you to understand why historians find Henry VIII and the momentous events of his reign so fascinating. It explores Henry's character, his thinking and how this impacted on events during his reign. It explains how Henry VIII and his chief minister, Thomas Wolsey, contributed to developments in government, foreign policy and religion. The rise and fall of Wolsey is examined, as are the problems faced by the king and his government due to political and religious change. These issues are examined as three key themes:

★ Henry VIII: character and aims

★ Wolsey: politics, government and foreign policy

★ The fall of Wolsey

Key dates

1509	Accession of Henry VIII		**1520**	The Field of the Cloth of Gold
	Henry married Catherine of Aragon			Pope awarded Henry VIII the title of 'Defender of the Faith'
1514	Wolsey became the king's chief minister			
1515	Wolsey appointed Lord Chancellor and made a cardinal		**1522**	The general proscription
			1526	Eltham Ordinances
1516	Henry's daughter Mary born		**1529**	Wolsey removed from power
1518	Wolsey appointed papal legate		**1530**	Wolsey died at Leicester while being taken under arrest to London
	Treaty of London (also known as the Treaty of Universal Peace)			

1 Henry VIII: character and aims

▶ *What were Henry VIII's personal attributes and qualities?*

Character and personality of the king

On 21 April 1509 Henry VIII became king of England. The succession passed without either incident or challenge. Although Henry was not yet eighteen (the age of majority was 21) his minority did not require the appointment of a **regent** or lord protector. In fact, from the very beginning of his reign, Henry was to demonstrate those qualities of decisiveness and ruthlessness that were to mark his kingship. Within days of his father's death, Henry announced his decision to

🔑 **KEY TERM**

Regent A member of the royal family who governs on behalf of the reigning monarch.

KEY TERM

Treason The act of betraying one's monarch and country.

honour his pledge to marry Catherine of Aragon. At the same time he ruthlessly disposed of his father's chief financial agents, the unpopular Sir Richard Empson and Edmund Dudley, who were tried and executed for **treason**.

Henry was certainly vain, which may explain, in part, why Empson and Dudley were used as scapegoats for the most unpopular aspects of his late father's policies, while marriage would demonstrate his fidelity, excite his subjects and strengthen his dynasty. The contrast between the aged Henry VII and his youthful successor could hardly have been more pronounced, which is why many commentators saw the change of monarch as a dawning of a new age.

SOURCE A

Study Source A. Why might the Venetian government have found this report useful?

This description of Henry VIII by the Venetian ambassador was sent to his government in Venice, 1515. Quoted in *Calendar of State Papers Relating To English Affairs in the Archives of Venice*, Volume 2, 1509–1519. Originally published by Her Majesty's Stationery Office, 1867, pp. 228–31.

After dinner, we were taken to the King [Henry VIII], who embraced us, without ceremony, and conversed for a very long while very familiarly, on various topics, in good Latin and in French, which he speaks very well indeed, and he then dismissed us, and we were brought back here to London …

Believe me, he is in every respect a most accomplished Prince; and I, who have now seen all the sovereigns in Christendom, and last of all these two of France and England in such great state, might well rest content.

Henry the man: strong or weak?

These actions so early in the reign suggest that Henry was a strong character whose behaviour bordered on the arrogant. On the other hand, they may also reveal a certain weakness in his personality for in both cases his aim appears to have been to court and enhance his popularity. This apparent contradiction has caused historians to disagree about what sort of man Henry was. The controversy has been over whether he was essentially strong or generally weak; whether he was the puppet or the puppeteer.

- Essentially strong: Henry was determined, self-assured and a good judge of character. He was the puppeteer who was responsible for appointing some of the most talented politicians and administrators of the period to lead his government: Thomas Wolsey (see page 64), Sir Thomas More (see page 113) and Thomas Cromwell (see page 90). The king was involved in policy making and the direction of government and foreign affairs followed the lines laid down by him.
- Generally weak: Henry was a ditherer and a bully and lacked a creative imagination. He was too easily manipulated by his ministers and mistresses. Henry was the puppet who did as his ministers advised. He was reactive rather than proactive in government and foreign affairs. Henry lacked vision, which meant that he did not control events: they controlled him.

Although no lasting consensus has emerged it is perhaps fair to say that the majority of the current generation of leading historians have concluded that Henry was essentially strong. Henry was human; he made mistakes, he occasionally vacillated, he could be cruel and vindictive but he never lost his authority or his power to dominate people or events. It must be remembered that both Wolsey and Cromwell were promoted and demoted by Henry, who did the same to their enemies such as Thomas Howard, the Duke of Norfolk, and Stephen Gardiner, the Bishop of Winchester (see page 172). This strongly suggests that Henry was the puppeteer rather than the puppet. Of course, is it worth stressing that Henry developed from a teenager to a mature man in the course of his long reign.

A man of conviction

Henry was a man of strong convictions. He was convinced that, as king, he had a divine right to rule and that to question his judgement was akin to questioning God. He believed strongly that all that he did was done with God's approval. He was observantly pious but was not deeply spiritual, being more practical and flexible in his religious belief. Henry was chivalrous and he adhered to a strict code and concept of honour that remained unchanged throughout his life.

Henry VIII's aims

Henry's reign was dominated by two key aims: securing the French crown and ensuring the succession. Both would develop into obsessions that came to dictate and shape Henry's actions.

The French crown

Unlike his father, Henry did not have to worry unduly about rival claims to his throne, nor did he have to worry about establishing the dynasty. Secure in his position as king, Henry pursued more chivalric, if indulgent, aims such as success on the battlefield and the conquest of France. Inspired by the exploits of his boyhood hero, Henry V, Henry VIII wished to emulate the English victory at Agincourt by leading a military expedition to claim what he believed to be his birthright, the French crown. Henry pursued this aim throughout his reign, confronting the French in three separate campaigns, in 1512–14, 1523–5 and 1543–6. Although Henry scored some notable successes such as victory at the Battle of the Spurs in 1513 and the taking of Boulogne in 1544, he failed to conquer France.

The succession

Henry's French obsession was overtaken, if not completely discarded, by his concern over the succession. By the late 1520s Henry had been married for over fifteen years and during this time he had fathered a daughter, Mary. His wife, Catherine of Aragon, was six years his senior and the prospect of her giving birth to a healthy son and heir diminished with each passing year. A number of miscarriages, stillbirths and infant deaths took their toll on the marriage and on

SOURCE B

Study Source B. Why might Henry VIII have commissioned this painting of himself and his father?

Henry VIII (left) and Henry VII (right): Hans Holbein's working drawing for a painting of c.1536.

Henry's mental well-being. He began to believe that his marriage to his brother's widow was cursed. Urged on by his desire to sire a healthy son he developed another obsession, the first target of which was Anne Boleyn, followed a decade later by Jane Seymour. These were young women who seemed to offer him the prospect of achieving his aim. Between 1526 and 1537 Henry ruthlessly pursued his aim, the consequences of which were to prove far reaching.

Image of a Renaissance prince

Standing over six feet (183 cm) tall, the new king was physically imposing, handsome and athletic. Henry revelled in competition and his chief interests were in jousting, tennis and hunting. His most famous portrait (reproduced on page 62) illustrates his physique and hints at the enormous pride he took in his appearance. In the courts of **Renaissance** princes, costume was an important and visible aspect of courtly magnificence, and the image projected by the king was greatly influenced by what he wore. The Venetian ambassador described Henry as being among 'the best dressed sovereign[s] in the world'. Henry wished his court to reflect his image as a Renaissance prince, a place of magnificence and munificence where scholars, artists, musicians and theologians were welcome and where they might seek the king's patronage. He continued his father's policy of spending lavishly on the court so as to underline his Renaissance credentials and impress foreign dignitaries and visitors. The politics of magnificence reached its height in 1520 with the so-called Field of the Cloth of Gold, when Henry erected a huge temporary palace near Calais, furnished with all manner of luxuries, to overawe his guest, the French king, Francis I.

Henry's interests

Henry's interests were more than just physical, they were also mental and intellectual. He embraced the ideals of the Renaissance, a cultural movement that in broad terms promoted the revival and development of classical learning in the arts, languages and sciences. Henry was well educated, sharp and inquisitive. His grandmother, Margaret Beaufort, supervised his studies and employed Cambridge scholars such as the poet John Skelton to tutor her grandson. Although Henry was proficient in Latin and French, and skilled in astronomy and mathematics, his real passion was in composing and playing music. Henry was certainly bright and able, and he surrounded himself with men of great scholastic reputation such as Sir Thomas More (see pages 111–13), Bishop John Fisher (see pages 110–11) and Archbishop Thomas Cranmer (see page 96). Henry VIII may not have been the 'universal genius' described by **Erasmus**, one of the most distinguished scholars of the day, but he was, arguably, among the most academically gifted monarchs in English history. He read widely, although claimed to find reading a chore, collected books to add to the library begun by his father, argued theology with distinguished theologians such as Erasmus and Cranmer, and debated points of law with skilled lawyers such as Cromwell and More.

 **KEY TERM**

Renaissance An intellectual and cultural movement dedicated to the rediscovery and promotion of art, architecture and letters. It promoted education and critical thinking and ranged across subjects such as politics, government, religion and classical literature. Its spread was encouraged by humanist scholars such as Erasmus.

KEY FIGURE

Erasmus (c.1466–1536)
A hugely significant figure in religious and educational thinking in Europe who played a pivotal role in the establishment of Humanism in universities. Erasmus's influence on the English episcopal and aristocratic patrons that came of age under Henry VIII was immense, especially in education.

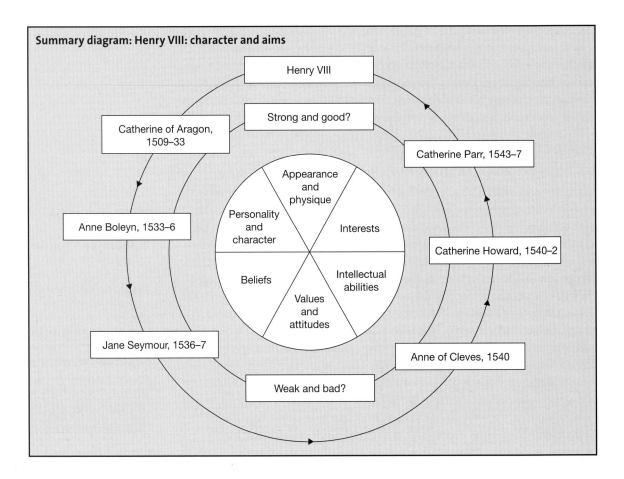

Summary diagram: Henry VIII: character and aims

Henry VIII

Strong and good?

Catherine of Aragon, 1509–33

Catherine Parr, 1543–7

Appearance and physique

Personality and character

Interests

Anne Boleyn, 1533–6

Catherine Howard, 1540–2

Beliefs

Intellectual abilities

Values and attitudes

Jane Seymour, 1536–7

Anne of Cleves, 1540

Weak and bad?

② Wolsey: politics, government and foreign policy

▶ *How significant was Wolsey's influence and impact on politics, government and foreign policy?*

Wolsey's career and rise to power

Thomas Wolsey was born the son of a butcher in Ipswich in *c.*1471. From these lowly origins he defied all the rules of social mobility by becoming the richest and most powerful man in England after the king. At the height of his influence, in the mid-1520s, his word was law and it was widely understood both at home and abroad that there was little point in attempting to secure any royal favour except through him. His court rivalled the king's in size and splendour and often outstripped it in day-to-day political importance. His palaces, especially Hampton Court and York House, were developed to be fit for a king.

The grammar school and university-educated Wolsey possessed a very fine mind and was to prove outstandingly able. He entered the Church, which he used as a vehicle for advancement knowing that his talent would enable him to forge a career. In an age of strict social hierarchy the Church, as close to a meritocracy as was possible at that time, provided opportunities for talented men of lowly origins to gain promotion and rise to positions of responsibility. Within ten years of being ordained a priest, in 1498, Wolsey had served as chaplain to Thomas Grey, Marquess of Dorset, and Sir Richard Nanfan, deputy governor of Calais, become Dean of Lincoln cathedral and, on the accession of Henry VIII, been appointed the new king's **almoner**.

Wolsey possessed the drive and confidence necessary to seize the opportunities that came his way. He did not fear failure and he was prepared to take calculated risks. In an age of patronage he was successful in attracting the support of important people such as Nanfan and Bishop **Richard Fox**; one of Henry VII's councillors. Wolsey was an interesting and attractive companion but, most important of all, he could be relied on to carry out whatever task was entrusted to him with exemplary skill and application. He thrived on hard and intensive work in an age when most people sought and found a gentle pace of life.

Royal councillor to king's chief adviser

Wolsey used the time spent working for Bishop Fox well. He gained experience of government and observed closely the working methods of royal councillors. When Henry VIII succeeded to the throne Wolsey noted that the headstrong and wilful king would, sooner or later, break free from the group of mature advisers he had inherited from his father. Whereas the experienced councillors tried to manipulate the young king into continuing his father's policies, Wolsey took advantage of the situation by giving the king the advice he wanted to hear, thus winning his approval. Wolsey was also helped by the fact that many of the leading figures from the previous reign either were removed from the scene, such as Empson and Dudley, or were pleased to seek a quieter life in political retirement, such as Archbishop William Warham and Bishop Fox. Wolsey was realistic enough to know that he would still have to prove himself worthy of the king's confidence.

Organising the French expedition

Wolsey's opportunity to prove his worth came in 1512–13. Aware of the king's desire to prove himself in war and to claim the French crown, he volunteered to organise the **expeditionary force** to France under Henry's leadership in the summer of 1513. The preparation, organisation, arming, feeding, supplying, transportation and paying of an army was a huge task and one fraught with problems. The biggest problem was in meeting the demands of a king who expected nothing less than success. Whereas more senior and experienced officials were reluctant to take on the task, fearing the consequences of failure, Wolsey embraced the challenge.

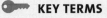 **KEY TERMS**

Almoner A priest in charge of distributing assistance or alms to the poor on behalf of the king.

Expeditionary force An army sent to fight in another country.

KEY FIGURE

Richard Fox (1448–1528)
A talented administrator and cleric who entered the service of Henry Tudor when the latter was in exile in France in 1484. After the victory at the Battle of Bosworth, Fox was promoted to the bishopric of Exeter and made a royal councillor. He became one of Henry VII's most trusted councillors and he soon entered the diplomatic service representing the king in negotiations with foreign princes. Following the accession of Henry VIII he continued to be an important member of the government but his power and influence were eclipsed by the rise of Wolsey.

SOURCE C

Study Source C. In your opinion, is the artist who painted this portrait sympathetic or hostile to Wolsey?

CARDINAL   WOLS

N.P.G. 32 THOMAS WOLSEY   P.U.

A contemporary painting of Cardinal Wolsey in his cardinal's robes by an unknown artist. Wolsey is holding a staff in his right hand and a scroll of paper in his left.

Wolsey proved to be an effective and efficient organiser. He antagonised most of those in authority, whom he either bypassed or ignored in order to achieve results, arguing that the king's wishes must take precedence over all other considerations. However, the more people complained to Henry about Wolsey's ruthlessness in getting done what was necessary, the more the king warmed to the servant who seemed able to overcome all obstacles in implementing his wishes. Henry rewarded Wolsey by appointing him, in rapid succession, Bishop of Tournai in France (particularly fitting for the man who had made its capture by Henry possible, although he was never able to make good his claim to this position), Bishop of Lincoln and Archbishop of York. The archbishopric was particularly significant because it made Wolsey the second most senior person within the Church in England. By the middle of 1514 Henry was referring almost all matters of business to Wolsey, in the certainty that they would be dealt with in the way that he desired.

Most powerful churchman in England

With the king's support Wolsey pressed on with his ambition of becoming the most powerful churchman in England. Knowing that Archbishop Warham would not make way for him to succeed to the most powerful position in the English Church, the archbishopric of Canterbury, Wolsey sought to put pressure on Pope Leo X to appoint him to a position that outranked Canterbury. Supported by Henry VIII, Wolsey orchestrated a campaign to exert pressure on the Pope to appoint him a cardinal, a position that outranked all churchmen except the Pope. Leo X succumbed to the pressure and in 1515 Cardinal Wolsey joined the ranks of the European clerical elite, becoming a 'prince of the Church'.

Lord Chancellor

As a further testimony of the king's faith in Wolsey he appointed him Lord Chancellor, the highest office of state, in place of Warham, who resigned the post. Three years later, in 1518, Wolsey was appointed to the highest category of papal representative – a ***legatus a latere* or papal legate**. This was a powerful position in which the office holder was invested with full papal powers. The **legatine powers** granted to privileged clerics like Wolsey were usually for specific purposes and for a limited period. However, by a combination of skilled diplomacy and royal influence Wolsey first obtained an extension of his legatine powers before securing the confirmation of his powers for life in 1524. This was a remarkable achievement made possible by the support offered by Henry VIII, who basked in the reflected glory of his subject and chief servant becoming one of the most powerful churchmen in the Continental Catholic Church.

Government and politics under Wolsey

Leading **humanists** throughout western Europe were arguing the case for radical changes in both the aims and the methods of government. To the majority of contemporaries, the duty of government was simply to defend the realm from attack and to maintain law and order. They did not wish or expect government to interfere in the normal course of events more than was absolutely necessary. Unlike his contemporaries, who generally seemed satisfied with his conduct in governing the kingdom, historians have been more critical of Wolsey's performance in government and politics.

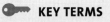 **KEY TERMS**

***Legatus a latere* or papal legate** A position normally awarded for a specific purpose so that a representative with full papal powers could be present at a decision-making occasion far distant from Rome.

Legatine powers The authority to represent and act on behalf of the Pope in England.

Humanists Scholars who question the belief systems of the Church and who embrace free thinking, culture and education.

Historians such as Stanley Bindoff and Geoffrey Elton criticised Wolsey for abusing his power and for not making much-needed reforms in either Church or State. They claim that in fifteen years' service as the king's chief minister Wolsey failed to use his considerable power and influence to reform those areas of government most in need of change, namely, the judicial system and the Crown's financial administration.

Wolsey and the judicial system

As Lord Chancellor, Wolsey was head of the judiciary. He was directly responsible both for the legal work of the King's Council and for the chief law courts, such as **Star Chamber**, **Chancery** and **Requests**. Wolsey seems genuinely to have desired to see justice better served in the kingdom by ensuring:

- That the courts were accessible to the poor. The common people stood little chance of challenging the rich and powerful in the local law courts, mainly because of the high legal fees which deterred many from pursuing cases. Thus, Wolsey often reviewed cases and if he found the complainant had been unfairly treated he transferred the case into one of his own courts, either Star Chamber or Requests, where a fresh hearing would take place. However, it is important to remember that Wolsey was determined to ensure that justice would be done. Whether rich or poor, the guilty would be punished.
- That the rich and powerful did not gain any legal advantage in the courts. The landowning class, the elites – the gentry and nobility – had long dominated proceedings in local courts either as judges or as the family and friends of those who presided over cases. With local justice firmly in the hands of the rich and powerful, Wolsey sought to ensure that the chief law courts would be fair and balanced to rich and poor alike. Court records reveal that Wolsey was not afraid to prosecute members of the nobility, especially for breaches of the laws against maintenance and affrays.

However, as historian Keith Randell (writing in 1993) has pointed out, Wolsey was 'unscrupulous in using the system to further his own interests, especially by overturning legal decisions that adversely affected him and by using the law to harry those against whom he had a grudge'.

Failure to reform the judicial system

According to S.T. Bindoff (writing in 1969), 'Wolsey's administration was a period of much promise [but] little performance.' The fact that Wolsey started a number of schemes to reform the law but failed to see them through suggests that he intended to do more than he achieved. It is important to stress that Wolsey attempted no institutional changes and he was quick to abandon his support of the commons whenever matters affected him personally or threatened his power.

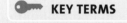 **KEY TERMS**

Court of Star Chamber Dealt with crimes such as disorder, riot, assault, fraud, corruption, municipal and trade disputes and disputes over the enclosure of land.

Court of Chancery Dealt with disputes over inheritance and wills, lands, trusts, debts, marriage settlements and apprenticeships.

Court of Requests Known as the 'poor man's court', it was intended to provide easy access for poor men and women to royal justice. Types of cases heard included title to property, forgery, perjury, forfeitures to the king and marriage contracts.

The author and historian John Stow, best known for his 1598 *Survey of London*, later commented that 'It was a strange matter to see, a man not trained up in the laws, to sit in the seat of judgement, to pronounce the law.' Wolsey's lack of training in either canon (Church) or civil law is sometimes cited as a reason to explain why he failed to reform the judicial system.

Wolsey and the financial system

It has been suggested that Wolsey's attempts to reform the king's Privy Chamber show that he tried to make permanent improvements in the system of financial administration he inherited. However, to suggest that Wolsey's interest in finance was confined to the king's household is unfair. In the opinion of John Guy, 'in the mainstream of finance Wolsey made a permanent contribution to government'. Guy believes that Wolsey innovated a more efficient system: 'the Tudor subsidy'.

The subsidy required Parliament to calculate its tax on property and income in a more accurate and realistic assessment of the wealth of individual taxpayers. In the preamble to the Subsidy Act of 1512 Wolsey justified the legislation by highlighting the necessity of devising a more efficient tax and one that could be levied 'as well in shorter time as in more easy, universal and impartial manner than the common tax of fifteenths and tenths'. The subsidy was flexible enough to accommodate changes. For example, in the subsidy of 1513 a tax was levied on the rank of individual noblemen together with a tax on the property of commoners. In 1514 the subsidy taxed wages as well as landed property without distinguishing between nobility and commoners.

Wolsey followed up the subsidy with the **Eltham Ordinances** of 1526 which attempted, in part, to reduce the cost of running the royal household. By making the household's financial administration more efficient and flexible, Wolsey hoped that he might need to rely less on Parliament to raise funds to finance government. Historians have accused Wolsey of wasting an opportunity to overhaul the Tudor financial system but this is unfair given the opposition to his plans from powerful vested interests and the sheer scale of the reforms that would be needed. The Tudor financial system was vast and complex and would require more than the decade and a half of Wolsey's service to change it.

The 'general proscription' and Parliament

In 1522 Wolsey organised a national survey, the so-called 'general proscription', to assess the population's taxable wealth. Armed with the information provided, he was able to levy some £200,000 by two forced loans in 1522–3. But still more was needed, and it became apparent that adequate finance required a Parliament. Wolsey made no secret of his dislike for Parliament, which may explain why, during his fifteen years in office, the institution was only summoned by the king twice, in 1515 and 1523. To Wolsey, Parliament seemed to be designed to stir up trouble for the government, and its members appeared

> **KEY TERM**
>
> **Eltham Ordinances** A set of instructions drawn up to reform the king's court and Privy Chamber, including its financial system.

never to understand that their prime function was to carry out the king's wishes.

Reluctantly, Wolsey allowed a Parliament to be summoned in 1523 because it was obvious to him that there was no other way of raising the large sum of money that the king needed to implement his interventionist policy in Europe. If he could have found some way of avoiding the necessity he would have done so, but his subsequent experience with the Amicable Grant confirmed that a vote from Parliament was the only practical way of securing the additional funds required to pay for a large army.

Thus, in April 1523, Wolsey sought a much larger grant from the Commons than had ever been demanded before – a subsidy to be levied at the rate of 4s. in the pound on property (20p in modern money) – to bring in as much as £800,000. In reality the Amicable Grant raised around £300,000, so Wolsey sought to make up the shortfall by taxing the Church, which brought in nearly £250,000. It is to Wolsey's credit that for the first time since 1334 the Crown was attempting to raise more realistic taxation.

Wolsey and the nobility

Wolsey knew that control of the nobility was essential for efficient and effective government. The Crown depended on the authority they possessed and Wolsey made it his duty to ensure that noble power, particularly in the localities, was used in the service of the king. The nobility had been strictly controlled by Henry VII, but this had been relaxed following his death. Wolsey's first use of his authority as chancellor was therefore to announce a stricter monitoring of the nobles' behaviour.

In 1516 Wolsey attended a meeting of Star Chamber in which he took the opportunity to announce what he termed the new law of Star Chamber. This stated that those responsible for administering justice and governing the localities, be they nobleman or gentleman, should not see themselves as being above the law. And as if to emphasise the point, on that same day the Earl of Northumberland was summoned into court for contempt of the council's jurisdiction and was subsequently committed to prison. Wolsey was making plain his intention to develop a system of centralised royal authority.

Wolsey the tyrant?

This led some to question Wolsey's motives, while others accused him of being a tyrant protected only by the trust and influence of the king. There is some truth in these accusations; for example, when Thomas Lucas, formerly Henry VII's solicitor-general, slandered the chancellor he was sent to the Tower without trial. Indeed, there is evidence to show that Wolsey also attempted to interfere in the marriage arrangements of the aristocracy, something they bitterly resented. Amid simmering noble discontent, shadowy rumours of a plot against Wolsey circulated.

The most spectacular clash between Wolsey and a nobleman was that involving the Duke of Buckingham. According to Sybil M. Jack (writing in 1996), Buckingham was no friend to Wolsey: 'The duke's royal blood, touchy personality, and penchant for wild talk were all likely to bring him under suspicion, even before it emerged that he had been speculating about what might happen should the king die.'

The duke was warned to conduct himself more discreetly, but he failed to do so. Buckingham was summoned to London in April 1521, charged and convicted of treason, and executed the following month. Foreign ambassadors reported that Buckingham lost his head because he 'murmured against the chancellor's doings'.

On the other hand, there is no clear evidence that Wolsey, any more than the king, was hostile to the nobility. In fact, the Earl of Worcester considered the chancellor to be a good friend. In general terms Wolsey's policy towards the powerful can be described as one of offering carrots as well as sticks. By holding out the prospect of desirable appointments he hoped to encourage them to become his clients. In the final analysis, the fact remains that as long as Wolsey had the king's backing most nobles worked well enough with him, and some of them accepted his authority.

Wolsey and foreign policy

It was once assumed that the king's chief minister was almost entirely responsible for the direction of English foreign policy in the period between 1514 and 1529. The king was regarded as a willing but largely passive participant in Wolsey's grand schemes. However, this is no longer the case. It is clear that Henry played a significant role in shaping the kingdom's foreign policy. Wolsey did not have a free hand to decide policy although he did exercise considerable influence over the king.

Wolsey's principal aim was to preserve the balance of power in Europe by ensuring that neither Charles V of Spain nor Francis I of France could act without taking into account the reaction and interests of England. To maintain the diplomatic balance Wolsey threatened to give his support to whichever side seemed likely to be attacked by the other. In an attempt to ensure that England retained a position of significance in international relations, Wolsey cultivated close links with the papacy. By actively supporting and promoting papal interests in England and elsewhere in Europe, Wolsey earned the trust of successive popes. His reward came in 1515 when Pope Leo X made him a cardinal and again in 1518 when he became a *legatus a latere* or papal legate.

By securing such a powerful position in the European Church, Wolsey was able to promote English diplomatic interests on a wider political stage. Wolsey's ecclesiastical promotions were encouraged and promoted by Henry VIII, who saw the advantage of having such a powerful English voice in Rome.

Critics of Wolsey's foreign policy

Some historians have accused Wolsey of deliberately subordinating English foreign policy to that of the papacy, but there is little evidence to support this. Henry VIII was too astute a politician to be so easily deceived. It is probably true to say that for much of Wolsey's period in office the interests of England invariably coincided with those of the papacy. Again, it has been claimed that Wolsey harboured ambitions of becoming Pope, but if this was the case he would only have done so with Henry's active encouragement. To have an Englishman as Pope would have reflected well on Henry VIII and enhanced his prestige and that of his kingdom.

Another accusation levelled at Wolsey is that he had no clear aims in his approach to diplomacy. Again this is unfair since Wolsey had to respond to a king who often changed his mind and who wished to follow a different path to the one mapped out by Wolsey. Wolsey was aware that Henry's twin ambitions were glory in war and securing the French crown. Besides being very expensive, these aspirations carried considerable risks both to the king and to the kingdom. Wolsey was no warmonger but he knew that his first duty was to serve the king. In the first decade of Henry's reign his council was split between the hawks (who wanted war) and the doves (who wanted peace). Wolsey used this division of opinion to his advantage by playing off one side against the other so as to suit his policy and satisfy the king. Therefore, it is fair to say that Wolsey's foreign policy was successful because it was so flexible and adaptable.

Diplomat and peacemaker

Wolsey's first and arguably most important role in Henry's service lay in diplomacy. However, before he could reach the dizzy heights of becoming the king's leading diplomatic adviser Wolsey had first to serve his apprenticeship. When England, in alliance with Spain, Venice and the Pope, Julius II, went to war with France in 1512 Wolsey gained his first experience of the duties and pitfalls involved in organising, financing, transporting and feeding an army. In spite of some early setbacks, the manner in which Wolsey had conducted himself in correspondence with Ferdinand of Aragon (Henry VIII's father-in-law) greatly impressed the king.

 **KEY TERM**

Quartermaster-general
The person responsible for feeding, arming and generally supplying the army.

In 1513, following a shuffling of alliances, England sent another large army to France with Henry in command. Wolsey, taking on the role of a **quartermaster-general** rather than as a war minister, was called on to manage the preparations. The success of the expedition – a French force was defeated near Therouanne, followed by the capture of that town and Tournai – enhanced Henry's reputation as a warrior and Wolsey's as a master organiser. By putting himself at the heart of royal affairs, Wolsey was given the opportunity to participate in the conduct of the king's business. His success was such that the queen and others in England were now routinely writing to him. The king's growing trust in Wolsey enabled the latter to shape English diplomacy, the guiding principle of which was to ensure that England was not left isolated against a **Valois–Habsburg** alliance.

When, in 1514, Louis XII of France became a widower, Wolsey seized the opportunity to propose a Valois–Tudor alliance to be sealed by the offer in marriage of Mary, sister of Henry VIII. With Henry's willing consent, the marriage went ahead and the ensuing treaty gave Wolsey's grateful master an annual income of 100,000 crowns and confirmed English possession of Tournai. Although the treaty was short-lived (the death of Louis early in 1515 put Francis I on the French throne), the success of the negotiations had enabled Wolsey to cement his place as the king's chief diplomat.

The Treaty of London

In the autumn of 1518 the Treaty of London (also known as the Treaty of Universal Peace) was signed by England, France, Spain, the Holy Roman Empire, the Netherlands, Burgundy and the papacy. The signatories agreed to commit to a policy of peaceful co-operation and to make war on any ruler that broke the terms of the treaty. This attempt to bind the leading states of Europe to a policy of perpetual peace was much admired at the time. Wolsey was praised for his negotiating skills while Henry VIII basked in the glory of his chief minister's diplomatic triumph.

The Field of the Cloth of Gold

Wolsey was to find that diplomatic triumphs have a tendency to fade very quickly. Within two years of the signing of the Treaty of London there was renewed tension in the alliance when Charles V of Spain competed with Francis I of France for the crown of the Holy Roman Empire; Charles won. Charles's election as Holy Roman Emperor in 1519 forced Wolsey to mediate between the two in an effort to preserve the peace. In 1520 he succeeded in persuading Charles and Francis to meet separately with Henry VIII. The first of those meetings took place in May 1520 when Charles briefly met Henry in England on his way from Spain to the Netherlands. It was cordial but did not amount to anything of significance. In order to impress a disappointed king, Wolsey planned a grander affair in the next meeting between Henry and Francis.

Wolsey's efforts were rewarded when a month later, in June 1520, Henry and Francis met at Ardres, near Calais. Known as the Field of the Cloth of Gold, the meeting was one of the most spectacular diplomatic events in early modern European history. A huge temporary palace of timber and canvas was erected, surrounded by pavilions, galleries and tilting grounds. Henry had nearly 5000 attendants to Francis's 3000 and both retinues were accompanied by hundreds of pounds' worth of velvet, satin, damask and other luxurious fabrics, furnishings and hangings. Following a stage-managed meeting the lavish festivities continued for a fortnight, but they were a victory of style over substance.

KEY TERM

Valois–Habsburg Names of the French (Valois) and Austrian (Habsburg) royal families.

For all the pomp and ceremony it seems that the meeting achieved nothing of lasting significance. If it was intended to improve Anglo-French relations it failed. The Venetian ambassador reported that Henry and Francis hated each other and they took part simply to try to out-do each other. If the Field of the Cloth of Gold was intended to advance the cause of European peace it failed because Charles V suspected that Henry was siding with Francis.

? Study Source D. Why do you think Henry VIII commissioned this painting?

SOURCE D

A painting depicting the scene at the Field of the Cloth of Gold (c.1520) by an unknown artist.

The Habsburg–Valois conflict

Charles V's election as Holy Roman Emperor in 1519 reignited a conflict between the Habsburg and Valois dynasties that had begun some 25 years earlier. The key factor in the dynastic quarrel was control of Italy. The Valois king of France, Francis I, wished to secure control of the Italian peninsula but he was opposed by the Habsburg Charles V. The simmering tension between these men was temporarily cooled by Wolsey's Treaty of London but this came to a dramatic end in 1521 when Francis declared war on Charles. Wolsey and Henry VIII feared the outcome of this conflict since a victory or defeat for either side would upset the balance of power.

Invoking the terms of the Treaty of London, Charles called on England and the other signatories to come to his aid against Francis, who had broken the terms of this agreement. After meeting Charles V in the Netherlands in 1521, Wolsey agreed to an Anglo-Imperial alliance sealed in the Treaty of Bruges. According to the terms of the agreement Wolsey pledged to send an English army to fight the French if Francis refused to make peace. Unlike Henry, who was keen to enter the war, Wolsey did all he could to delay English involvement. He hoped that the conflict would resolve itself without the need for a costly English intervention.

Unfortunately for Wolsey, Francis ignored the warnings he had been given and in 1523 an English army was sent to France. Much to Henry's frustration the war did not go well, and without a decisive victory and with the expenses of war piling up the king urged Wolsey to withdraw English support for Charles. Wolsey's betrayal of Charles coincided with the latter's stunning victory over the French at the Battle of Pavia in 1525. Not only was the French army totally destroyed, Francis and most of his nobles were captured. Henry VIII now urged Wolsey to seal a new agreement with the victorious Charles whereby France would be divided between them but with Henry taking the title of King of France.

The Tudor–Habsburg alliance breaks down

Henry's plan was but wishful thinking, for Charles rejected the proposal. Since Henry had forsaken their alliance, Charles did not fully trust Henry who, he believed, would become too powerful and less pliable if he extended his power on the Continent. Charles preferred to release Francis and restore him to the kingship of France, thinking that he could control him. However, Charles had miscalculated: although Francis was forced to swear an oath concerning his future conduct, and had to provide his own sons as hostages, he launched fresh attacks on Charles within a year of his release. Francis was assisted by the Pope, Clement VII, who released him from his oath to Charles on the grounds that it had been extorted under pressure. This angered Charles, who vowed to revenge himself on Clement. With the eyes of the Catholic world on him, Charles did not dare harm his royal hostages.

KEY FIGURE

**Edward Hall
(1497–1547)**

A lawyer and historian, Hall also represented Much Wenlock and later Bridgnorth, Shropshire, in Parliament.

? Study Source E. What methods were employed by the royal commissioners in collecting the revenues due under the Amicable Grant?

The 'Amicable Grant' 1525

Given his own past behaviour, it is perhaps ironic that Henry was enraged by what he believed was Charles's duplicity. He determined to launch an attack on France but was forced to abandon this when he was unable to raise the huge sums necessary to fund an army. To help raise the money demanded by Henry, Wolsey devised a scheme known as the 'Amicable Grant' in which he sent out commissioners to demand a non-parliamentary tax. This tax demand proved to be very unpopular, as demonstrated by **Edward Hall** in Source E.

SOURCE E

Edward Hall recounts the reaction of the people to Wolsey's demand for money in his book *The Union of the Two Noble and Illustrious Families of Lancaster and York*, commonly known as *Hall's Chronicle* and published in 1542.

Throughout all the realm this demand was utterly denied so that the commissioners could achieve nothing, and yet they tried both by fair means and foul. Some spoke fair and flattered whilst others spoke cruelly and threatened, and yet they could not achieve their purpose. In Kent Lord Cobham was commissioner and he handled men roughly, and because one John Skudder answered him clownishly he sent him to the Tower. As a result the people muttered and grumbled against Lord Cobham and said that they would not pay.

In Essex the people would not assemble before the commissioners and in Huntingdonshire several resisted the commissioners and they were apprehended and sent to the Fleet prison.

The League of Cognac 1526

The failure of the Amicable Grant did not deter Wolsey from promoting another less expensive scheme. If war was beyond England's financial resources then clever diplomacy would have to suffice. Wolsey took advantage of Henry's rage against Charles V to set up an anti-imperial alliance, known as the **League of Cognac**, in 1526, in which England's allies would help to shoulder the financial burden of war. With sufficient allies on board, England declared war on Charles in 1528, although Wolsey never intended to put an English army into the field. Unable to fight a conventional war, Wolsey turned his skills to fighting a diplomatic war and it brought its reward in the Treaty of Cambrai. Although not initially involved in the discussions between Francis and Charles, Wolsey managed to negotiate his way into the terms of the treaty of peace, in which England's place as a major power was acknowledged.

It is fair to say that England's foreign policy under Wolsey had enjoyed more successes than failures. Certainly after the campaign of 1513 Henry knew that he was internationally regarded as a figure of splendid chivalric kingship, an image bolstered by events such as those at the Field of the Cloth of Gold in 1520. However, if the primary aim of his foreign policy was to secure the French crown then it can be regarded as a spectacular and expensive failure.

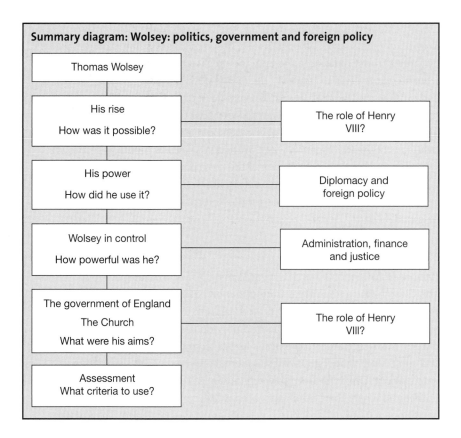

The summary diagram contains:

Summary diagram: Wolsey: politics, government and foreign policy

- Thomas Wolsey
- His rise — How was it possible?
- The role of Henry VIII?
- His power — How did he use it?
- Diplomacy and foreign policy
- Wolsey in control — How powerful was he?
- Administration, finance and justice
- The government of England — The Church — What were his aims?
- The role of Henry VIII?
- Assessment — What criteria to use?

3 The fall of Wolsey

▶ *How did the state of the Church and the annulment crisis contribute to Wolsey's fall from power?*

The traditional account of the Reformation

The traditional story regarding the Reformation in England is that it took place largely because Henry VIII wished to obtain a divorce from his first wife (Catherine of Aragon) so that he could marry his second (Anne Boleyn). It was believed that Henry fell uncontrollably in love with Anne Boleyn soon after he learned that Catherine of Aragon would no longer be able to bear him children, and would therefore not be able to provide him with the son he so desperately desired. In these circumstances divorce became an urgent necessity because:

- Anne Boleyn refused to accept the king's sexual advances until they were married, which drove him almost to distraction.
- Henry was astute enough to recognise that, in any case, a son born to Anne out of wedlock would at best have a contested claim to succeed him.

Only the Pope could dissolve marriages, and he remained stubbornly unwilling to do so in Henry and Catherine's case, despite years of persuasion followed by threats from England. In the end, the only way in which Henry could get what he wanted was to take over the Pope's powers within his own kingdom and arrange the divorce himself. This he did, and the Reformation took place (in essence the establishment of an independent Church of England) as an unintended side effect of political and personal necessity. One of the main casualties of the Reformation was Cardinal Wolsey. His failure to secure the divorce led to his downfall. As one of the most powerful churchmen of his day, Wolsey's fall inevitably impacted on the Church. Indeed, because historians tend to emphasise the political reasons for the Reformation they tend to neglect the religious.

The Church

The pre-Reformation Church appeared to be powerful, stable and popular. The Church was a huge organisation that had a presence in virtually every village, town and city throughout the kingdom. It ministered to the needs of its parishioners on a daily basis and provided essential services such as burials, marriages and christenings. Its parish priests offered advice, guidance and community leadership while its monks provided charity, education and employment. Unlike in Germany, where the Reformation began under Martin Luther and where the Church appeared weak, corrupt and neglectful of its parishioners, the English Church was generally well regarded. The English Church was not free of corruption and abuses such as **pluralism**, **nepotism**, **non-residence** and simony, but these were not as widespread, and the Church was not as unpopular, as to produce a ruthless reformer like Luther in Germany. Apart from the Lollards, a radical dissenting sect dating from the late fourteenth century, hard-core anticlericalism had little support in England. Most parishioners readily acknowledged their obligations to their Church and the majority seemed genuinely happy with the quality of their religious experience. However, it is important to note that the religious experience offered through the Church was not necessarily of a universally high quality and that the average parishioner did not think deeply about his or her religion.

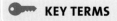 **KEY TERMS**

Pluralism When priests served more than one parish.

Nepotism The promotion or employment of family members and friends to important offices.

Non-residence When priests did not live in their parish.

? Study Source F. What does the author mean by the phrase 'community Christians'?

SOURCE F

From historian Glanmor Williams, _The Reformation in Wales_, Headstart History Publishing, 1991, p. 2.

The mass of the people were what might be described as 'community Christians' rather than individual believers. It was the customs which they absorbed from the community in which they were brought up much more than their own convictions which determined their religion. When they went to the parish church they worshipped as a communal group and were content to leave it to their priests to conduct services and administer the sacraments on their behalf in Latin, a language that most of them did not understand.

This suggests that much of their belief and practice was of necessity imitative and unthinking; in short, habit rather than conviction.

The relationship between the English Church and the Church in Rome

The relationship between the English Church and the Church in Rome was stable and generally harmonious. Indeed, the pre-Reformation Church enjoyed a fair degree of independence from Rome. Its senior leaders, archbishops and bishops, were chosen not by the Pope but by the monarch, often as a reward for loyal service. The Pope had the power to object to and block senior appointments in the Church, but this was rare. The good diplomatic relations established by Henry VII between the English Crown and the papal tiara served both parties well. Thus, the papacy could expect to receive regular payment of its clerical taxes and to receive the appeals of English litigants to its courts in Rome. The faithful took a great interest in events in Rome and when news of a papal election reached London it was celebrated by a procession to St Paul's, where a service of thanksgiving would take place.

Only gradually did the influence of Continental Humanism make its presence felt in England. The works of the Dutch humanist Erasmus (see page 63), the greatest scholar of his day, and Luther, began to impact on the thinking of the literate. The spread of literacy and the impact of the printing press provided greater access to religious literature, which encouraged debate and growth in dissension. The paradox is that the Church encouraged education, which promoted free thinking and debate, but it steadfastly refused to accept criticism.

The Church was certainly ripe for reform but not of the kind initiated by Henry VIII. English kingship was, in part, a religious office. Through his anointment at his coronation Henry VIII received God's blessing. As king, Henry was expected to set an example of piety and to protect the Christian faith and Church. Unlike his father Henry VII, Henry was an amateur theologian who could not resist meddling in the affairs of the Church, which stemmed from his belief in the divine right of kings. Until the divorce the relationship between the Crown and the Church had been cordial and respectful but, thereafter, it deteriorated, becoming tense and fractious.

The annulment

The annulment or, as contemporaries came to call it, the king's 'great matter', has helped influence and shape attitudes to and concepts of the Reformation. It is widely believed that the Reformation of the Church in England took place mainly because Henry VIII wished to obtain an annulment of his marriage to his Spanish wife, Catherine of Aragon, so that he could marry his English mistress, Anne Boleyn. The reason why this became such an issue is that only the Pope had the power to dissolve marriages and he appeared unwilling to do what Henry had requested. Given that the Catholic Church never granted divorce, only annulment, the Pope's reluctance is understandable. It was Wolsey's failure to get an annulment that left divorce (and a consequent break with Rome) the only option for Henry.

Despite years of debate, legal challenges and, ultimately, threats, it became clear to Henry that the only way in which he could obtain an annulment was to take over the Pope's powers within his own kingdom and arrange the separation for himself. This led to the Reformation, which was an unintended side effect of political necessity and personal desire.

Catherine's failure to produce a son and heir weighed heavily on Henry's mind. He firmly believed that a female could never rule England and that, if Mary succeeded him as queen, the kingdom would be plunged into dynastic civil war such as had happened during the Wars of the Roses. Believing that his marriage was cursed, Henry turned to Anne Boleyn, who promised him an heir. Henry recognised that a son born to Anne out of wedlock would be likely to have a contested claim to succeed him. Annulment became an urgent necessity. The man given the task of securing this was the king's chief minister, Wolsey.

SOURCE G

Study Source G. What reasons did Henry give for seeking an annulment?

Henry VIII's speech to Parliament explaining his reasons for seeking an annulment, quoted in Edward Hall, *The Union of the Two Noble and Illustre Families of Lancastre and Yorke*, 1542.

When we remember our mortality and that we must die, then we think that all our doings in our lifetime are clearly defaced and worthy of no memory if we leave you in trouble at the time of our death. For if our true heir be not known at the time of our death, see what mischief and trouble shall succeed you and your children … And although it has pleased God to send us a fair daughter of a noble woman and me begotten to our great comfort and joy, yet it hath been told us by divers great clerks that she is neither our lawful daughter nor her mother our lawful wife, but we live together … in open adultery. Think you that these words touch not my body and soul, think you that these doings do not daily and hourly trouble my conscience and vex my spirits, yes, we doubt not that if it were your own cause every man would seek remedy when the peril of your soul and the loss of your inheritance is openly laid to you.

The influence of biblical texts

Henry claimed that his doubts about the validity of his marriage stemmed from an Old Testament text of the Bible (*Leviticus* chapter 20, verse 21), the translation, from the Latin, of which reads:

If a man shall take his brother's wife, it is an unclean thing: he hath uncovered his brother's nakedness; they shall be without children.

To an amateur biblical scholar like Henry, this was ample proof that his lack of surviving legitimate male children was God's punishment for marrying in defiance of divine law. This was because Catherine had previously been married to his elder brother, Arthur, whose early death in 1502 had made her a widow after five months of married life. However, it was pointed out to Henry that the Levitical tract did not apply because he had fathered a child, Mary, with Catherine. Having convinced himself that his marriage was cursed, Henry sought clarification in the Hebrew original, which he took to mean 'sons' rather than 'children'. In the opinion of historian Virginia Murphy (writing in 1995), 'By substituting the Hebrew for the Latin, Leviticus was thus cleverly made to fit Henry's situation exactly.' However, the majority of historians believe that the king's cynical manipulation of biblical texts did his cause more harm than good for it only served to antagonise his theological critics.

Apart from his infatuation with Anne Boleyn, the most plausible explanation for Henry's decision to free himself of Catherine appears to have been his unshakeable belief that he had been living in sin for some seventeen years. It is possible that Henry believed that as punishment for this sinfulness his soul would suffer the torment of eternal damnation.

Wolsey and the king's 'great matter'

Henry's confidence in a swift and painless resolution to his 'great matter' suffered a serious setback when negotiations in Rome for the annulment became mired in legal arguments. What had been expected to be a formality, lasting no more than a few weeks, dragged on for months without any prospect of being resolved in the short or medium term. It became clear that the Pope, Clement VII (1523–34), was deliberately stalling, which caused a frustrated Henry to blame Wolsey for the delay. In the opinion of historian J.J. Scarisbrick (*Henry VIII*, 1997), Henry believed 'that it was not only his right to throw away his wife, but it was also his duty – to himself, to Catherine, to his people and to God'. Encouraged by Anne Boleyn and her allies at court, Henry demanded that Wolsey pursue a more aggressive policy in dealing with the Pope. In these pressured circumstances Wolsey adopted a dual strategy to persuade the Pope to grant the annulment:

- The primary strategy: Wolsey asserted that the original dispensation, issued by Pope Julius II and accepted by both England and Spain, was insufficient in law. Henry's legal advisers claimed that no pope had the right to set aside divine law and nor could he simply ignore the biblical text of Leviticus.
- The secondary strategy: this was more straightforward and its success hinged on Wolsey's powers of persuasion. His intention was to persuade the Pope to transfer the case to England and delegate responsibility for the case to Wolsey.

As papal legate, Wolsey certainly had the status and power to preside over the case. Aware of the wider diplomatic situation, Wolsey sought to ease the pressure being brought to bear on the Pope by Charles V, by removing Clement from any personal involvement in the decision-making process.

After some delay in reaching his decision, Pope Clement appeared to favour this solution but he insisted that the case must be tried by two papal legates and he reserved the right to either accept or reject the judgement reached by the legatees.

Campeggio and the Legatine Court at Blackfriars, London

It took seven months for the Legatine Court to finally meet at Blackfriars in May 1529. The delay was caused, in large part, by Campeggio's insistence that the case be tried according to the detailed procedures set out in canon law. As prescribed by law, Campeggio interviewed Henry and Catherine in turn before drawing up the necessary papers to conduct the case in open session. In his report to Pope Clement, Campeggio stated that Henry was so certain that his marriage was invalid that 'an angel descending from Heaven would be unable to convince him otherwise'.

Wolsey's attempts to speed up the process served only to antagonise Campeggio, who responded by delaying still further the legal procedure. An increasingly desperate Wolsey resorted to bribery and blackmail, both of which were resisted by the **cardinal protector**. By the time the case opened on 31 May, Henry had not only come to distrust Campeggio but also lost faith in Wolsey. It took nearly three weeks before Catherine was summoned to appear in court, and when she did, she refused to recognise its right to hear the case. Registering her right to appeal directly to Rome, Catherine then withdrew. After one further brief appearance on 21 June, Catherine refused to attend or acknowledge the authority of the court. Four days later, on 25 June, she was charged with contempt of court.

Urged by Henry to continue the case in her absence, Campeggio reluctantly carried on for a further three weeks, until late July, when he suspended proceedings. On Wolsey's insistence, Campeggio agreed to resume the case in October but it was a futile gesture. Henry realised that Campeggio would never reach a verdict. A month before the court was due to reconvene at Blackfriars Pope Clement recalled Campeggio and summoned the case to Rome.

Wolsey's fall from power

In truth, Wolsey's failure was due, in large part, to events beyond his control. Certainly the political situation in Europe did not work to his advantage. Queen Catherine was Charles V's aunt and the emperor would never accept the humiliation of a member of his family. In 1527 Charles sacked Rome and had Pope Clement at his mercy so that when Henry's annulment petition was received at the papal Curia, Clement was put in an impossible position. According to one English envoy, Clement was a weak, old man who was unlikely ever to come to a decision. Wolsey became frustrated by Clement's dithering but he could do little to persuade the Pope to act.

Clement dared not grant Henry's petition for the annulment of his marriage but, instead, he played for time. Time was against Wolsey, as were Anne Boleyn and

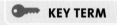

KEY TERM

Cardinal protector
A cardinal appointed to speak for and defend the rights of the Church in a particular country at the papal Curia in Rome.

her family, who brought pressure to bear on the king. The growing influence of the Boleyn faction at court did much to undermine Wolsey, contributing to his problems which in turn multiplied until he could no longer control events either at home or abroad.

Wolsey's failure

Wolsey's greatest failure was his inability to secure for Henry the annulment of his marriage to Catherine of Aragon. This lost him the king's favour and support. It seems that this was the issue at the forefront of the king's mind for the whole of the two years prior to Wolsey's fall. The minister had promised that this would be a matter easily resolved because of his influence with the papacy, from which all annulments of marriages must come, but every attempt had resulted in disappointment.

In the circumstances, Henry had been very patient. Anne Boleyn was refusing to have sex with him until he could guarantee to make 'an honest woman' of her by marrying her. It was obvious to everybody at court that this caused Henry great frustration. And Henry was increasingly aware that the passage of time was endangering his aspiration of passing his crown to an adult male when he died. It is an indication of the depth of Henry's faith in Wolsey and the skill with which the minister explained away the delays that the breakdown in their relationship was so long delayed. When the final failure of Wolsey's efforts to secure the annulment became apparent, the king turned on his once faithful and most trusted servant.

Wolsey's arrest

Wolsey was arrested and all his possessions were confiscated. However, he was soon released and allowed to live in modest comfort away from court. It was only some months later that he was rearrested and taken towards London from his archdiocese of York, to which he had been 'exiled' by Henry. But his health was broken and he died at Leicester on 29 November 1530. During the period of his disgrace he had done all he could to engineer his reinstatement. He had sent a stream of pleading letters to the king and had attempted to gather support among his 'friends' throughout Europe. But all had been to no avail. Henry had slowly become convinced that his long-time leading servant must suffer the only fitting end to his period of dominance: death as well as disgrace. Wolsey's premature end at Leicester had in fact spared him from the show trial and execution that almost certainly awaited him in London.

That Wolsey managed to survive all attacks on his position for fifteen years is remarkable. This was due in large part to two factors: the minister's outstanding abilities and the king's trust in him. Thus, the relationship between Henry VIII and Wolsey was a real (if very unequal) partnership that depended on the achievements of both parties for its success. Wolsey's failure to deliver the one thing most desired by the king – the annulment – resulted in the dissolution of that partnership.

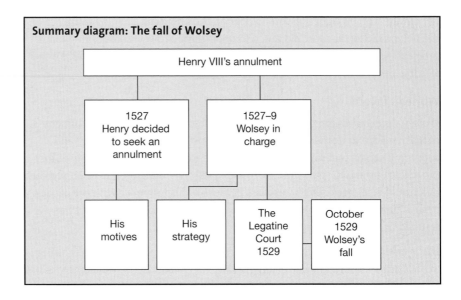

Summary diagram: The fall of Wolsey

Henry VIII's annulment

- 1527 Henry decided to seek an annulment
  - His motives
  - His strategy
- 1527–9 Wolsey in charge
  - The Legatine Court 1529
  - October 1529 Wolsey's fall

Chapter summary

Henry VIII possessed a forceful and powerful personality and he did much to influence events during his reign. His appointment of Thomas Wolsey as chief minister proved to be a masterstroke and together they did much to improve the government of England. Their conduct of foreign policy was far more energetic and interventionist than that of Henry VII. Under Wolsey, England became a significant player on the international stage. The period is marked by the change in the relationship between the king and Wolsey primarily because of Henry's desire for a male heir. Henry's love for Anne Boleyn was matched by his determination to obtain an annulment from Catherine. The international and religious ramifications of the annulment issue led to difficulties abroad and tensions at home. The status, power and wealth of the Church were put under the spotlight and moves were made to reform it. The beginning of the Reformation was more political than religious in intent as the king sought to pressure clerics into supporting him in his conflict with Pope Clement VII, who was reluctant to issue the annulment. Wolsey's failure to secure the annulment led to his fall from power.

Refresher questions

Use these questions to remind yourself of the key material covered in this chapter.

1 How effectively did Wolsey manage politics and government?

2 What kind of relationship did Wolsey have with the nobility?

3 How effective was Wolsey's foreign policy?

4 Why did Henry VIII experience a difficult relationship with Francis I?

5 Why did relations between Henry and Charles V change so frequently?

6 How popular and healthy was the church in pre-Reformation England?

7 Why did Henry want an annulment?

8 What steps did Wolsey take to obtain an annulment?

9 Why did Wolsey fail to secure the annulment?

10 How influential a role did Pope Clement VII play in the annulment crisis?

11 How and why did Wolsey fall from power?

12 What was the nature of the relationship between Wolsey and King Henry?

Question practice

ESSAY QUESTIONS

1 'The pre-Reformation Church was considered ripe for reform by many contemporaries because of the existing abuses of it.' Explain why you agree or disagree with this view.

2 To what extent can Wolsey be blamed for failing to resolve the king's 'great matter'?

3 'Habit rather than conviction best sums up the religious motivation of the masses.' Assess the validity of this view.

4 'Cardinal Wolsey was the architect of his own downfall.' Assess the validity of this view.

5 How far was religious change in the years 1529–54 driven by the personal religious beliefs of successive monarchs?

6 How accurate is it to say that Wolsey's foreign policy between 1519 and 1529 was a complete failure?

7 Assess the reasons for Wolsey's fall from power.

INTERPRETATION QUESTIONS

1 With reference to Extracts 1 and 2 (page 86) and your understanding of the historical context, which of these two extracts provides the more convincing interpretation of Wolsey's fall from power?

2 Using your understanding of the historical context, assess how convincing the arguments in Extracts 3–5 (pages 86–7) are in relation to the causes of the Reformation in religion.

EXTRACT I

Adapted from P. Gwyn, *The King's Cardinal: The Rise and Fall of Thomas Wolsey*, Pimlico, 1990, p. 596.

The evidence for Wolsey being destroyed by an aristocratic faction is slight. Wolsey got on perfectly well with individual nobles such as Norfolk and Suffolk, but also with the nobility as a group. This was not particularly because Wolsey was a 'nice guy', but because he was a good politician, who could see no advantage in antagonizing people upon whom the good government of the kingdom depended, and who, if he got on the wrong side of them, could have made things very difficult for him.

It was Henry who had made Wolsey, and it was Henry who destroyed him, just as he was to make and destroy Thomas Cromwell. Henry made all the important decisions and appointments. In every sense the king ruled.

EXTRACT 2

From the introduction by G.R. Elton to A.F. Pollard, *Wolsey*, Collins, 1965, p. vii.

Anyone with eyes in his head could see that Wolsey had tried to do the impossible, to rule as king when he was not the king, to ignore the legal and constitutional traditions of England and substitute for them his own self-confident judgement, to do a highly professional job in a very amateur manner. He lasted so long because in two things he was not amateur at all: he knew how to promote himself, and for most of the time he knew how to keep Henry satisfied.

For fifteen years he impressed England and Europe with his grandeur, his hard work, his skill and intelligence, and his very positive action in the affairs of this world. He often achieved what he set out to do, even if subsequent events showed his aims to have been mistaken and his solutions to have been patchwork.

EXTRACT 3

From J.J. Scarisbrick, *Henry VIII*, Eyre Methuen, 1968, p. 242.

Despite what has sometimes been said or implied, it is probable that the English Church was in no worse condition, spiritually speaking, in 1529 than it had been fifty, a hundred, or a hundred and fifty years before. The picture of a slow, steady decline into oblivion is suspect. Not only is it factionally questionable (for it is arguable that on the eve of the Reformation the English Church, though still largely wretched, was in some ways in better case than it had been for decades); worse, it misguides. For the really significant thing that had happened was not so much any change within the Church as a rise in standards of society, lay society, without it. What had been tolerated before and patiently accepted as part of the given order, though often bitterly mocked, would be tolerated no longer.

EXTRACT 4

From G.R. Elton, *Reform and Reformation: England 1509–1558*, Harvard University Press, 1977, p. 187.

All was not well with the Church in England, there were without doubt problems though we should guard against the folly of exaggeration. Nevertheless, there is evidence to suggest that the clergy attracted more dislike than love. The state of the Church was widely believed to be rotten. Popular anticlericalism thrived on tales of gluttonous monks, lecherous friars, ignorant and dishonest parish priests, ambitious and corrupt bishops, pregnant nuns, and other such scandalous stories of sin and debauchery. Satirists unquestionably exaggerated the evils in the Church, but they had enough reality to draw on to carry widespread conviction. The Church was showing all the signs of an institution in danger but unaware of its peril. If the Church was to survive reformation was essential.

EXTRACT 5

From C. Haigh, *The English Reformation Revised*, Cambridge University Press, 1987, p. 58.

Relations between priests and parishioners were usually harmonious, and the laity complained astonishingly infrequently against their priests. There were local tensions, certainly, but they were individual rather than institutionalised, occasional rather than endemic. In a frantic search for the causes of Reformation, we must not wrench isolated cases of discord from their local contexts, and pile them together to show a growing chorus of dissatisfaction: we must not construct a false polarisation between the Church and the people it served. The English people had not turned against their Church, and there was no widespread yearning for reform. The long term causes of the Reformation – the corruption of the Church and the hostility of the laity – appear to have been historical illusions.

CHAPTER 4

Henry VIII: Cromwell and the revolution in Church and State 1530–47

This chapter explains how Henry VIII and his chief adviser Thomas Cromwell contributed to the changes in religion and government. The rise and fall of Cromwell is examined, as are the problems faced by the king and his government by those who opposed the unprecedented, if not 'revolutionary', political and religious changes. These issues are examined as the following themes:

★ Reformation in religion

★ Revolution in government

★ Opposition and the fall of Cromwell

The key debate on *page 122* of this chapter asks the question: Was there a revolution in government?

Key dates

1529–36	Reformation Parliament	1536	Cromwell appointed Lord Privy Seal
1532	Emergence of Thomas Cromwell as the king's chief minister		The Ten Articles
			Pilgrimage of Grace
1533	Henry married Anne Boleyn and daughter Elizabeth was born		Execution of Anne Boleyn
		1537	Henry VIII's son Edward born
	Act in Restraint of Appeals		Publication of *The Bishops' Book*
1534	Cromwell appointed Chancellor of the Exchequer	1538–40	Closure of the larger monasteries
	Act of Supremacy and Treason Act	1539	Act of Six Articles
1535	Execution of John Fisher and Sir Thomas More	1540	Cromwell executed on a charge of treason
	Valor Ecclesiasticus	1547	Death of Henry VIII

Reformation in religion

▶ *What was the nature and scale of the reformation in religion?*

Cromwell's career and rise to power

It may be argued that Thomas Cromwell (*c*.1485–1540) was one of the three most powerful politicians to exercise power in sixteenth-century England. The other two were his employer, mentor and friend, Thomas Wolsey (*c*.1471–1530), and his 'natural' successor, **William Cecil**. These men held the highest posts in the royal administration, and were responsible for formulating policy and for the direction and management of government. That Cromwell may be counted among this elite list is all the more impressive when we realise that he served for the shortest period in office, a mere eight years, compared to Wolsey's fifteen and Cecil's incredible 40.

Yet before the publication of Geoffrey Elton's pioneering work, *The Tudor Revolution in Government* in 1953, very few scholars had concentrated on Cromwell. Controversial and compelling, Elton's research suggested that the 1530s witnessed a revolution in government and that the man most responsible for this was Cromwell. Cromwell was a master tactician who planned and skilfully guided England through the political minefield of the Reformation and who reformed government, making it more bureaucratic and thus more efficient. Whether one agrees with Elton's interpretation or not (and many historians do not), there is no doubt that something very significant did happen in the 1530s, which included the following:

- the break with Rome
- the closure of the monasteries
- the role of Parliament in the Reformation.

Cromwell was at the heart of it.

Rise to prominence

Cromwell's rise to prominence and power began in the early 1520s when he first came to the attention of Cardinal Wolsey while acting as a legal agent for Charles Knyvett, formerly surveyor to Edward Stafford, third Duke of Buckingham. Wolsey was impressed by Cromwell's legal expertise and in 1524 he appointed him to be his legal adviser. Between 1526 and 1529 Cromwell became one of the cardinal's most senior and trusted advisers. His instinct for survival ensured that he left Wolsey's service before his master's sudden fall from power in 1529. Nevertheless, Cromwell displayed a commendable degree of loyalty to his old master and he did all he could to defend Wolsey, short of endangering his own rising position in the king's household.

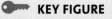

KEY FIGURE

William Cecil (1520–98)

A talented administrator who first gained promotion to the government in the reign of Edward VI. He was a Protestant who supported the Henrician and Edwardian changes in religion and who retired from public life during the reign of Catholic Queen Mary. He won the confidence of a young Princess Elizabeth, who appointed him her chief minister at the start of her reign. He served until his death 40 years later.

Thomas Cromwell

1485	Born the son of Walter Cromwell of Putney, a blacksmith and cloth merchant
1503–14	Served on the Continent as a mercenary soldier, trained in banking and traded as a cloth merchant
1520	Established in London mercantile and legal circles
1523	Entered the House of Commons for the first time
1524	Entered the household of Cardinal Wolsey
1530	Became a member of the King's Council
1534	Confirmed as Henry VIII's principal secretary and chief minister
1535	Appointed the king's vicegerent (vicar-general) and oversees the dissolution of the monasteries
1540	Tried and executed for treason

Cromwell lived in Europe for eleven years. He fought at the battle of Garigliano in Italy before entering the household of Italian banker, Francesco Frescobaldi.

He later left for the Netherlands where he traded as a cloth merchant in Antwerp. He returned to England to trade as a cloth merchant before setting up a legal practice in London. Cromwell's legal and political talents were spotted by Wolsey who took him into his service. He rose through the ranks to become Wolsey's principal adviser.

Cromwell left Wolsey's service before the latter's fall from power and entered the royal household. He again rose quickly through the ranks to become the king's chief legal and political adviser before being appointed master of the king's jewels. By 1534 Cromwell had become Henry VIII's principal secretary and chief adviser. He secured the annulment of the king's marriage to Catherine of Aragon, piloted the legislation responsible for the break with Rome and managed the dissolution of the monasteries.

Cromwell is credited with promoting the Reformation by orchestrating England's break with Rome and with wide-ranging reforms in government, the core of which was his restructuring of the revenue system.

Cromwell came to the attention of the king, as he had done previously to Wolsey, by his expertise in legal matters. How Cromwell moved from being one of the king's many legal advisers to becoming his chief minister is not known. It took three years before Cromwell emerged from the shadows of the royal household to take his place on the King's Council in 1531 and a further twelve months before he secured his first major office, the mastership of the king's jewels. In 1533 he temporarily replaced Bishop Stephen Gardiner (see page 170), who was absent on business abroad, as Henry's principal secretary. He must have greatly impressed the king, for on Gardiner's return Cromwell was retained and his position was made permanent in 1534.

Serving the king

Cromwell's transformation from king's councillor to principal secretary and chief minister in less than three years was almost certainly due to his ability to convince Henry that he had a solution to his 'great matter': how to end the king's marriage to Catherine of Aragon so that he could he could wed Anne Boleyn. Wolsey's failure to secure the annulment enabled Cromwell to manipulate the king and push him in a direction that he had not, hitherto, considered. If Pope Clement VII was reluctant to grant the annulment then pressure would

SOURCE A

A portrait of Thomas Cromwell painted by Hans Holbein (the Younger), court artist to King Henry VIII, in 1532–3.

Study Source A. Why was it considered so important that Cromwell be painted sitting next to a book and a collection of letters?

be applied to the Church in England to persuade him to do as Henry wished. However, what began as pressure soon grew into something altogether much bigger. The scale and ruthlessness of Henry's attack on the Church, for that is what it became, gathered momentum until it reached a logical conclusion: schism.

Henry VIII's motives in breaking away from Rome were much more political, and personal, than religious. The English Reformation put the Church firmly under the control of the State. It also removed England from the authority of the Pope, a source of outside interference which was resented. The resulting royal supremacy made Henry VIII more independent and, arguably, more powerful than any monarch in English history. It enabled him to rule an undivided kingdom where Church and State were merged into a single sovereign state. This 'constitutional' revolution in the relationship between Church and State and the monarch's position and power within it was accompanied by a reform in government.

On the surface, the Crown was the main beneficiary of the English Reformation. Henry VIII was able to reduce the political power of the Church and exploit its vast wealth. Ecclesiastical riches replenished the Exchequer, which had been almost bankrupted by Henry VIII's unsuccessful wars. On the other hand, once religion had come to the forefront of the political arena, it created problems for the monarchy. For example, religious differences deepened the rift between political factions at court, which meant that Henry VIII had to tread a cautious path between the conservative Catholic and progressive or reforming Protestant parties.

Resolving the king's 'great matter'

The annulment proceedings stalled following Wolsey's fall and death. They were not resumed during the period in office of his successor as Lord Chancellor, Sir Thomas More (see page 113). More was in favour of maintaining the *status quo* and was opposed to any pressure, let alone attack, on the Church. During his short period in office (1530–2) matters were allowed to drift. However, an increasingly frustrated king was determined to press on but had no clear idea on how to proceed.

Thomas Cromwell provided the king with the idea and the plan to make it work. In his opinion, the Pope would never be persuaded to rule in Henry's favour and the only way forward was to remove the Pope's power in such matters and to give it to someone who would do as the king wished. This 'someone' was preferably a senior cleric within the English Church who had the status and power to mount a credible challenge to the Pope on religious as well as jurisdictional terms. Unfortunately, the head of the Church, the Archbishop of Canterbury, William Warham, was opposed to the annulment and little could be done until he was replaced. Cromwell calculated that this need not take too long as the archbishop was over 80 years of age but, in the meantime, to satisfy an impatient king, other avenues would be explored. One of those avenues was Parliament.

Cromwell's blueprint for success

Cromwell's key decision was to use Parliament to pass laws restricting papal powers by recognising that these powers in fact resided in the Crown of England, and stipulating the punishments that would be meted out to those who opposed or acted contrary to the new arrangements. The uniqueness of the approach suggested by Cromwell appealed to Henry. At the time it was generally accepted that Parliament was a rarely and briefly used component of political life (it had played no significant part in the first twenty years of Henry's reign) whose main functions were to grant extraordinary taxes and to pass new laws. The idea of using it to bring about a revolution in the relationship between Church and State was highly innovative. It was also very shrewd. It ensured that the representatives of the landed and merchant classes, on whom the king depended to exercise his authority throughout the country, would be fully involved in, and beneficiaries of, whatever was done.

The passing of two pieces of vital parliamentary legislation marked the first official steps in the process of reducing the Pope's influence in England:

- the Act in Restraint of Annates (1532)
- the Act in Restraint of Appeals (1533).

The Act in Restraint of Annates forbade the payment to the Vatican of up to 95 per cent of **annates**. Henry hoped that this financial penalty would encourage the Pope to reconsider his position in regard to the annulment or risk losing the payment of annates entirely.

Act in Restraint of Appeals

Pope Clement did not respond, so greater pressure was applied the following year with the passing of the Act in Restraint of Appeals, which declared that final authority in all legal matters, lay and clerical, resided in the monarch and that it was therefore illegal to appeal to any authority outside the kingdom on any such matters. This was a significant measure because:

- it ensured that the final verdict on the validity of Henry and Catherine's marriage would be taken out of Rome's hands
- in order to justify the change, the right of the Pope to make decisions affecting Henry and his subjects was publicly denied.

The fact that Anne Boleyn had become pregnant – either by design or having given in to Henry's demands – injected a sense of urgency into the work of securing the passage of this necessary legislation, which explains why it passed swiftly through both Houses of Parliament and received the royal assent.

SOURCE B

From the preamble to the Act in Restraint of Appeals 1533, justifying what was being done.

… that this realm of England is an empire, and so hath been accepted in the world, governed by one supreme head and king having the dignity and royal estate of the imperial crown of the same, unto whom … all sorts and degrees of people divided in terms of spirituality and temporality, be bounden and owe to bear next to God a natural and humble obedience to the king …

Forcing the Church to submit to royal authority

To get to this point the Church had been browbeaten into submission. Parliament could only do so much without the consent of the senior clerics in the Church, so Cromwell, with the king's active encouragement, set about ensuring a clerical acceptance of the 'reforms' proposed. Growing anticlericalism was exaggerated by Cromwell and used as an excuse to justify reform of the Church.

KEY TERM

Annates Money equivalent to about one-third of the annual income paid to the Pope by all new holders of senior posts within the Church in England and Wales.

Study Source B. Why might the Pope object to this Act?

For those within the Church who resisted, Cromwell responded by charging the entire clerical class with **praemunire**. The indictment was phrased in such a way – acknowledging Wolsey's authority as papal legate without seeking the king's permission – that it was virtually impossible for any cleric to escape punishment under the law. A precedent had been set in the toppling of Wolsey when he, too, had been charged and found guilty of *praemunire*. Henry reasoned that what had succeeded against one cleric, especially one so mighty, could also be applied to them all.

The relentless pressure applied by Henry finally took its toll and the Church caved in. When Convocation met in January 1531 the majority of its members were eager to compromise. The price of their pliancy was high. They were informed that the king would withdraw the indictment of *praemunire* in return for the following:

- a grant of £118,000
- the awarding to him of the title of 'sole Protector and supreme Head of the English Church and clergy'.

The Pardon of the Clergy

After some hard bargaining both sides managed to reach a compromise. Negotiating on behalf of Convocation, Bishop John Fisher (see pages 110–11) failed to achieve a reduction in the huge sum demanded but he did persuade the king to accept payment over five years. Arguably Fisher's most significant achievement was in amending the title Henry had claimed for himself. Convocation agreed to accept the king as their 'supreme head' but only on condition that a qualifying clause was added to the title, namely 'as far as the law of Christ allows'. This concession made it possible for each cleric to interpret for himself what (if anything) the king's new title meant in practice.

The agreement between the Crown and the Church was enshrined in an Act of Parliament passed in January 1531. The Pardon of the Clergy absolved the church of any wrongdoing and the indictment was withdrawn. Despite Fisher's concessions, there was only one winner in this contest and that was the king.

Supplication against the Ordinaries

If the clergy thought that the king's pardon had ended the conflict between Church and Crown, they were mistaken. A year later, early in 1532, it seems that Parliament took the lead in attacking the Church when the House of Commons presented the king with a petition known as the Supplication against the Ordinaries (senior clergy such as bishops). The petition's attack on the Church was two-fold:

- it claimed that the Church was riddled with corruption
- it challenged the Church's right to have its own courts and laws independent of the Crown and State.

The petitioners urged the king to root out this corruption and end the legal and legislative independence of the Church by bringing it firmly under the control of the State. There is some dispute among historians regarding the origin of the Supplication but the majority believe that it was probably engineered by Thomas Cromwell and pushed through Parliament in order to give the impression that the king had the support of his people.

Henry agreed to consider the petition and passed a copy to Convocation requesting them to respond to the complaints. Henry was cynically manipulating events by pretending, in the opinion of historian Keith Randell (1993), 'to be the impartial judge in a dispute between two groups of his subjects'. Convocation responded by rejecting completely the complaints and countered by asserting the Church's ancient right to enact and enforce canon law. The defiant tone of the reply angered the king, who abandoned the pretence of impartiality and aligned himself with the Commons. Henry demanded that Convocation agree to respect his kingly authority and to acknowledge his right to govern the Church as he did the State. With the legislative independence of the Church under threat, the more militant bishops in Convocation urged their fellow clerics to resist the king's demands. Unfortunately for them, the Archbishop of Canterbury, William Warham, was weak and indecisive, and he failed to provide the kind of leadership required to resist the Crown.

Submission of the clergy

Henry pressed home the attack by demanding the submission of the clergy. Unable to resist the pressure any longer, in May 1532 Convocation reluctantly agreed to the terms of the submission. The Church did the following:

- surrendered its right to make ecclesiastical laws independently of the king
- promised not to issue new laws currently being drafted without royal licence
- agreed to submit existing laws to a royally appointed committee for revision.

The terms of the submission were confirmed in an Act of Parliament. The clergy's will to resist had been crushed. At this point, Sir Thomas More, a defender of the Church's right to autonomy, resigned as Lord Chancellor.

A new Archbishop of Canterbury: Thomas Cranmer

Not content to browbeat the clergy into submission, Henry decided that the next head of the Church would be his personal appointment and a man who would do as he was told. The aged Archbishop of Canterbury, William Warham, had proved awkward and less pliant than Henry would have wished so, when he died in 1532, the king chose Thomas Cranmer to take his place.

Cranmer appeared to have all the right attributes to lead the Church. He had shown a marked lack of personal ambition, was intellectually very able and had shown himself to be strongly in favour of the annulment. He had already been useful to the king, carrying out his instructions to the letter, whether it was in writing a book supporting Henry's case (in 1529), acting as an agent buying

Thomas Cranmer

1489	Born in Nottinghamshire, the younger son of a lesser gentry family
c.1529	Became chaplain to Thomas Boleyn, Earl of Wiltshire, father of Anne
1530	Appointed English ambassador to Charles V (1530–3)
1533	Chosen by Henry VIII to succeed William Warham as Archbishop of Canterbury
1547	Took leading part in the Edwardian regime both in government and in the Church. Issued Protestant *Book of Homilies*
1549	Issued the blandly reformist first *Book of Common Prayer*
1552	Issued the more extreme second *Book of Common Prayer*
1556	Burned at the stake for withdrawing an earlier promise to accept some key Catholic doctrines

Cranmer studied at Cambridge University where he joined the 'White Horse' group, radical Protestants who met at the tavern of the same name to discuss the new ideas coming from Europe such as Lutheranism. He supported Henry VIII's divorce. While in Europe on royal business he secretly married the niece of the Lutheran Church leader of Nuremberg in Germany.

Cranmer presided over Henry VIII's divorce from Catherine of Aragon, promoted the marriage with Anne Boleyn and declared Henry VIII to be head of the Church in England. He presided over Henry VIII's divorce from Anne Boleyn and promoted his marriage with Jane Seymour. He worked with Cromwell in government and in turning England towards Protestantism; for example, he was responsible for *The Bishops' Book* of 1537. Cranmer unsuccessfully opposed the conservative Act of Six Articles, he was forced to separate from his wife but refused to resign his office. He took no part in the destruction of Cromwell. He became one of the leading members of the reformist party at court. Henry VIII's support enabled him to survive conservative attempts to destroy him in the early 1540s. His contribution to religious reform during Edward's reign was the high point of his career. When Mary came to the throne he was arrested, stripped of his title as Archbishop of Canterbury and imprisoned for heresy.

Arguably, Cranmer played a greater role than any other single churchman in establishing and shaping the Church of England. He was not as timid as some historians believe but was willing to accept gradual change in the Church. He was fiercely loyal to the Crown and he proved to be an able government minister and churchman. His greatest strength lay in his refusal to support religious extremism; he advocated toleration and preached against persecution.

support in European universities (in 1530), or, as now, serving as England's ambassador at the court of Charles V.

Cranmer's 'reformist views' had led to his becoming a junior member of the Boleyn faction, thus making him acceptable to the queen-in-waiting. Once the Act in Restraint of Appeals had become law there was a need for rapid action. Anne Boleyn, convinced that the annulment would soon be achieved, had finally consented to share her monarch's bed at some time in 1532. By January 1533 she knew that she was pregnant, and Cranmer was instructed to perform a secret marriage ceremony. It was now important that the annulment be finalised and the new marriage declared legal before the baby was born in the early autumn. The king's 'great matter' had now become the king's 'private matter'. Cranmer acted with speed, tact and efficiency. A hearing of the case was arranged for late May and, when Catherine refused to attend, a swift judgement was delivered against her. It was announced that the papal dispensation had been invalid, that Henry and Catherine had therefore never been legally married, and that the secret marriage of Henry and Anne was legal. The king was well satisfied and pleased that six years of endeavour on his 'great matter' had ended in victory.

The break with Rome and the royal supremacy

It is to Cromwell that historians turn to explain why the decision to break completely with Rome was eventually taken. Cromwell may well have used the argument that this was the only way of being sure that the annulment would be granted. Cromwell's first success was in persuading Cranmer to support him so that the two of them might better influence the king. The royal supremacy asserted that the King of England had a God-given right of **cure of souls** of his subjects, was head of the national Church and owed no obedience to the 'Bishop

KEY TERM

Cure of souls An ancient practice of nourishing and defending the souls of parishioners by sermons, rituals and confession.

SOURCE C

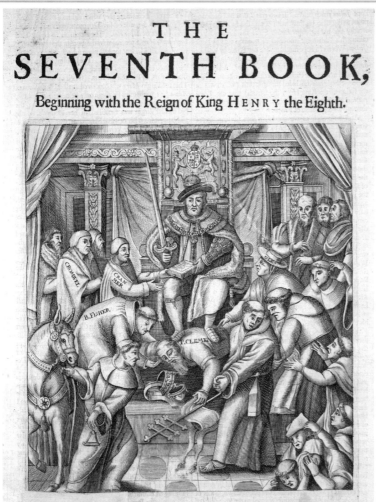

The 'Seventh Book'. An illustration of an allegory of the Reformation from John Foxe's *Book of Martyrs*, first published in 1563. The image represents the views of later reformers on the religious changes introduced by Henry VIII in the 1530s.

Study Source C. Why might the Pope condemn the illustration on the front cover of this book?

of Rome'. This was based on the premise, expounded in the Act in Restraint of Appeals, that 'this realm of England is an empire … governed by one Supreme head and King'. It claimed this had always been so and that the papacy had usurped jurisdiction over the English Church.

Thus, the Act of Supremacy sought to re-establish the king's territories as a 'sovereign empire' within which no other ruler could exercise any control. Much of the force of the argument underpinning this policy lay in the word 're-establish'. Those who urged the king in this direction believed that the rulers of England had enjoyed sole power in their kingdoms until some time in the early Middle Ages, when the Pope had established a variety of legal and financial claims because of his headship of the western Church. These, it was argued, should be rejected out of hand.

When Cromwell finally prevailed on Henry to assent to the passing of the Act in November, a complete break with Rome was achieved. Cromwell's success was only possible because the Pope was not prepared to bow to any threat, thus enabling Henry to be persuaded that it was only by throwing off allegiance to Rome that his annulment could be achieved. Once it had been accepted by the king that there could be no going back, the task of those who wished to see an end to papal power in England for reasons unconnected to Anne Boleyn became much more straightforward.

Supremacy and vicegerent (vicar-general)

The terms of the Act of Supremacy empowered the king 'to reform and redress all errors, heresies and abuses' in the Church. This was significant because the routine management of the Church in spiritual as well as temporal matters passed from clerical into lay hands. Henceforth, it would be the king and his representatives rather than the Archbishop of Canterbury and the clerical hierarchy who would direct the nation's religious affairs.

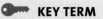

KEY TERM

Vicegerent King's deputy in Church affairs.

Henry wasted little time in exercising his new powers and one of his first acts as supreme head was to appoint his representative to oversee the Church. In January 1535 Cromwell was appointed as the king's **vicegerent** in spiritual matters. This gave him enormous power since it meant that he was in a position to exercise the authority that legally belonged to the king. Much to their dismay, the senior clergy found Cromwell to be an energetic and intrusive vicegerent. Any hopes that they had that the royal supremacy would be a distant, light-touch affair were soon dispelled when Cromwell involved himself in day-to-day matters. Even Cranmer, as Archbishop of Canterbury, found himself subject to the forceful opinion of the vicegerent on such matters as clerical appointments.

Act Extinguishing the Authority of the Bishop of Rome

Cromwell sought to eradicate every vestige of papal authority in England. Through his careful management of the Reformation Parliament, a number of Acts were passed that, collectively, led to the enhancement of royal authority and the extinction of papal power. The most important of these Acts was the aptly named 'Act Extinguishing the Authority of the Bishop of Rome' (1536), under the terms of which the Pope was denied:

- access to and collection of clerical taxes
- the power of appointment to Church offices
- the authority to determine matters of religious doctrine
- the right to grant dispensations and personal exemptions
- the use of his title in England, being known, henceforth, as the Bishop of Rome.

Any clerics who persisted in recognising or defending papal authority were deemed to be traitors and were dealt with by means of the Treason Act (see page 109). Drawn up by Cromwell immediately after the Act of Supremacy, the Act made it treason to deny or question the validity of the king's supremacy. For those who broke the law by daring 'to slanderously and maliciously publish and pronounce, by express writing or words, that the king should be heretic, schismatic, tyrant, infidel or usurper', there was only one punishment: death.

In the opinion of historian W.J. Sheils (writing in 1989), the significance of the royal supremacy is that it 'came to be exercised by the King in Parliament, rather than by the King in his own right'. It was, he continued, 'essentially a personal supremacy' that involved 'Parliament not only in matters of jurisdiction but also in matters of doctrine'. To some historians such as G.R. Elton, this amounted to a constitutional revolution because it redefined the Crown's relationship not just with the Church but with Parliament also. The Church became subject to the power of the State and the king's authority over the Church was expressed through legislation enacted in Parliament.

The royal supremacy in action: the dissolution of the monasteries 1536–40

The majority of historians agree that the principal reason for the dissolution of the monasteries was financial. The Crown was in dire need of an additional permanent source of income. Henry and Wolsey had struggled to finance the French war of 1522–3 when taxpayers resisted what they considered to be excessive financial demands. The monasteries were thought to be an easy target because they were already in crisis and it was rumoured that the monastic orders preferred papal primacy to royal supremacy. Humanists had condemned them as a drain on the **Commonwealth** and the monastic vocation had declined to such an extent that many houses were staffed by dwindling numbers of inmates. Fewer than 10,000 monks, friars and nuns, inhabiting over 800 monastic institutions, were sustained by perhaps one-fifth of the cultivated land in England and Wales. As events were to prove, the closure, confiscation of goods and subsequent sale and lease of monastic land did much to enrich the English Crown.

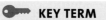 **KEY TERM**

Commonwealth A term derived from 'commonweal', meaning the wealth, health and good of the community.

As early as 1533 there had been talk of the Crown assuming control of Church property and estates, both monastic and secular, and of employing bishops as salaried officials. There was a generally held perception that the monasteries no longer commanded enough respect to justify the great wealth with which they were endowed. The fact that Wolsey met with no opposition when he dissolved some 29 houses in the 1520s might be cited as proof of this. However, it was not until 1535, after Henry had become head of the Church, that a plan was put forward to survey the wealth and possessions of the monasteries before any subsequent action was taken. That action would be taken against the monasteries was inevitable, given the cutting remark by Ambassador Chapuys that Cromwell's rise to power was due to a promise he made Henry that he would make him 'the richest king in Christendom'.

Visitation and the *Comperta Monastica*

In 1535 Cromwell began exercising his powers as the king's vicegerent. His first objective was to assess the state of the monasteries, so he assembled a team of agents who were entrusted with the task of visiting the vast majority of the nation's religious houses. Monastic visitations were nothing new; they had a long history and were an accepted part of Church administration. Traditionally, such visitations had been conducted either under the authority of the bishop in whose diocese the particular monastic community was located or by the head of the religious order to which the clerics belonged. The difference between the more traditional visitations and those ordered by Cromwell was the searching nature of the enquiry and the attitude of the agents delegated to compile the reports.

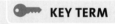 **KEY TERM**

Comperta Monastica
'Monastic discovery'. A book compiled by Cromwell's agents which contained lists of transgressions and abuses admitted by monks and nuns.

Much of the work done in compiling the ***Comperta Monastica*** (also known as the *Compendium Compertorum*) was carried out by some of Cromwell's most trusted 'servants', Thomas Legh, Richard Layton, John ap Rhys, John Tregonwell and John Vaughan. They were handpicked by Cromwell because they were able and ambitious and supported his reformist agenda. They were mainly secular clergy who had expressed doubts about the value and quality of the monastic vocation. Rhys and Vaughan, Cromwell's Welsh agents, were especially dismissive of relics, pilgrimages and miraculous tokens. In addition, the commissioners were instructed to record whether or not the monasteries were complying with the Oath of Supremacy and to detail any alleged offences against the Crown. Clearly, these were men in whom Cromwell had complete trust.

Valor Ecclesiasticus of 1535

The *Valor Ecclesiasticus* (translated as 'church list') represented Cromwell's most ambitious project to date. It was the greatest survey of ecclesiastical wealth and property ever undertaken and has been described a kind of Tudor Domesday Book. The *Valor* valued taxes paid to the Crown from ecclesiastical property and income that had previously been paid to the Pope. Unlike the handpicked commissioners who worked on the *Comperta*, the work of the *Valor* was undertaken by local gentry.

In what was a colossal undertaking, every parish and every monastic institution in England and Wales was visited. As a result of their work the government gained a solid understanding of the scale of the wealth of the Church as a whole and of the monasteries in particular. According to the *Valor*, the net annual income of the Church was put at between £320,000 and £360,000 when omissions are taken into account (in today's values this would range from £103 million to £122 million).

The impact of the *Valor Ecclesiasticus* and *Comperta Monastica*

The *Valor* and the *Comperta* provided the ammunition for those determined to close the monasteries. The *Valor* provided a list of itemised expenditure as well as income, which Cromwell manipulated and then used to show evidence of widespread corruption. Cromwell was able to demonstrate the bankruptcy of monasticism by revealing that in spite of the considerable income enjoyed by the religious orders only three per cent was regularly allocated to charitable works. The misapplication of funds, fraud and clerical corruption were highlighted by Cromwell, who managed to convince an initially sceptical king of the necessity and value of the exercise.

Even more damning, and certainly more sensational, were the tales of widespread immorality and sexual perversion contained in the *Comperta*. To help ensure that the reports compiled by his agents would be believed, Cromwell was able to provide the signed confessions of monks and nuns who had admitted breaking their vows of chastity. The more lurid tales dwelt on the stories of monks taking part in homosexual practices and nuns who had borne children.

The dissolution of the smaller monasteries 1536

The test of Henry's supremacy over the Church was whether it could be imposed on the people and in the localities. The work of Cromwell's commissioners fuelled rumours that the government intended to close the monasteries and to seize their wealth. These fears were realised in part by the passing, in March 1536, of the Act for the Dissolution of the Smaller Monasteries. According to the preamble of the Act, the smaller monasteries were being closed because of the 'manifest sin, vicious, carnal and abominable living [that] is daily used and committed among the little and small abbeys, priories and other religious houses'.

As the Act made clear in a later, more significant, section the real reason for their dissolution was financial. The test of their fitness to continue was whether they had an annual income of more than £200. Those houses that failed to meet this financial target were to be dissolved and their property to pass to the Crown. As a consequence, 399 houses were suppressed, with the inmates given two options:

- to continue their vocation by transferring to a larger monastery
- to abandon their vocation and rejoin society.

To avoid protest or opposition, the heads of the dissolved houses were more generously provided for by being pensioned off. Some religious houses, 67 in total, were exempted from dissolution but the price of their continued existence was that they had to pay a heavy financial penalty.

Resistance to the dissolution

In some parts of England, most notably in the north, there was a violent reaction against the closures. There were far fewer petitions to buy or lease monastic property in the north, such as Lancashire, Yorkshire and Northumberland, mainly because the religious houses were held in greater esteem. In some instances, Cromwell's commissioners were prevented from conducting their business by angry mobs determined to defend the monasteries.

Pilgrimage of Grace 1536–7

Those commissioners who continued to operate in the face of local protests were partly responsible for stirring up the Pilgrimage of Grace in October 1536. This was a widespread popular revolt that took place between late 1536 and early 1537 in the north of England. Some 40,000 people joined the rebellion, which proved to be the largest and most serious in the sixteenth century. It was caused mainly by resentment over the changes in the Church and the dissolution of the monasteries. The rebellion never seriously threatened the king but it did threaten the maintenance of law and order in the north.

The size and geographical scale of this rebellion – Lincolnshire, Yorkshire, Cumberland and Westmorland – shocked Henry and for a while the dissolution process was halted. Once the situation had settled and the ringleaders were dealt with, the dissolution began again. The first to be closed were those houses that had supported the rebels but this gave way to a more widespread dissolution that took no account of size, wealth or whether they had been obedient or not.

The destruction of the remaining monasteries 1538–40

In 1539 an Act of Parliament was passed making legal what had already occurred, namely the closure of the remaining monasteries. Following the suppression of the Pilgrimage of Grace the process of dissolution was revived but conducted piecemeal. Cromwell's commissioners were instructed that all monasteries regardless of their size, wealth or powerful connections were to be closed and their property seized. The majority of the remaining religious communities went quietly but for those who resisted the only possible outcome was death.

Among those who suffered under the terms of the unforgiving Treason Act was Richard Whiting, Abbot of Glastonbury, head of one of the richest monasteries in the country. His execution at his abbey was followed by those of his colleagues at the abbeys of Colchester and Reading. Even as the last of the monasteries were being closed, the Crown was denying the destruction that was taking place. In a confidential report sent in May 1539 to Francis I by the French ambassador, Marillac, it was said that Parliament was 'discussing the reduction of certain abbeys of which they wish to make bishoprics, the foundation of schools for children and hospitals for the poor'. By 1540 every one of the 800 monastic houses had been closed but only a small percentage of them had been transformed into the 'bishoprics', 'schools' and 'hospitals' mentioned by Marillac.

Reaction of the monasteries to the dissolution

Apart from those few institutions which lent support to the Pilgrimage of Grace, the majority of the religious houses accepted their dissolution. Indeed, after the initial dissolution of the smaller monasteries, the evidence suggests that many of the larger monasteries were expecting to be dissolved in the near future and were dispersing their assets among friends and well-wishers so that they would not fall into the king's hands. This seems to have caused Cromwell to amend his judgement that the richer religious houses would be too powerful to destroy without risking widespread political unrest. The piecemeal closures of late 1538 and early 1539 were probably intended to test the resolve of the remaining monastic communities. Much to Cromwell's relief, he found that most were willing to surrender to the Crown without a struggle.

Violent action was necessary only against the few who resisted, such as the abbots of Glastonbury, Reading and Colchester. In any event, Cromwell, the highly skilled, pragmatic politician, made it difficult for the monasteries to resist because he opted to pursue a policy of a piecemeal process of closure. This denied his potential enemies time to plan or organise any serious resistance.

Lack of opposition to the dissolution

In the final analysis, the monasteries offered little opposition to their dissolution because Henry had the law on his side. As supreme head of the Church, the king had the power to deal with them as he wished, a position that the monks and nuns had accepted by swearing the Oath of Supremacy in 1535. Moreover, the majority of the senior clerics, the abbots, priors and other heads of houses, had been bought off, which deprived the rank and file of the leadership they needed to resist. The truth is the will to resist had been broken when Convocation caved in to royal pressure in the Submission of the Clergy. The abbots outnumbered their secular counterparts, the bishops, in Convocation, so that monastic submission to the will of the king was already well established by the time the dissolutions took place. Although some received support from a number of northern monasteries it was really a rebellion of the laity rather than of the clergy.

Social and economic consequences

It has been claimed by some historians that the dissolution of the monasteries amounted to a revolution in land ownership. There were also social and economic consequences since the monasteries had been employers of large numbers of farm workers and had provided a stimulus to the local economy. Religious houses also offered hospitality for pilgrims and charity for the old and infirm. Monasteries had also supplied alms for the poor and destitute, and it has been argued that the removal of this and other charitable resources, amounting to about five per cent of net monastic income, contributed to the legions of 'sturdy beggars' that plagued late Tudor England, leading to crime and social instability.

On a more positive note, the dissolution did witness the survival of some of the more impressive abbey churches which were transformed into cathedrals in newly created dioceses such as Bristol, Gloucester, Chester and Westminster. Many others were purchased by their local communities to serve as parish churches, such as in Abergavenny, Bath and Tewkesbury. By the same token, the loss of such great abbeys as Glastonbury, Fountains, Rievaulx and Tintern cannot be so easily explained or excused and may amount to what some historians have described as 'cultural vandalism'.

Historians have traditionally focused attention on the effect of the disappearance of the monasteries on the wealth of the Crown. This is because the seizures made between 1536 and 1540 had the potential to virtually double the king's regular income. That this did not happen was because vast amounts of monastic property were sold quickly and at far less than their market value. Henry wanted to solve his immediate financial problems and had no long-term plan to put the Crown's finances on a more secure footing. In the opinion of historian Denys Cook (writing in 1980), the sale of monastic property might have been an example of 'poor economics' but, politically at least, it was 'a master stroke ensuring the permanence of the Henrician Reformation by the simple expedient of selling shares in it'.

Cromwell: architect of the Henrician Reformation?

There is no doubt that Cromwell played a pivotal role in the Henrician Reformation. As the king's vicegerent in religious affairs, he exerted the most significant influence of any individual (with the possible exception of Thomas Cranmer) on the life of the Church. As a reflection of Cromwell's powerful influence in royal circles, he was described by his enemy, Cardinal Reginald Pole, as 'an agent of Satan sent by the devil to lure King Henry to damnation'. Denying that Cromwell held genuine evangelical convictions, Cardinal Pole claimed that he was moved instead by greed and a **Machiavellian** desire to serve the king. Indeed, Cromwell may even have agreed in part with Pole's assessment, for he maintained to the end that his beliefs always took second

---

KEY TERM

Machiavellian Cleverly deceitful and unscrupulous. Named after an Italian political writer and thinker, Niccolo Machiavelli (1469–1527) of Florence.

place to his loyalty to his master, and that he would have followed whatever religion he had been instructed to. Within months of his minister's death, a regretful Henry VIII was convinced of the truth of this claim, and most historians have subsequently come to the same conclusion.

This is not to suggest that Cromwell had no religious beliefs. Cromwell, like Cranmer, was a religious reformist who favoured some aspects of the Lutheran faith. Nor can he be accused of being uninterested in religious issues because – from his letters – it is evident that he was. It is just that his first priority was always to prove his unswerving loyalty to Henry. Unlike Sir Thomas More, Cromwell was prepared to carry out whatever instructions he was given by the king, even if these ran counter to either his policy objectives or his personal beliefs. Indeed, in the opinion of More, Cromwell's biggest error was in telling the king what he could do rather than what he ought to do. Nevertheless, it is clear that Cromwell sometimes took risks by pursuing a reformist agenda and passing measures through Parliament of which Henry might not necessarily approve, such as the Ten Articles.

Role and power as vicegerent

Cromwell used his authority as Henry's ecclesiastical deputy to the full. He was helped in this regard by a willing Cranmer who, as Archbishop of Canterbury and thus the leading churchman in England, brought the authority of the Church to his aid. Aware of the delicate balance that existed in Convocation between the reforming and conservative bishops, Cromwell followed a policy of divide and rule. He enlisted the help of the reformers, who included Cranmer, to devise statements on religious doctrine that could be issued in the king's name and enforced throughout the Church.

Cromwell justified his actions by declaring that he was simply following the king's instructions and that those who proposed to do otherwise might be guilty of treason. Thus, Cromwell demanded that an episcopal consensus be reached so that a measure of uniformity in religious beliefs and practices could be achieved. To counter the opposition of the more militant conservatives, he pursued a policy of threat and intimidation. In this way, Cromwell was able to secure a working majority in Convocation, which became a useful tool in his quest to control the Church. Thus, he was able to persuade the bishops to agree to more radical measures, such as the publication of a Bible in English and its distribution across the kingdom.

To ensure that his measures and instructions were followed, Cromwell issued several sets of highly detailed injunctions or orders. Traditionally, injunctions had been issued either by individual bishops to deal with issues within a diocese or collectively in Convocation if the need was more national than local. Under the authority vested in him as vicegerent, Cromwell decided to bypass the episcopacy and to issue the injunctions himself. The first set of Royal

Injunctions, issued in the summer of 1536, was used to enforce the Crown's doctrinal and anti-papal measures, such as the following:

- erasing any reference to the Pope in religious services
- defending the royal supremacy in sermons
- removing superstitious images in churches
- encouraging the preaching of scripture
- discouraging pilgrimages.

Cromwell's greatest success: the Ten Articles

Cromwell's greatest success in securing a movement away from the existing beliefs and practices of the Church came with the passing of the Act of Ten Articles in 1536. In a clear move towards Protestantism, the central doctrine of the Catholic Church – the Seven Sacraments – was rejected, leaving only three – baptism, penance and the Eucharist. Cromwell was able to do this mainly because the king was distracted by the turmoil of his domestic life. At times of personal crisis Henry was more susceptible to Cromwell's persuasion because he wanted his chief minister to prepare a case for his divorce from Anne Boleyn. For some time the king had been reflecting on the biblical prohibitions of marriage, and having cast one wife (Catherine) aside via the annulment he wished to rid himself of another (Anne) by divorce. Cromwell's doctrinal arguments might suggest a way of justifying his actions.

Cromwell intended to follow up the Ten Articles with a much fuller explanation of what was permissible, in a revised doctrine. He planned to enlist a dedicated group of bishops and theologians who would work under his authority but follow the guidelines set out by Cranmer and Edward Foxe. After six months' work, a draft text had been completed, the details of which showed a distinct shift towards a more strongly Lutheran position. The text was entitled *The Godly and Pious Institution of the Christian Man* (also known as *The Bishops' Book*), and Cromwell ordered that a copy be given to the king.

The Bishops' Book

According to Cranmer, it was usual for Henry to rely on others to read books for him, so he tended to get his ideas second hand. However, on this occasion the king was too busy even to employ a reader so the book went unread for some months. Pressed for a decision by Cromwell, the king agreed to its publication but only on condition that the book be clearly marked as carrying only the bishops' authority. He was willing to write a short introduction but he made plain to the readership that he had only 'taken as it were a taste of this your book'. *The Bishops' Book,* as it was popularly known, appeared in July 1537 and although it was not the definitive doctrinal statement that Cromwell had sought – there was evidence of conservative influence – he was satisfied with the results. In the opinion of historian Keith Randell, 'the publication bore all the signs of being a step in the "softening up" process that was such a typical and successful strategy of Cromwell's'. It took Henry until 1543 before he was ready to consent to the publication bearing his name, resulting in the *King's Book*.

The Injunctions

In 1538 the vicegerent published his second set of Royal Injunctions. To ensure that these were not ignored, as some bishops had chosen to do with the first set in 1536, Cromwell enlisted the help of justices of the peace (JPs) to police the process of compliance. Any bishop who refused to implement the instructions was to be reported to Cromwell. These injunctions were more specific and reformist in tone than those of 1536. Instead of merely stipulating that superstitious practices should be discouraged, they stated that objects of dubious veneration, such as the relics of saints, should be removed from churches and that people should be actively discouraged from undertaking pilgrimages. To assist this process, Cromwell ordered the destruction of Thomas Becket's shrine in Canterbury Cathedral.

Although many bishops dragged their feet in putting these policies into effect, not all did. Among the most active in implementing Cromwell's Royal Injunctions was William Barlow, bishop of St David's. Barlow ordered that the bones of Saint David, the patron saint of Wales, should be removed from public view to discourage pilgrimage and then quietly buried. His enthusiasm for religious reform caused a rift with his clergy and he was advised, for his own safety, to stay away from his diocese. This so-called 'Protestant experiment' in St David's contrasts with the truculence displayed by Barlow's neighbour, the strongly conservative bishop of Llandaff, George de Athequa. Although an absentee bishop, Athequa's reluctance to enforce Cromwell's injunctions in his diocese is more fully understood when we consider the fact that he had been the loyal chaplain to his fellow Spaniard, Queen Catherine.

Arguably the most significant of Cromwell's Royal Injunctions was that a register of births, marriages and deaths should be kept in every parish. The unintended consequence has been the accumulation of one of the richest sources of evidence for the study of family history.

Reversing the drift towards Protestantism

If Cromwell thought he had secured the future direction of the nation's religion he was mistaken. The drift towards Protestantism was brought to an abrupt end in 1539 when Parliament passed the Act of Six Articles. This marked the beginning of a conservative ascendancy in both Church and State as the Duke of Norfolk, supported by Stephen Gardiner, Bishop of Winchester, and Cuthbert Tunstall, Bishop of Durham, sought to undermine Cromwell's reformist agenda. They were helped by the deteriorating international situation which witnessed an alliance between Francis I and Charles V. Henry feared that they might respond to Pope Paul III's call for a Catholic crusade against the recently excommunicated king of England. In addition, an ageing Henry began to think of his mortality and was persuaded that the process of religious reform had gone too far.

The Act of Six Articles

Referred to by Protestants as 'the bloody whip with six strings', the Act was a step back towards conservative Catholicism. Formally titled 'An Act Abolishing Diversity in Opinions', the Six Articles reinforced existing heresy laws and reasserted traditional Catholic doctrine as the basis of faith for the English Church. For example:

- **consubstantiation** was rejected and **transubstantiation** reintroduced
- clerical celibacy was enforced
- private masses were allowed
- **confession** was reintroduced.

It has been suggested that the Act of Six Articles was a 'panic measure' by a king reacting to international pressures. His excommunication in 1538 by Clement's successor, Pope Paul III (Henry snubbed the new Pope and refused to repeal the Act of Supremacy), was followed by the threat of invasion made possible by the conclusion of peace between Francis I of France and Charles V of Spain and the Holy Roman Empire. There is a further suggestion that the Act was inspired by Henry's declining health and increasing fear of death, which contributed to his desire to confirm his standing as a 'good Catholic'.

The doctrinal position of the Church in England by 1547

The doctrinal position of the Church in England owed much to, and was shaped by, Henry VIII's personal religious outlook. The problem was that the king's religious beliefs were somewhat ambivalent. On the one hand, he appeared to be conservative, opposed heresy and desired uniformity but, on the other, he embraced the role of a religious reformer by rejecting pilgrimage, superstition and the monastic ideal. The Reformation took a decidedly conservative path after Cromwell's fall in 1540 but the continued influence of Cranmer as archbishop, aided by the king's pro-reformist final wife, Catherine Parr (1512–48), ensured that some Lutheran principles were never completely abandoned.

⚷ KEY TERMS

Consubstantiation
The belief that the wine and bread taken at communion were symbolic and merely represented the blood and body of Christ.

Transubstantiation
The belief that the wine and bread taken at communion were actually the blood and body of Christ when they were blessed.

Confession Where parishioners confess their sins to a priest in order to receive absolution.

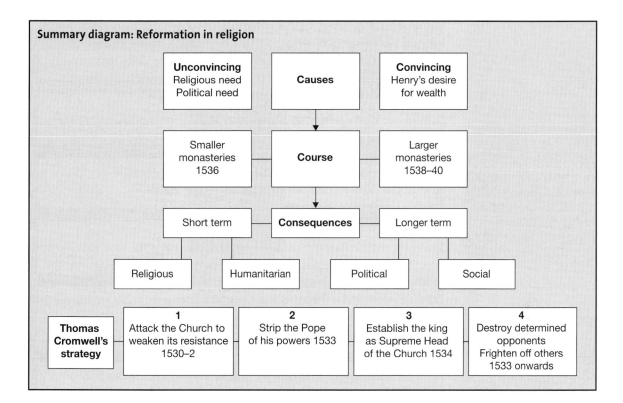

Summary diagram: Reformation in religion

Opposition and the fall of Cromwell

▶ *How serious was the opposition to religious change and did it contribute to the fall of Cromwell?*

Opposition and the Treason Act

Henry and Cromwell were acutely aware that the political and religious policies they were pursuing were likely to be unpopular. What they could not anticipate was the potential scale and seriousness of that opposition. Cromwell had calculated that the opposition would come from a minority of hardliners who would refuse to accept the changes and who preferred martyrdom to submission. This group was likely to consist of devout clerics, like Bishop John Fisher, and politicians of conscience, such as Sir Thomas More. The king's chief minister, Cromwell, believed that with a little 'persuasion' the majority of the population would accept the changes without protest. To ensure that the reaction of the Crown would be seen to be proportionate and legally justified, he drew up the Treason Act, which he steered through Parliament in 1534.

The key clause in the Act specified that any person who 'do maliciously wish, will or desire by words or writing, or by craft imagine, invent, practise, or attempt any bodily harm to be done or committed to the king's most royal person, the queen's [Anne Boleyn] or their heir's apparent [Elizabeth]' was guilty of high treason for which they would be put to death.

Not only were people forbidden to speak or write anything that might be critical of the king and his policies, they were also obliged, if required by a magistrate or judge, to swear oaths accepting the changes and pledging their allegiance to the Crown. Cromwell was confident that the terms of the Act would be sufficient to deter all but the most determined of the king's opponents.

John Fisher, Bishop of Rochester

Two of the most influential and determined opponents of the king were Bishop John Fisher and Sir Thomas More (see page 113). Their harsh treatment at the hands of the king shocked contemporaries, who blamed both Anne Boleyn and Thomas Cromwell for their trial and execution. They were both canonised (made saints) by the Catholic Church in 1935.

Fisher was one of the most senior and well-respected clerics in the English Church. He was a humanist scholar and theologian of international repute. He was a particular favourite of Henry VIII's grandmother, Margaret Beaufort, and he gave the oration at Henry VII's funeral. As a young man, Henry VIII admired the charismatic and learned bishop, but this turned into a deep loathing once the depth of Fisher's opposition to the annulment became clear. He was the only bishop in Convocation who, from the beginning, consistently opposed the king and his policies. Described as unskilled in politics, he nonetheless vigorously opposed the anticlerical legislation passing through the Reformation Parliament.

Initially, Henry tolerated Fisher's theological and intellectual arguments against accepting the annulment and for rejecting the invalidity of the papal dispensation. Henry even granted Fisher's request to serve as one of Queen Catherine's legal counsel at the annulment tribunal at Blackfriars. However, Fisher's increasing outspokenness, both in public and in print, on the matter of the annulment caused Henry to abandon the restraint he had shown thus far.

Enemy of the king

Henry was furious when Fisher declared his supporter for the Holy Maid of Kent, **Elizabeth Barton**. Barton had attracted the attention of the government when she denounced Henry's attempts to annul his marriage. Fisher believed that Barton's visions and prophesies were divinely inspired. However, when Barton began prophesying that if Henry remarried he would die shortly thereafter and go straight to hell, Fisher distanced himself from her. Fisher was not prepared to go as far as to discuss in public the king's mortality or any sin he may have committed, but in private he began corresponding with Charles V, whom he encouraged to invade England and remove Henry. When Barton

KEY FIGURE

Elizabeth Barton (1506–34)
Known as the Holy Maid of Kent, Barton was a nun at St Sepulchre's Convent in Canterbury. She was known for her prophecies and claims to be in contact with the Virgin Mary. Barton had a remarkably wide following among the English clergy and nobility.

publicly stated that Henry 'should no longer be king of this realm … and should die a villain's death' she was arrested, tried and convicted of heresy. In April 1534 she was executed at Tyburn (which is in present-day London).

In the same month that Henry disposed of Barton he moved against Fisher. Henry realised that he could not simply punish Fisher without just cause as this might encourage protest both at home and abroad, so he charged him with treason on two counts:

- meeting with the heretic Elizabeth Barton and failing to disclose the treasonous nature of her prophesies
- refusing to swear the Oath of Supremacy accepting the annulment of the king's marriage and the succession of his offspring by Anne Boleyn.

Fisher was imprisoned in the Tower and Henry was prepared, at first, to leave him there. However, this changed when Pope Paul III (1534–49), Clement's successor, appointed Fisher a cardinal. It is thought that Pope Paul did this in an effort to save Fisher's life by deterring Henry from punishing a newly appointed 'prince of the Church'. It had the opposite effect. Henry resented the pontiff's attempts to interfere in the internal affairs of England. On being informed of Fisher's promotion, Henry is reported to have said that he would 'give Fisher a red hat of his own, or else see that he had nowhere to put it'. Fisher was tried for treason and executed in 1535.

Sir Thomas More

Sir Thomas More was a lawyer by trade and a scholar by inclination. His literary activities had earned him a reputation as one of Europe's leading scholars. He attracted the attention and patronage of Henry VIII, who came to regard him as a friend. His political interests drew him to court, where Henry employed him as an advisor and diplomat. However, in the cut and thrust of Tudor politics More's strict moral code prevented him from doing the things needed to become a front-line political figure. This explains why many of his contemporaries were surprised when Henry offered him the post of Lord Chancellor. To succeed Wolsey at such a critical juncture in the annulment process was very risky. More could offer no solution to the problem. Like Fisher, he was not convinced by the king's reasons for seeking the annulment but unlike his clerical friend, More was willing to remain silent.

During his two-year tenure as Lord Chancellor (1530–2), More worked behind the scenes to frustrate Henry's cause but to little practical effect. However, it was not the annulment itself that caused him to resign but the king's mounting attack on the independence of the Church. Henry's bullying of Convocation followed by the Pardon of the Clergy and Parliament's Supplication of the Ordinaries caused More to feel uncomfortable about remaining in office. He did not believe that the Church's best interests would be served if it passed into the hands of laymen.

SOURCE D

Study Source D. Why might More have commissioned this portrait?

A portrait of Sir Thomas More wearing his chain of office as Lord Chancellor, painted in 1530 by Hans Holbein (the Younger).

More's resignation and execution

More's resignation coincided with the Submission of the Clergy because he felt no longer able to serve a king who had so offended against the laws of God and the Church. He intended to retire from public life and protect himself by remaining silent. Unfortunately for him, Henry was not satisfied and he requested that More swear to the Oath of Succession. Like Fisher, More refused and he joined the bishop in the Tower. He was later tried and was found guilty on a legal technicality, aided by the perjury of Cromwell's agent Richard Rich. More was executed in July 1535, a month after Fisher.

Sir Thomas More

1478	Born the son of a lawyer, Sir John More, in London
1504	Entered Parliament
1510	Appointed under-sheriff of London
1518	Admitted to the King's Council as an adviser to the king
1521	Knighted by Henry VIII. Co-author with the king of *Defence of the Seven Sacraments*, a rejection of Luther and Protestantism
1530	Appointed Lord Chancellor (king's chief minister)
1532	Resigned from government after refusing to support king's annulment and for opposing the king's attack on the Church
1535	Tried and found guilty of treason. Executed by beheading

More was educated at St Anthony's School, London, and served as a teenage page in the household of Archbishop John Morton. Between c.1494 and 1496 he attended Oxford University, after which he was admitted to Lincoln's Inn to study law. In 1501 More became a barrister-at-law. In 1505 he became friends with Desiderius Erasmus, the international scholar and humanist. In 1511 his first wife died in childbirth and he married for a second time.

- In 1515 More joined the royal delegation to Flanders to negotiate new agreements on the wool trade.
- In 1518 he was appointed to the King's Council.
- Henry VIII appointed More Speaker of the House of Commons.
- In 1525 he was appointed to government office as Chancellor of the Duchy of Lancaster.
- He reached the peak of his power in 1530 when he was appointed to succeed Wolsey as Lord Chancellor.

However, More could not support the king's divorce and opposed the attack on the Church so he resigned. In 1534 he refused to swear to the Act of Succession and Oath of Supremacy, for which he was committed to the Tower of London.

More was a reluctant martyr and Henry VIII a reluctant executioner. More's last words on the scaffold were: 'I die the king's good servant, but God's first'. He is important because he is seen as a man of conscience and he refused to compromise or betray his principles.

Cromwell's fall from power

Religious differences deepened the rift between political factions at court. The most notable casualty of this rivalry was the 'architect of the Reformation', Thomas Cromwell. Cromwell's greatest achievement was in planning and piloting the legislation responsible for the break with Rome. His survey, closure and eventual destruction of the monasteries represent a model of administrative speed and efficiency. Unfortunately, his skill and effectiveness in government, his promotion of the key aspects of Protestantism, and his leadership of the religious reform movement at court caused jealousy and made him powerful enemies. When he made mistakes, such as arranging the marriage between Henry VIII and Anne of Cleves, his enemies pounced and ruined his reputation with the king. The man most responsible for bringing Cromwell down was Thomas Howard, Duke of Norfolk, leader of the conservatives at court.

Barely three months after being ennobled as Earl of Essex, Cromwell was executed on trumped-up charges of treason in July 1540. In the opinion of historian Diarmaid MacCulloch, 'Cromwell was destroyed by noblemen who considered themselves the natural rulers under the king'. Cromwell was especially hated because 'he was a self-made man in a world of hierarchy, where nearly everyone believed God had put them in their place'. Cromwell was regarded as an example of a man seemingly defying God's will.

After Cromwell's fall, Henry had to tread a cautious path between the conservative Catholic and reforming Protestant parties. By 1546 he had decided that the safest way to protect the succession and the royal supremacy was to give control of the Privy Council to Somerset and the reformers.

SOURCE E

From William Roper, *The Life of Sir Thomas More* (c.1550). Roper was More's son-in-law.

Master Cromwell you are now entered into the service of a most noble, wise and liberal prince. If you will follow my poor advice, you shall, in your counsel-giving unto his grace, the king, ever tell him what he ought to do but never what he is able to do. So shall you show yourself a true, faithful servant and a right worthy counsellor. For if a lion know his own strength, hard were it for any man to rule him.

> ? Study Source E. What do you think is the meaning of the advice given to Cromwell?

The decline and death of Henry VIII

Henry VIII died in January 1547. It was not a sudden event. He had been seriously ill for nearly a decade. He suffered from excruciatingly painful swelling of his legs, which periodically broke out into horrible sores. Henry was massively overweight, with a waist of over 50 inches (127 cm). This huge bulk seems to have increased the severity of the pain that he would, in any case, have suffered. Unsurprisingly, there were critical moments when both his doctors and his court had expected that their patient and monarch would soon be dead. Given his health problems it is perhaps remarkable that Henry survived into his fifty-fifth year. Indeed, he had already outlived many of his contemporaries in an age when a person reaching 40 was thought to be entering old age rather than middle age.

Faction struggle: conservatives and reformers

There was never any doubt that Henry's successor would be his only son, Edward. However, since it was recognised that it was highly likely that Edward would still be a minor when his father died (he could not be declared 'of age' until he reached 21 in 1558 at the earliest), all interest at court centred on the arrangements to be made for the government of the realm in the years before the new king attained adult status. It was well understood that whichever faction secured the dominant position during Edward's minority would be able both to exercise enormous power and to acquire considerable wealth at the expense of the monarchy.

The two contending factions, although they were anything but settled in their composition, were the conservatives, headed by the Duke of Norfolk, and the reformers, led by Edward Seymour, Earl of Hertford, who was Jane Seymour's brother.

Contending court factions

- The conservative faction led by Thomas Howard, Duke of Norfolk, and Bishop Stephen Gardiner.

- The reform faction led by Edward Seymour, Earl of Hertford, and Archbishop Thomas Cranmer.

- The 'conservatives' have been so called because they both favoured keeping the teachings and practices of the Church of England as traditional as possible and believed that the king should seek advice from his leading nobles rather than from men of common birth as had tended to happen since 1485. The most politically able of their active members was Stephen Gardiner, the Bishop of Winchester, whose plotting had been behind most of the attempts to discredit individual reformers ever since he had lost the struggle with Thomas Cromwell to win the king's favour in the early 1530s.

- The reformers had been identified with Cromwell during his period of dominance. Since his fall in 1540, they had naturally been somewhat in disarray. Perhaps their obvious new leader might have been Thomas Cranmer, Archbishop of Canterbury, as he had long been known to be sympathetic to their leanings towards Protestantism in religion. However, Cranmer was interested neither in politics nor in seeking greater power for himself. His competitive spirit was minimal. It was, therefore, left to Edward's relations on his mother's side to set about rebuilding the fortunes of the faction that favoured change.

The succession

Although Henry VIII's final years were marked by failing health, he managed to maintain the authority of the Crown and preserve the unity of the realm. Apart from the wars with Scotland and France, which had begun in 1542 and 1544, respectively, Henry VIII's major concern in his last years was the succession. Since 1527 he had been obsessed with the need to safeguard the dynasty by leaving a male heir to succeed him. The birth of Prince Edward in 1537 had seemed to achieve this objective. By 1546 the king's declining health made it clear that his son would come to the throne as a minor. To avoid any possible disputes, Henry made a final settlement of the succession in his will of 1546. This replaced the Succession Acts of 1534, 1536 and 1544, although the terms of the will were similar to the Act of 1544.

In the event of Edward dying without heirs, the succession was to pass first to Mary, the daughter of Catherine of Aragon. If Mary died without heirs, her sister Elizabeth, daughter of Anne Boleyn, was to succeed. The major change to the previous settlement was that if all Henry's children were to die without heirs, the throne was to pass to his niece, Frances Grey. Lady Frances was the elder daughter of Henry VIII's sister Mary from her marriage to Charles Brandon, Duke of Suffolk (Mary's first husband, King Louis XII of France, had died in 1515). This clause meant that the other possible claimant to the English throne, the infant Mary, Queen of Scots, was excluded. Mary was the descendant of Henry VIII's sister Margaret, who had married James IV of Scotland. Henry was anxious to preserve the royal supremacy, hence the inclusion of the Protestant Grey family and the exclusion of the Catholic Stuart dynasty. Although the will had replaced the earlier succession settlements, the Acts of 1534 and 1536, which had made Mary and Elizabeth illegitimate, were not repealed.

Henry's last will and testament

Henry's major concern in his will was to secure the peaceful succession of his son and safeguard the royal supremacy. By the middle of 1546 it had become clear that the surest way to achieve this, and to prevent a power struggle, was to give authority to Seymour and the reform faction. The disgrace of Howard and omission of Gardiner from the will had made the position of Seymour and his supporters more secure. Seymour's authority was further strengthened by adjustments to the terms of the will right up to the time of Henry VIII's death.

The will was drafted towards the end of December 1546 but it was not authorised to be signed until a month later, when the king knew that he was about to die. The explanation that has most often been given for this sequence of events is that the existence of the unsigned will, of which those named in it were aware, was a ploy by Henry to intimidate his leading subjects further. The fact that the document was unsigned was a clear threat that if those named in it did not please him in every detail, the wording of the will would be altered to their disadvantage before it was made final.

SOURCE F

From the last will and testament of Henry VIII, 1546.

As to the succession of the Crown, it shall go to Prince Edward and the heirs of his body. In default, to Henry's children by his present wife, Queen Catherine, or any future wife. In default, to his daughter Mary and the heirs of her body, upon condition that she shall not marry without the written and sealed consent of a majority of the surviving members of the Privy Council appointed by him to his son Prince Edward. In default, to his daughter Elizabeth upon like condition. In default, to the heirs of the body of Lady Frances, eldest daughter of his late sister the French Queen. In default, to those of Lady Elyanore, second daughter of the said French Queen. And in default, to his right heirs. Either Mary or Elizabeth, failing to observe the conditions aforesaid, shall forfeit all right to the succession.

Study Source F. Why was Henry VIII's will so politically significant?

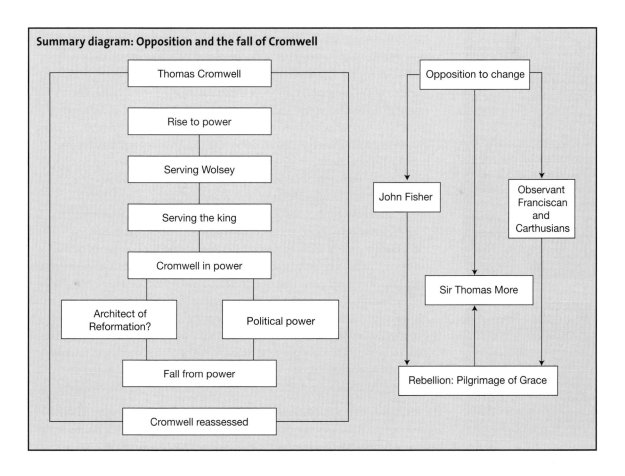

Summary diagram: Opposition and the fall of Cromwell

③ Revolution in government

> ▶ *What was the nature and scale of the revolution in government?*

Elton's 'revolution in government' theory

In the opinion of historian G.R. Elton, 'a revolution in government' took place between 1532 and 1540, when Cromwell was Henry's chief minister. Elton's main contention was that during these years a series of changes were made that in their totality marked a transition from medieval household to modern bureaucratic forms of government.

Elton's theory can be broken down into four component parts:

- The structure and organisation of central government. The 'administrative revolution' was responsible for a radical change in the structure and organisation of central government. The major part of this recasting of central administration revolved around the reorganisation of the financial departments and the creation of the Privy Council. The result was that *government by the king* was replaced by *government under the king*.
- The role of Parliament and the scope and authority of statute law. The essential ingredient of the Tudor revolution was the concept of national sovereignty and the creation of a sovereign law-making Parliament. In using Parliament to enforce the Reformation, the Crown was emphasising that nothing lay outside the competence of parliamentary statute. The result was that *king and Parliament* had been replaced by *king-in-Parliament*.
- The relationship between Church and State. By bringing the Church firmly under the control of the king, the royal supremacy had initiated a 'jurisdictional revolution' in the relationship between Church and State. The independence of the Church had been quashed and the balance of power between Church and State had tipped firmly in favour of the latter. The result was that *Church and State* had been replaced by *Church-in-State*.
- The extension of royal authority in the regions. By bringing the outlying regions of the kingdom under the control of the central government, Cromwell was aiming to create a nation that was a jurisdictional entity. He gave more authority and purpose to the Council of the North and reformed the government of Wales by empowering the Council of Wales and the Marches. Although short-lived, he also set up a Council of the West.

The result was that a *fragmented polity* was replaced by a *unitary state*. Elton argued that, as these developments were one of the major turning points in the history of British politics, they well deserved the title of revolution.

Defining medieval and modern government

Elton's argument turned on his definition of medieval and modern forms of government and his assessment of what happened in the 1530s.

SOURCE G

From G.R. Elton, *The Tudor Revolution in Government*, Cambridge University Press, 1953, p. 75.

In every way, then, the great restoration of government after the civil wars of the fifteenth century, the work of Edward IV and Henry VII, represented the restoration of medieval government at its most efficient. A financial administration based on the king's chamber and the somewhat informal means adopted for audit and control, the extended use of the signet [the king's private seal] and the rise of the secretary, and government through individual councillors rather than a council, all these marked the triumph of household methods in administration.

Elton was quite specific about the features that typified medieval government. He argued that modern forms of government were very different from medieval methods of administration. Medieval systems of government were based on royal officers working within the household and accountable only to the king. Modern systems of government were bureaucratic, being based on 'departments of state' staffed by professional salaried officials who worked according to agreed procedures. In this way the bureaucratic 'departments' could function efficiently without the constant supervision of the monarch, who might be lazy, weak or, in the case of Edward VI, a child. Therefore, the 'system' was paramount.

Elton concluded that because of the nature and scale of the changes that took place in the structure of government in the 1530s the English administrative system crossed the line that divides the medieval from the modern. He identified two changes as being of particular importance.

First change: the replacement of a household system of finance by a bureaucratic system

- In the medieval system most of the king's income was received by individual officers whose conduct was not properly regulated and whose accounts were not regularly audited. These officials worked informally within the royal household. Many of these officials were appointed to the offices because of their family connections and patronage and not on merit or administrative ability.
- In the modern system legally constituted and properly regulated departments received and paid out money and were efficiently audited. They were staffed for the most part by professionally trained administrators who owed their promotion to merit and ability rather than patronage. The most important of these 'new' departments were the Court of First Fruits and Tenths and the Court of Augmentation. They were tasked with administering the king's income and assets from the Church.

Study Source G. What were the key features of medieval government?

Second change: the establishment of the Privy Council

Elton argued that at some time in the 1530s (probably in 1536, to deal with the Pilgrimage of Grace, see page 102) the informal medieval system of a large council, with between 70 and 90 members, was replaced by a more formal Privy Council system in which an elite group of about twenty trusted permanent councillors assumed responsibility for running the government. Elton summarised his argument by claiming that 'when an administration relying on the household was replaced by one based exclusively on bureaucratic departments and officers of state, a revolution took place in government'.

According to Elton, the Privy Council's small size and the eminence and competence of its members enabled it to function effectively during periods of crisis such as the rebellion known as the Pilgrimage of Grace and even during the royal minority of Edward VI. The creation and importance of the Privy Council by 1540 are not in doubt but some historians have rejected Cromwell's part in its creation. Responding to criticism from historians who claim that the Privy Council was structured along lines prefigured by Wolsey in his Eltham Ordinance of 1526 (see page 69), Elton pointed out that the cardinal's chief adviser at the time was none other than Thomas Cromwell. Cromwell's death in July 1540 did not witness the end of the Privy Council, which continued to evolve after his death.

SOURCE H

Study Source H. How might Elton's critics use this source to undermine his claim that Cromwell was responsible for a revolution in government?

From the minutes of a Privy Council meeting in August 1540. This recorded the appointment of Sir William Paget as the Council's first secretary to keep the minutes of every meeting. Quoted in J.R. Dasent, editor, *Acts of the Privy Council of England*, Volume 1, Her Majesty's Stationery Office, 1890.

The 10th day of August in the 32nd year of the reign of our sovereign lord King Henry VIII … an order was taken and determined by his Majesty by the advice of his Highness' Privy Council that there should be a clerk attendant upon the said Council to write, enter and register all such decrees, determinations, letters and other such things as he should be appointed to enter in a book, to remain always a ledger.

The role of Parliament and the relationship between Church and State

Elton claimed that Cromwell's work radically enhanced the power of the State and the competence of Parliament within the State. It is claimed, with some justification, that Cromwell not only paved the way for royal government to take control of the English Church, but also masterminded the method through which this could best be achieved: by means of parliamentary statute. By making Henry VIII the Supreme Head of the Church in England, Cromwell had created a revolution in the relationship between Church and State. In using Parliament to enforce the Reformation, Cromwell had established the principle that king-in-Parliament constituted the highest form of authority in the kingdom. To support his case, Elton compared the volume of legislation passed during Henry VIII's reign, some 37 years, with that passed between 1258, the middle of the reign of Henry III, and 1509, around 251 years. For example, in the printed *Statutes of the Realm* the laws passed by Henry VIII filled 1032 pages but the laws passed between 1258 and 1509 filled 1094 pages. Clearly, the workload of Parliament had increased dramatically.

The extension of royal authority in the regions

It is perhaps in the area of regional and local government that Elton's thesis is most vulnerable to criticism. Elton's argument here turned more on what Cromwell intended than on what he achieved. Cromwell may have intended to extend royal authority into the wilder and remoter parts of the kingdom but his success was limited. He had no choice but to depend on the unpaid co-operation of local gentry acting as JPs and on the willingness of powerful noble landowners or influential clerics who invariably filled the offices of president of the regional Councils of the North, West and Wales.

Only in respect of his reform of the government and administration of Wales and the Marches can anything approaching an Eltonian 'revolution' be detected. Between 1536 and 1543 the semi-independent power of the Marcher Lordships was swept away, Wales was divided into shires as in England, and the Welsh were given representation in Parliament for the first time. In addition, the Council of Wales and the Marches, which had been a household institution of the Prince of Wales, was bureaucratised and given statutory authority to govern this region of the realm whether there was a prince or not.

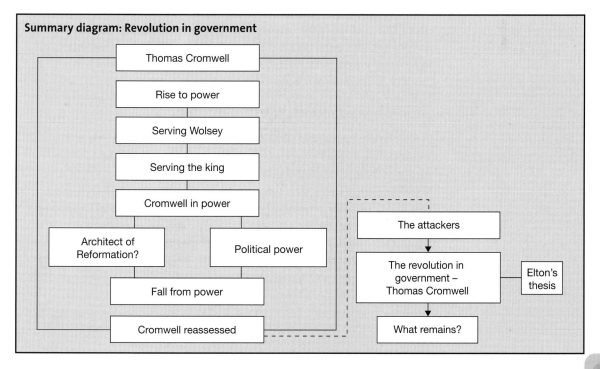

Summary diagram: Revolution in government

4 Key debate

▶ *Was there a revolution in government?*

Arguably, the most important debate on Tudor history was started by G.R. Elton in the early 1950s. Since its publication in 1953, Elton's *Tudor Revolution in Government* has been the focus of fierce debates about the nature, structure and operation of Tudor government. He identified the reign of Henry VIII, and more specifically the 1530s under the influence of Thomas Cromwell, as the time when revolutionary changes took place in the way England was governed. His claim was that the period marked the transition from 'medieval' to 'modern' forms of government that transformed and enhanced the power and authority of the Crown and central government. Such was the brilliance and freshness of Elton's work (which he continued to build on for more than 30 years) that few historians of the period have subsequently been able to distance themselves from the storm of controversy that has surrounded the issue ever since.

Elton's 'revolution' thesis concentrated on highlighting significant change in the following key areas. The structure and organisation of central government was part of what Elton called the 'administrative revolution' which was concerned with the reorganisation of government financial departments. The most significant element of this 'administrative revolution' was the creation of the Privy Council. The role and competence of Parliament were greatly enhanced. King and Parliament had subtly shifted to become king-in-Parliament, which constituted the highest form of authority in the kingdom. The revolution here lay in the implication that Parliament was competent to deal with any matter. The essential ingredient of the revolution in government was the concept of national sovereignty. This is part of what Elton called the 'jurisdictional revolution' in which royal government extended its control of the English Church as well as the State to be uniformly powerful throughout the kingdom.

Elton's 'revolution in government' theory

In Elton's opinion, the fact that Henry VII had ascended the throne of a 'medievally-governed kingdom', while Elizabeth I was able to hand to her successor, James I, a country 'administered on modern lines', was indicative of radical change in the structure, machinery and operation of government. This transition from 'medieval' household government, whose efficiency and effectiveness depended on the personal energy and ability of the monarch, to a more 'professional' and 'modern' national bureaucracy which could function efficiently without the close supervision of the monarch, was, in Elton's view, done in accordance with Cromwell's blueprint in the eight years between 1532 and 1540.

EXTRACT 1

From G.R. Elton, *The Tudor Revolution in Government*, Cambridge University Press, 1953, pp. 424–5.

When an administration relying on the household was replaced by one based exclusively on bureaucratic departments and officers of state, a revolution took place in government. The principle then adopted was not in turn discarded until the much greater administrative revolution of the nineteenth century, which not only destroyed survivals of the medieval system allowed to continue a meaningless existence for some 300 years, but also created an administration based on departments responsible to parliament – an administration in which the crown for the first time ceased to hold the ultimate control. Medieval government was government by the king in person and through his immediate entourage. Early modern government was independent of the household, bureaucratically organised in national departments, but responsible to the crown.

The revisionist interpretation: revolution or evolution?

Few historians would deny that the middle decades of the sixteenth century witnessed remarkable changes in royal authority and in the government of the kingdom, but most are reluctant to go as far as Elton in claiming that a 'revolution' took place. The problem lies in the use of the term 'revolution' for some historians, notably David Starkey, who totally reject the idea that anything approaching a 'revolution' took place.

EXTRACT 2

From C. Coleman and David Starkey, editors, *Revolution Reassessed: Revisions in the History of Tudor Government and Administration*, Oxford University Press, 1986, p. 30.

Government in the sixteenth century, unlike government in the fifteenth, did not need and did not get a radical overhaul. Within its limits it worked very well; some modifications were of course required, and they took place. But they happened ad hoc and without great drama. It is always a pity to drive a great idea, Coriolanus-like, off the stage, but it must be done: Tudor readjustment in government indeed, but no revolution.

Modifying the 'revolution in government' theory

John Guy does not entirely reject the use of the label 'revolution' to describe the changes that occurred during the 1530s, but he does question the authorship and causes of these changes. To him, Cromwell was no visionary reformer but a 'pragmatist', someone who operated in the realm of the politically possible. He prefers to see the changes in terms of an 'evolutionary' process spanning a longer period and involving more people than simply Cromwell and his tight-knit group of servants.

EXTRACT 3

From John Guy, *Tudor England*, Oxford University Press, 1988, p. 156.

It has been argued over the last thirty years that Cromwell achieved a 'revolution in government' during the 1530s, though this interpretation has been attacked. The 'revolution' thesis maintains that Cromwell consciously – that is, as a matter of principle – reduced the role of the royal household in government and substituted instead 'national' bureaucratic administration within departments of state under the control of a fundamentally reorganized Privy Council. Such argument is, however, too schematic. The thesis that a Tudor 'revolution in government' took place is comprehensible when the periodization of change is extended to Elizabeth's death, though whether the word 'revolution' is appropriate – as opposed to 'readjustment' or straightforward 'change' – is a matter of judgement. If 'revolution' is supposed to designate permanent change, it will not do.

?️ 'Revolution' or 'readjustment'? According to Extracts 1–3, which label better describes the changes in government during Henry VIII's reign?

Chapter summary

Henry VIII and his chief minister, Thomas Cromwell, are credited with introducing significant changes in religion and government during the 1530s. The Reformation was a significant process that witnessed the gradual shift away from Roman Catholicism to a form of Anglo-Catholicism that included elements of Continental Protestantism. The compilation of the *Valor Ecclesiasticus* and subsequent closure of the monasteries are regarded as yardsticks of the considerable changes that occurred over a decade. The revolution in religion was, according to some historians, accompanied by an equally revolutionary change in government. The Reformation Parliament brought the Church and State together in an unprecedented attempt to shape the constitutional relationship between the two. Cromwell has been identified as the prime mover in these momentous changes. The problems and challenges faced by the king and his government came mainly from those who opposed the unprecedented, if not 'revolutionary', political and religious changes. The most significant casualty of these changes was Cromwell himself, who was brought low by his enemies, led by the Duke of Norfolk. Cromwell was the victim of envy, faction fighting and an unreliable king who sacrificed, arguably, the most talented minister in his government.

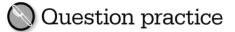 Refresher questions

Use these questions to remind yourself of the key material covered in this chapter.

1 What was Cromwell's 'new idea' to break the deadlock between King Henry VIII and the Pope?

2 How significant was Cranmer's role in the annulment issue?

3 Why did the Crown attack the Church?

4 How was the king's 'great matter' resolved?

5 What was meant by the royal supremacy and how was it achieved?

6 What impact did court faction have on the progress of the Reformation?

7 What caused the break with Rome?

8 How significant was the royal supremacy?

9 How significant were the visitations and the *Valor Ecclesiasticus*?

10 What motivated Cromwell to close the monasteries?

11 What were the short- and long-term effects of the dissolution?

12 Can Cromwell be described as the architect of the Henrician Reformation?

13 What did Elton mean by his use of the term 'revolution in government' and how significant was Cromwell's part in it?

Question practice

ESSAY QUESTIONS

1 'Every monastic institution in England and Wales was closed down during the reign of Henry VIII because of the King's urgent need for money.' Explain why you agree or disagree with this view.

2 'Protestantism was so popular by 1547 that England was more a Protestant than a Catholic nation.' Assess the validity of this view.

3 How important was Cromwell's contribution to the reformation of religion in England?

4 How accurate is it to say that Parliament became one of the most important parts of Tudor government in the years 1529–54?

5 How accurate is it to say that the Church was less popular by the end of Henry VIII's reign in 1547 from its position at the beginning of his reign in 1522?

INTERPRETATION QUESTIONS

1 With reference to Extracts 1 and 2 (page 126) and your understanding of the historical context, which of these two extracts provides the more convincing interpretation of a revolution in government?

2 Using your understanding of the historical context, assess how convincing the arguments in Extracts 3–5 (pages 126–7) are in relation to the causes of the dissolution of the monasteries.

EXTRACT 1

From G.R. Elton, *The Tudor Revolution in Government*, Cambridge University Press, 1953, pp. 424–5.

When an administration relying on the household was replaced by one based exclusively on bureaucratic departments and officers of state, a revolution took place in government. The principle then adopted was not in turn discarded until the much greater administrative revolution of the nineteenth century, which not only destroyed survivals of the medieval system allowed to continue a meaningless existence for some 300 years, but also created an administration based on departments responsible to parliament – an administration in which the crown for the first time ceased to hold the ultimate control. Medieval government was government by the king-in-person and through his immediate entourage. Early modern government was independent of the household, bureaucratically organised in national departments, but responsible to the crown.

EXTRACT 2

From John Guy, *Tudor England*, Oxford University Press, 1988, p. 156.

It has been argued over the last thirty years that Cromwell achieved a 'revolution in government' during the 1530s, though this interpretation has been attacked. The 'revolution' thesis maintains that Cromwell consciously – that is, as a matter of principle – reduced the role of the royal household in government and substituted instead 'national' bureaucratic administration within departments of state under the control of a fundamentally reorganized Privy Council. Such argument is, however, too schematic. The thesis that a Tudor 'revolution in government' took place is comprehensible when the periodization of change is extended to Elizabeth's death, though whether the word 'revolution' is appropriate – as opposed to 'readjustment' or straightforward 'change' – is a matter of judgement. If 'revolution' is supposed to designate permanent change, it will not do.

EXTRACT 3

From J.J. Scarisbrick, *Henry VIII*, Eyre Methuen, 1968, p. 337.

1536 saw the first stage of the dissolution of English monasticism. That vast enterprise, the Valor Ecclesiasticus, *a survey of the wealth of the English Church, had been drawn up in 1535; next year the first act of dissolution of monasteries of less than £200 annual value was passed. Tudor England was about to embark on its most massive single enterprise. English monasticism was a huge and urgent problem; that radical action, though of precisely what kind was another matter, was both necessary and inevitable, and that a purge of the religious orders was probably regarded as the most obvious task of the new regime – as the first functions of a Supreme Head empowered by statute 'to visit, extirp [destroy] and redress'. The real question was not whether the monks should be hammered but whether the purging of monasticism should not be included in a much larger programme which tackled the problem of redisposing the wealth of the entire Church.*

EXTRACT 4

From Glanmor Williams, *The Reformation in Wales*, Headstart History Publishing, 1991, p. 7.

Welsh monasteries at this time had little capacity to withstand impending dissolution themselves or to inspire others to resist on their behalf. All of them were severely reduced in the number of their inmates from what they had been in their heyday. Of the forty-seven houses in Wales only Tintern had the thirteen monks usually thought to be necessary to keep up the full round of monastic worship and prayer. The average number of monks to a house ranged between five and eight, but a number of smaller houses had only two or three inmates. Some were heavily in debt and most of them were, for all practical purposes, under the control of powerful families of local gentlemen. Monks and friars were not wicked or corrupt, generally speaking, although occasional scandals did occur in their midst: Robert Salusbury, abbot of Valle Crucis, was reported to be a highway robber and a monk at Strata Florida was accused of counterfeiting money. Yet it has to be recognised that their moral condition mattered far less in accounting for their dissolution than the political and economic needs of the king.

EXTRACT 5

From W.J. Sheils, *The English Reformation 1530–1570*, Routledge, 1989, p. 27.

Though there had been much humanist criticism of monastic life in the early sixteenth century, the influence of these critics in England did not extend beyond the universities and court circles before the 1530s. The monasteries and friaries were spread unevenly throughout England: only fourteen were in Lancashire, but Lincolnshire contained sixty-six religious houses in 1535. As is likely with such diversity, standards varied greatly. At Carishead in North Lancashire the prior in the 1530s was suspected of murder, but at Evesham in Worcestershire the monks appear to have maintained an intellectual and spiritual life which also involved nearby houses. Between these extremes, however, most monasteries shared the characteristics of the Lancashire houses which, though not disreputable, had declined in moral authority as a result of over-involvement in local secular affairs.

CHAPTER 5

Edward VI: Somerset, Northumberland and the royal minority 1542–53

This chapter is designed to help you to understand the key features of the reign of Edward VI by reference to the experiences of the Dukes of Somerset and Northumberland, who ruled the kingdom on behalf of the boy-king, and Archbishop Cranmer, who established Protestantism as the State religion. The chapter examines the political, religious, social and economic problems that faced the Edwardian regime. These issues are examined as four key themes:

★ Henry VIII's legacy: a kingdom in turmoil?

★ Edward VI: minority government under Somerset and Northumberland

★ Cranmer and the Protestant revolution

★ A nation in crisis? The impact of social, economic and religious change

Key dates

1542	Armed raid on Scotland led by Duke of Norfolk	1547	Edward Seymour created Duke of Somerset and Lord Protector
1543	Treaty of Greenwich with Scotland	1549	Rebellion in East Anglia and the West Country. Fall of Somerset
1544	Invasion of France; Boulogne captured		
	Act of Succession passed in Parliament	1551	John Dudley created Duke of Northumberland and Lord President of the Council
1545	Attempted French invasion of England failed		
1546	Treaty of Ardres between England and France	1552	Execution of the Duke of Somerset
	Henry drafted his last will	1553	Edward VI changed line of succession in favour of Lady Jane Grey
1547	Death of Henry VIII and accession of Edward VI		Death of Edward VI, brief reign of Lady Jane Grey and succession of Mary

1 Henry VIII's legacy: a kingdom in turmoil?

▶ *Was Henry VIII's legacy a kingdom in turmoil?*

Henry VIII's legacy has been hotly debated. The traditional interpretation of Henry's final five years in power presents him as an increasingly incompetent and unscrupulous tyrant who stumbled from one disaster to another. It has been maintained that he left behind him difficulties so serious that they threatened to harm the interests of the monarchy, its subjects and the kingdom. The implicit judgement has often been that it might have been better for all concerned if he had died somewhat earlier than he did. Herein lie the origins of the so-called 'mid-Tudor crisis', the period between the perceived decline in Henry VIII's reign from *c.*1542 to the accession of Elizabeth I in 1558.

A mid-Tudor crisis?

Until comparatively recently, historians have tended to underestimate the reigns of Edward VI and Mary because they appeared to be riddled with insoluble problems and bedevilled by almost permanent crisis. Given that Edward was a child and Mary was a female, the twin evils of rebellion at home and an unwinnable war abroad worked to undermine an already fatally weakened monarchy. Evidence of social unrest, economic collapse, religious division and political faction all conspired to convince historians that the term 'mid-Tudor crisis' was indeed an apt description of the period. Geoffrey Elton summed it up best when he wrote: 'After the rule of factions in the reign of a child, the accession of the wrong kind of Queen nearly completed the ruin of both dynasty and country.'

This is no longer considered to be the case. Revisionism has redressed the balance by accepting that while there were periods of crisis during the combined eleven-year reign of Edward and Mary, there were positive achievements also. The fact that the dynasty survived and that Elizabeth I inherited a fully functioning political system is certainly evidence of that. Led by Jennifer Loach, Robert Tittler and David Loades (writing between 1991 and 2012), the revisionists pointed out that the reigns of Henry VII, Henry VIII and Elizabeth could also furnish numerous examples of crises, some of which were every bit as serious as those that plagued Edward and Mary. Further, they point to the fact that Northumberland was a 'remarkably able governor' whose initiatives in government reveal a highly professional attitude, while Mary's ministers devised a scheme for recoinage and drew up a new Book of Rates which increased customs revenue. Historian G.D. Ramsay described the latter initiative as 'a major achievement in Tudor fiscal administration'.

Henry VIII's legacy

The kingdom that Henry VIII bequeathed to his successor, Edward VI, was plagued by political, religious, economic and social problems. But these problems were not insurmountable and they did not plunge England into a permanent state of crisis. Arguably, the most serious difficulties facing the new Edwardian regime arising out of Henry's legacy were in politics, religion and foreign diplomacy.

Political legacy

The political difficulties of Edward's reign stemmed mainly from the fact that he was a minor when he ascended the throne. This was hardly the fault of Henry VIII, who did as much as he could to ensure stability and continuity in royal government. Henry's last will and testament made arrangements for the government of the kingdom after his death. Henry was well aware of the struggle for power that was taking place around him and his fear was that the government would become a battleground for contending factions, each keen to secure the dominant position during his son's minority. The successful faction would be in a position both to exercise enormous power and to acquire considerable wealth at the expense of the monarchy.

To avoid this, Henry's will stated that the country should be ruled after his death by a Regency Council, whose members were named and whose membership could not subsequently be changed. It was also stated that the Council's decisions must be corporate, with no member being given greater prominence than any other. This attempt to stop the emergence of a leader, together with the fact that the Council appeared to be composed of equal numbers of 'conservatives' and 'progressives', shows that Henry was trying to ensure a political equilibrium until his son was old enough to take charge of government and decide for himself what changes, if any, were to be made.

Court factions

Broadly speaking, the contending factions were the 'conservatives', headed by the Duke of Norfolk, and the 'progressives', led by the Earl of Hertford, Edward's uncle. Although aligned on religious grounds the main aim of each faction was political power:

- The conservatives favoured keeping the teachings and practices of the Church of England as traditionally Catholic as possible and believed that the king should seek his advice from his leading nobles rather than from men of common birth as had tended to happen since 1485. The most politically able of their active members was Stephen Gardiner (see page 172), the Bishop of Winchester.
- The progressives favoured religious reform and the adoption of significant aspects of Continental Protestantism. The most able member of this faction was Thomas Cranmer, Archbishop of Canterbury, who, unlike Gardiner, was more interested in religious reform than either political power or personal enrichment.

The peaceful and stable political landscape intended by Henry's meticulous planning proved impossible to achieve. The arrest and detention of Norfolk by the king had weakened the conservatives and given the progressives a major boost in their quest for power. Nevertheless, the fact remains that when Henry's guiding hand was removed from the tiller, the ship of state ran aground on the rocks of personal ambition, political rivalry and bitter recrimination. It is ironic that the most serious threat to the political stability of the realm came not from infighting between the conservatives and the progressives but from a factional split among the latter.

Religious legacy

As soon as Henry made himself head of the English Church in 1534 he came under pressure to formulate an acceptable doctrine. The progressives, inspired by Cranmer, advocated the introduction of moderate Lutheran ideas but the pro-Catholic conservatives, led by Gardiner, favoured a policy of minimum change to the basic Catholic doctrines. For twelve turbulent years, from 1534 to 1546, royal favour swung between the two factions. The first major statement of doctrine, the Act of Ten Articles, came in 1536. This Act was passed when the reformers were in the ascendancy, and introduced a number of Lutheran doctrines into the Church of England such as belief in consubstantiation. Three years later, in 1539, the conservatives regained royal favour and the Act of Six Articles was passed to remove many of the Lutheran beliefs.

SOURCE A

Deathbed portrait of Henry VIII together with his son Edward VI, the Pope and members of the Royal Council, *c*.1570. Painted by an unknown artist.

> Study Source A. What message is the painting trying to convey? **?**

Such shifts of policy meant that by 1547 the doctrines of the Church of England were a compromise and contained many inconsistencies which were unacceptable to progressives and conservatives alike. Ultimately, Henry's religious legacy was a toxic mix of diluted Lutheranism fused with enlightened Catholicism that provided fertile ground for further bitter conflict. In short, the religious problems remained unresolved.

Diplomatic legacy

During the last five years of Henry's reign his grasp of England's foreign policy was slipping. Peaceful diplomacy had been abandoned in favour of military confrontation. The charge against Henry is that his final years were marked by war on two fronts – France and Scotland – in which he needlessly squandered his wealth and endangered the financial strength of his successors by attempting to win military glory. In fact, the cost of the war was enormous and by 1546 over £2 million, mainly raised by the sale of monastic lands, had been spent, thus adding to the growing financial crisis enveloping the Crown. His failure to achieve lasting success in France or to remove the ever-present threat of a Scottish invasion led to serious security problems for his successor.

On the other hand, it has been argued that he succeeded in maintaining England's position as a major player at the centre of international diplomacy, while securing the northern frontier by defeating the Scots at the Battle of Solway Moss in 1542 and safeguarding Calais by capturing Boulogne in 1544. However, this caused a great deal of resentment in France and Scotland, and the tension between England and its nearest neighbours only required a spark to ignite another conflict. Thus, Henry's legacy was one of uneasy peace and costly defence.

? Study Source B. What problems might Henry VIII bequeath to his son and successor, Edward VI?

SOURCE B

From a report on Henry VIII's political and religious legacy, sent to King Francis I of France by the French ambassador at the English court, Charles de Marillac, 1543. Quoted in _Letters and Papers, Foreign and Domestic, Henry VIII_, Volume 18, Part 1, January–July 1543. Originally published by Her Majesty's Stationery Office, 1901, pp. 212–13.

Thence proceeds … distrust and fear. The King, knowing how many changes he has made, and what tragedies and scandals he has created, would fain keep in favour with everybody, but does not trust a single man, expecting to see them all offended, and he will not cease to dip his hand in blood as long as he doubts his people.

Hence every day edicts are published so bloody that with a thousand guards one would scarce be safe. Hence too it is now with us, as affairs incline, he makes alliances which last as long as it makes for him to keep them.

Lightnesss and inconsistency proceeds from the nature of the nation, and has perverted the rights of religion, marriage, faith and promise, as softened wax can be altered to any form.

Summary diagram: Henry VIII's legacy: a kingdom in turmoil?

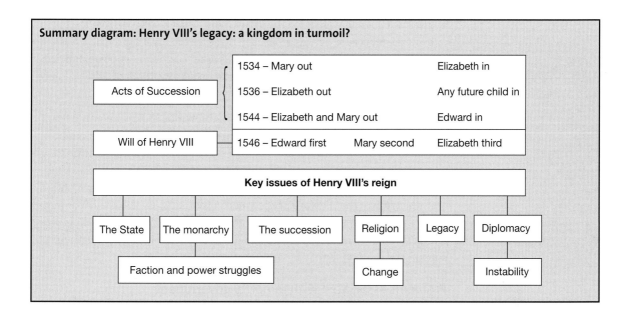

② Edward VI and minority government

▶ *How well did Somerset and Northumberland govern the kingdom?*

The boy-king and the succession

Henry VIII's major concern in his last years was the succession. Since 1527 he had been obsessed with the need to safeguard the dynasty by leaving a male heir to succeed him. The birth of Prince Edward in 1537 had seemed to achieve this objective. However, by 1546 the king's declining health made it clear that his son would come to the throne as a minor. To avoid any possible disputes Henry made a final settlement of the succession in his will of 1546. The terms of the will outlined the succession:

- In the event of Edward dying without heirs, the succession was to pass to Mary, the daughter of Catherine of Aragon.
- If Mary died without heirs, her sister Elizabeth, daughter of Anne Boleyn, was to succeed.
- If all Henry's children were to die without heirs, the throne was to pass to his niece Frances Grey. Lady Frances was the elder daughter of Henry VIII's sister Mary, who first had married King Louis XII of France and then Charles Brandon, Duke of Suffolk.

- Henry deliberately excluded the infant Mary, Queen of Scots from the line of succession because he was anxious to preserve the royal supremacy. Although Mary was the descendant of Henry VIII's sister Margaret, who had married James IV of Scotland, the Stuart dynasty was fiercely Roman Catholic, hence the inclusion of the moderately Protestant Grey family.

To ensure a smooth succession, Edward VI's coronation took place only a few days after his father's funeral. The coronation ceremony was cut short out of consideration for Edward's youth. Archbishop Cranmer used the occasion to urge the nine-year-old supreme head of the Church to quicken the pace of his father's religious reforms and to ensure the destruction of Catholic superstition and idolatry. Not that Edward needed much prompting, for it was evident that, partly as a result of his schooling and partly from conviction, the new king was a Protestant. Even at so tender an age a brief perusal of his diary is sufficient to support the contention that he was a Protestant.

Problems associated with minority government

Minority governments are always afflicted by uncertainty, which is why the plan put in place by Henry VIII had intended that Edward would take charge of the government when he attained the age of eighteen. In the event, Edward remained a minor throughout his reign but it would be wrong to conclude that he was simply a spectator. Edward was well educated and intelligent and, as he grew older, became more involved in affairs of State. Therefore, although government was directed and policy decided by men whom Edward had inherited and been surrounded by after his succession, they could not simply ignore his wishes. For example, to the embarrassment of his advisers, in March 1551 the thirteen-year-old king told his Catholic sister, Mary, that he would no longer tolerate her hearing mass in her household. Later that year Edward began attending meetings of the Privy Council during which he wrote various papers showing his close interest in the making of policy. Perhaps Edward's most significant act of kingship was the *'devise* for the succession' (see pages 115–16) which he drew up shortly before his death, omitting his sisters, Mary and Elizabeth, and appointing his cousin, Lady Jane Grey, as his successor.

Somerset's *coup d'état*

As the old king lay dying, the Earl of Hertford, **Edward Seymour**, and Sir William Paget, secretly agreed that, regardless of Henry's wishes for a balanced Regency Council, the earl would take power as Lord Protector. By bribing the other councillors with titles, offices and financial rewards, Hertford took power in a bloodless *coup d'état*.

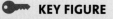

KEY FIGURE

Edward Seymour (c.1500–52)

Earl of Hertford and later Duke of Somerset. He was Edward VI's uncle and a member of Henry VIII's Royal Council. After a coup, Seymour governed England as Lord Protector 1547–9. Owing to his autocratic rule and unpopularity with the nobility, he was removed from power by Northumberland and later executed in 1552.

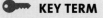

KEY TERM

Coup d'état French term to describe a sudden and illegal seizure of a government.

SOURCE C

Hertford's success is reflected in the disapproving opinion of the Venetian ambassador's diplomatic dispatch, 1547. Quoted in *Calendar of State Papers, Foreign*. Originally published by Her Majesty's Stationery Office, 1861, p. 17.

To secure his son and the crown the late king gave equal authority to sixteen regents, not making any of them chief, that they might rule the realm. Which was in truth well judged, had not all his orders, by some misfortune unknown to the reporter, been altered after his death, so that his last will and testament was published in another form than the true one, and everything is daily going from bad to worse.

Study Source C. Why did the Venetian ambassador disapprove of Hertford's seizure of power?

Somerset's government and administration

Advanced to the title of Duke of Somerset, Seymour set about the task of governing the realm. Somerset's government was not markedly different from that of the last years of Henry VIII. The Privy Council was made up of men who had risen to power under Henry VIII and who were using the same methods and machinery of government to cope with similar problems. The real differences were the lack of effective leadership and the fact that existing problems had grown worse. Economic and financial expedients and a half-hearted religious reform policy created only confusion and uncertainty among both the landed elites and the general public. While there is no evidence that Somerset tried to corrupt the government, it is equally true that he introduced no real reforms. What can be said is that he failed to show the leadership necessary to compensate for the absence of an adult monarch.

Short-term problems

The new regime inherited three pressing short-term problems from the previous reign. Immediate decisions had to be made about:

- whether or not to continue the wars against Scotland and France
- the question of religious reform
- finding ways of raising more revenue.

Long-term problems

As well as these immediate political and administrative difficulties, the government faced a number of serious long-term economic and social problems. Population continued to increase, and this presented a major threat to the government. Increasing population was the main cause of inflation because greater demand for goods pushed up prices. Not only did this add to the cost of administration, but it also threatened most people's living standards at a time when wages were not increasing. In addition, it meant that more people were available for employment. This, in turn, caused more poverty because it also raised the number of vagrants looking for work. It has been estimated that the population of England was growing at a rate of one per cent a year. This resulted in a rise in population of some 700,000, pushing the figure up from 2.3 million in 1520 to 3 million by 1550.

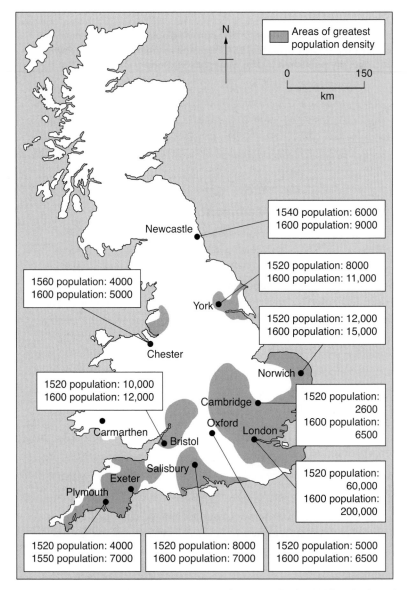

1540 population: 6000
1600 population: 9000

1520 population: 8000
1600 population: 11,000

1560 population: 4000
1600 population: 5000

1520 population: 12,000
1600 population: 15,000

1520 population: 10,000
1600 population: 12,000

1520 population: 2600
1600 population: 6500

1520 population: 60,000
1600 population: 200,000

1520 population: 4000
1550 population: 7000

1520 population: 8000
1600 population: 7000

1520 population: 5000
1600 population: 6500

Areas of greatest population density

Newcastle

York

Chester

Norwich

Cambridge

Oxford London

Carmarthen

Bristol

Salisbury

Exeter

Plymouth

Figure 5.1 Population distribution in sixteenth-century England. What do these figures show about where most people lived?

Somerset was faced with a dilemma. He had to continue the war for the sake of national prestige and to retain the support of the nobility. If Somerset maintained the war effort the country would be plunged further into debt. However, if he raised taxes this would be unpopular with the landed elites and other taxpayers. At the same time, Somerset had to take some action over religious reform if he was not to lose the support of the Protestant activists. Such a loss of support might allow a Catholic revival which would endanger Somerset's hold on power. Yet if he went too far, the reformers might provoke the Catholics into open rebellion.

Somerset was well aware that there was rising discontent among the people over the worsening economic conditions. He feared that this might lead to popular uprisings, but he was uncertain how to tackle the economic problems. Whatever action he took, it was likely to cause as many problems as it solved. In the event, it appears from Somerset's actions over the next two years, that his main objective was to continue the wars. At the same time he cautiously introduced some religious reforms and tried to damp down popular discontent.

Parliament and the Treason Act 1547

When Somerset had established himself he summoned Parliament to meet in November 1547. One of its first actions was to pass a new Treason Act. This repealed the old heresy, treason and censorship laws, and thus:

- allowed people to discuss religion freely without fear of censorship or arrest
- enabled the printing, publishing and circulation of books and pamphlets on religion
- permitted the importation of Lutheran and **Calvinist** literature from the Continent.

The removal of the restrictive laws encouraged widespread debate over religion, particularly in London and other large towns. Public meetings frequently ended in disorder and riots, with attacks on churches to break up statues of saints and other Catholic images. At the same time, the repeal of the old laws left the county and urban authorities with much less power to deal with such situations. Consequently, the government had helped to promote the very disorder that it was trying to avoid.

Parliament and the Proclamation Act of 1539

Somerset also repealed the Proclamation Act of 1539, which stated that royal **proclamations** should be obeyed as if they were Acts of Parliament, providing that they did not infringe existing laws. Although Tudor monarchs had used, and would continue to use proclamations, the Proclamation Act had been regarded with suspicion because it was feared that it would allow the monarch to rule without Parliament. However, the repeal of the Act did not mean that proclamations could not be used. Indeed, because the limitations previously imposed by the 1539 Act had been removed, it has been suggested that Somerset was trying to give himself more freedom to rule without Parliament. There is no evidence to suggest that this was his real intention, although there was a considerable increase in the use of proclamations during his period of office. Under Henry VIII proclamations were, on average, used six times a year. During Edward VI's reign they averaged nineteen a year, and of these, 77 – well over half – were issued by Somerset.

Parliament and the Chantries Act of 1547

The Chantries Act of 1547 might be seen as another measure of religious reform. Undoubtedly it was a logical step, after the dissolution of the monasteries,

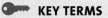

KEY TERMS

Calvinist Follower of the radical religious reformer John Calvin of Geneva who attacked Catholicism and promoted the Protestant faith.

Proclamations Official or public announcements issued by the Crown that included the right to make laws.

Chantries Religious foundations or chapels (often located in churches or cathedrals), sometimes with land attached, established by wealthy patrons and endowed with money to employ a priest to sing masses for the souls of the dead.

to close the **chantries**. Yet, in reality, this Act was a device to raise money to pay for the wars. A similar plan had already been discussed by Henry VIII and his advisers in 1545. Commissioners were sent out early in 1548 to visit the chantries, confiscate their land and property, and collect all the gold and silver plate attached to them. The latter was then melted down to make coins. Simultaneously the royal mints were ordered to reissue the coinage and reduce the silver content by adding copper. The coinage had already been debased in 1543 and there were to be further debasements until 1551, by which time the silver content had been reduced to 25 per cent. Although these measures provided much needed revenue, they created further problems. By increasing the number of coins in circulation the government was adding to inflation. Prices, particularly for grain, rose rapidly, fuelling discontent among the poor.

Foreign policy

Foreign policy during the first part of Edward VI's reign was strongly influenced by the legacy left by Henry VIII. The young king's minority created fears over national security and the succession. There were major concerns over the possibility of renewed French intervention in Scotland and the end of the fragile peace.

Scotland

Affairs in Scotland were of paramount importance because of Henry VIII's desire to see his son Edward married to the infant Mary, Queen of Scots. Under the terms of his will, Henry had set aside the English claim to the Scottish throne. This might be seen as a way of encouraging the Scots to accept the proposed marriage between Edward and Mary. On the other hand, Mary, Queen of Scots, as a legitimate claimant to the throne, could be used by either the French or the Habsburgs as a means of gaining control of England in the cause of the Catholic faith.

Somerset decided to try to isolate the Scots by negotiating with France for a defensive alliance. However, the death of Francis I and the accession of the more aggressive Henry II ended any hopes of a compromise with the French. Somerset strengthened the defences at Calais, Boulogne and Newhaven, and the fleet was sent to patrol the English Channel. Henry II renewed the Franco-Scottish alliance, and in June 1547 sent a fleet of warships with 4000 troops to Scotland. Somerset was left with no alternative but to intervene directly in Scottish affairs on the pretext of arranging the marriage between Edward and Mary that had been arranged by Henry VIII in 1543.

In September 1547 a joint land and naval invasion of Scotland was launched. Somerset and Dudley led an army to Berwick, from where they advanced towards Edinburgh to confront the Scots. At the Battle of Pinkie the Scots were defeated. After this victory Somerset was able to occupy all the main border strongholds. This gave England control of the border, but the success was not

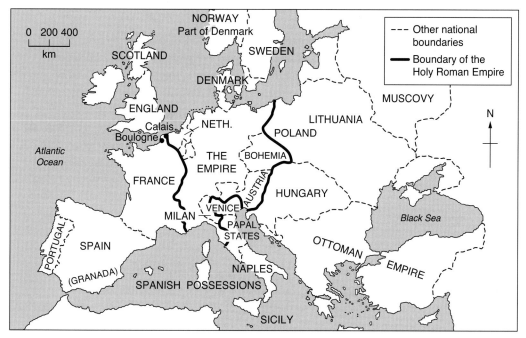

Figure 5.2 Map of Europe c.1550. How does the map suggest that England was vulnerable to attack?

as decisive as it appeared because the English army was not strong enough to occupy the rest of Scotland.

French intervention

Defeat united the Scottish nobles on the Royal Council, which decided to ask the French for help. A French fleet landed an army in Scotland, and Mary, Queen of Scots was taken to France to be educated. The French king, Henry II, proclaimed that France and Scotland were one country. Fortunately for Somerset, the threat of a united France and Scotland did not last as the French soon tired of the expense of garrisoning Scotland and the Scottish nobles came to resent the French presence.

Somerset too was facing crippling costs and he was forced to withdraw troops from the north, and to recall the fleet to guard the English Channel against possible French attack. This caused the English to abandon their hard-won strongholds north of the border. The French withdrew from Scotland and redeployed their forces to threaten English-controlled Calais and Boulogne. Without support, the Scots were too weak to launch a major attack on the north of England but, conversely, at home the French grew in strength and they tightened their siege of Boulogne. Given the Franco-Scottish alliance, England's weakening military position in France and the chronic shortage of money, Somerset had done his best but he knew that, in the long term, this was a war that could not be won.

Somerset's fall from power

Somerset's preoccupation with war abroad had distracted him from mounting problems at home. His failing leadership led to his government becoming increasingly ineffective and in 1549 the country drifted into what was potentially a major crisis. Somerset seemed unable, or unwilling, to take decisive action to suppress well-supported popular uprisings in the West Country and East Anglia. His unwillingness to act has traditionally been interpreted as showing sympathy for the plight of the poor commons, but it seems more likely that the initial delays were caused by the reluctance of the local ruling elites to intervene without government support. Lack of money made it difficult to raise a new mercenary army, and Somerset, as commander-in-chief, was reluctant to withdraw troops from his garrisons in Scotland and France. It was only when the Privy Council realised the seriousness of the situation and provided additional troops that Lord Russell in the West Country and **John Dudley**, Earl of Warwick, in East Anglia were able to defeat the rebels.

A major consequence of the rebellions was the fall of Somerset, whose colleagues quickly abandoned him as a man who had failed to prevent anarchy and revolution. When his chief rival, John Dudley (later to become Duke of Northumberland), fresh from his victory in Norfolk, detained Somerset in October 1549 there was no opposition. Although Somerset was released early the following year and rejoined the Privy Council, within a year he was accused of plotting against the government. He was executed in January 1552.

SOURCE D

Francis Burgoyne, letter to John Calvin, 22 January 1552, relating the events that led to Somerset's execution. Quoted in J.A. Froude, *History of England from the Fall of Wolsey to the Defeat of the Spanish Armada*, Longman, Green & Co., 1893, Volume V, p. 46.

Somerset was the head of a conspiracy against the whole Council and the Duke of Northumberland, whom he pursued with much hatred, since Northumberland had been foremost among those who deprived him of the rank of Lord Protector. Somerset and his supporters agreed that Northumberland should be murdered and that they, with Somerset restored to the office of Protector, should take over the government of the kingdom.

Northumberland's *coup d'état*

Even before his arrest, it was clear that Somerset was discredited and had lost control of the political situation. Many members of the Privy Council were offended by his arrogance in using his own household instead of the Council to conduct business. He had undermined the confidence of the aristocracy and the gentry because of his inept handling of the popular uprisings, while his religious reforms had alienated even moderates among the conservative party.

KEY FIGURE

John Dudley (1504–53)

Earl of Warwick and later Duke of Northumberland. He was a member of Henry VIII's Royal Council. He removed Somerset from power and ruled England as Lord President of the Council 1549–53. Removed from power by Mary I and executed in 1553.

? Study Source D. Why might historians consider this account to be biased?

A power struggle soon developed in which Northumberland was a leading contender. Northumberland crushed the rebel army in Norfolk and returned to London. This gave him a distinct advantage because, as the commander of the main army in England, he controlled the capital. Almost immediately he began to negotiate with Henry Fitzalan, Earl of Arundel, and Thomas Wriothesley, Earl of Southampton, leaders of the conservative party. In desperation Somerset issued a proclamation ordering all troops in England to return to their duties in Scotland and France. There was no response, and Somerset removed the royal household from Hampton Court to Windsor Castle for security.

Meanwhile the Privy Council protected its own position by issuing a proclamation blaming Somerset for the rebellions. All parties were anxious to avoid civil war. Eventually, Somerset agreed to negotiate on honourable terms, and in October 1549 he was taken into custody. At this point Northumberland showed his considerable ability as a politician. By pretending to be a Catholic sympathiser, he successfully conspired with the conservatives. This gave him control of the Council. However, the conservatives were secretly planning to seize power, appoint Princess Mary as regent and have Northumberland arrested along with Somerset.

Northumberland's alliance with Cranmer

At the same time Northumberland was plotting with the progressives, particularly Archbishop Cranmer, who had considerable influence in the royal household. With Cranmer's help he gained control over the administration of the royal household, which gave him immediate access to Edward VI. This enabled him to win the confidence of the king, and by February 1550 he was in a strong enough position to have the conservatives expelled from the Council. To secure his position he became Lord President of the Council. In April he was made General Warden of the North, which gave him military command. However, he achieved complete power only in October 1551 when he had Somerset re-arrested, and assumed the title of Duke of Northumberland. In spite of his reputation for greed and ruthlessness, historians are beginning to recognise Northumberland as an ambitious, but able, politician. In marked contrast to Somerset, he introduced a series of significant and lasting reforms.

Northumberland's government and administration

Northumberland had learned from Somerset's mistakes, and saw that control of the Council was the key to political power. As Lord President he was able to appoint and dismiss councillors at will, and had complete control over procedure. Able supporters of Somerset, such as Paget and William Cecil, who had been arrested, were released and allowed to return to their posts. Under their guidance the Council and its procedures were restored to the pattern established in the period 1536–47.

In order to increase his authority, Northumberland enlarged the membership of the Council to 33, selecting councillors on whose loyalty he could rely. Whenever possible he chose men of military experience, so that in the event of further rebellions, he, unlike Somerset, could be sure of immediate armed support. To make the Council more efficient and stable Northumberland created a smaller, inner committee with a fixed routine to conduct business. Seeing the danger arising from Somerset's frequent bypassing of the Privy Council, Northumberland restored it to the centre of government. For similar reasons he made less use of proclamations, preferring to use Parliament to confirm legislation whenever possible. The political difficulties facing the new government were the same as those which Somerset had failed to resolve. The most pressing problems were in revenue, finance and foreign policy.

Revenue and finance

Royal revenue remained a serious problem. By 1550 the government was virtually bankrupt. Somerset had spent £1,356,000 on the war, and sold Crown lands to the value of £800,000. The government even had to borrow to raise the £50,000 a year needed to maintain the royal household. Ending the war drastically reduced expenditure, but a number of expedients had to be adopted to keep the government solvent. In May 1551 the coinage was debased for the last time. Although inflation rose still further, the government made a profit of £114,000 to pay immediate expenses and short-term loans. Even so, a further £243,000 had to be borrowed from Continental bankers.

Sir William Cecil, restored as Secretary of State, was put in charge of financial planning. He recommended the sale of chantry lands and church goods to start paying off the government's debts. In March 1552 the coinage was reissued with the silver content restored to that of 1527. This helped to slow the rise in inflation and restore confidence in the currency. Strict economies were made in government spending, and Northumberland paid off the remainder of his mercenary troops. By these means most of the overseas debts were liquidated and a 'privy coffer', a contingency fund, was established.

By 1553 the financial situation had been stabilised. Even so, another £140,000 worth of Crown lands had to be sold to replace the revenue taxes, voted unwillingly by Parliament, which were not collected because they were so unpopular. The most pressing need was to streamline the collection of royal revenue and to find ways of increasing government income. In 1552 a commission recommended that to avoid corruption and inefficiency the number of revenue courts should be reduced from five to two – the Exchequer and the Office of Crown Lands (see pages 38–9). Northumberland had shown considerable political coolness and skill in resolving a serious financial crisis. Unlike Somerset, he had displayed the ability to delegate authority and skill in selecting the right people for the task.

Foreign policy, 1549

By the autumn of 1549 foreign affairs had reached a critical point. The war had become increasingly unpopular with both the nobility and the general public. High levels of taxation were undermining the economy and provoking hostility towards the government. For some time the Privy Councillors, such as Paget, had been advocating peace as a means of restoring financial and economic stability. Although Northumberland was much more sympathetic to these views than Somerset had been, during the winter of 1549 he was fully occupied in gaining control of the government.

Relations with France

The French took advantage of this power vacuum to build up their forces around Boulogne. They were able to break English lines of communication between Boulogne and Calais, which threatened to isolate the garrison of Boulogne. However, an English fleet decisively defeated a strong force of French ships in a battle off the Channel Islands. This gave England control of the Channel, and meant that Boulogne could be supplied by sea. However, as the government was virtually bankrupt, Northumberland was unable to raise an army to lift the siege.

In January 1550 Northumberland sent a delegation to France to negotiate peace. The Treaty of Boulogne was signed in March. Under the terms of the treaty the English had to withdraw from Boulogne in return for a ransom of 400,000 crowns. At the same time they had to remove their remaining garrisons from Scotland, and agree not to renew the war unless provoked by the Scots. Finally, there was to be a perpetual defensive alliance between England and France. Boulogne was handed over to the French on 25 April, and the English garrison was sent to reinforce Calais. Although the Treaty of Boulogne removed the danger of French invasion and ended the crippling expense of the war, the potential crisis still remained.

The humiliating peace and alliance with a traditional enemy was seen as a national disgrace, and added to Northumberland's unpopularity. In spite of this, peace was restored and the Crown's financial situation improved, as did the economy when trade between England and France was resumed. Nevertheless, England's international position remained weak, and was made worse because lack of money forced Northumberland to reduce the size of the army and the navy.

Relations with the Holy Roman Empire

England's improved relations with France led to a deterioration in relations with the Holy Roman Empire. Apart from being an enemy of France and disliking the Anglo-French alliance, Charles V was particularly annoyed by the attempts of the English reformers, including King Edward, to force Princess Mary to abandon her Catholic faith. A consequence of this cooling of relations was a breakdown in commercial contacts with the Netherlands, which had been protected by the ***Intercursus Magnus*** since 1496.

> **KEY TERM**
>
> ***Intercursus Magnus*** Used to describe the protection of commercial contacts between England and the Netherlands in an agreement of 1496.

KEY TERM

Catholic Inquisition
Institution set up in 1478 by the Catholic Church to search for and destroy heretics or non-conformists. There were a number of different inquisitions and the operation was often in the hands of the secular authorities assisting the Church.

In April 1550 Charles issued an edict allowing the **Catholic Inquisition** to arrest any heretics in the Netherlands. This outraged many English merchants. Although the edict was modified to exclude foreigners, it helped to bring about the collapse of the Antwerp cloth market, as many Flemish cloth-workers fled to England to avoid persecution. It was not until December 1550 that Charles made any attempt to restore good trading relations, and then only from fear that England would be driven into a closer alliance with France.

Relations with Scotland

Anglo-Scottish relationships were in an equally poor state. When Northumberland withdrew the remaining English garrisons from Scotland he left the French in control. However, the Scottish nobles and the Protestant lowlanders were becoming increasingly hostile towards the French, fearing that Scotland would become a mere province of France. The fall of Somerset had left a confused situation on the English side of the border. Lord Dacre and the Earl of Rutland at Carlisle and Berwick had no clear policy to follow. In 1550 Northumberland decided to take personal control of affairs along the border by making himself General Warden of the North, with Lord Wharton as his deputy.

To end the constant minor disputes which threatened the uneasy peace, Sir Robert Bowen was ordered to survey the border. He reported that an area fifteen miles by four miles (24 km by 6.5 km) was under dispute. After strengthening Berwick and Carlisle, Northumberland returned to London, leaving Lord Dacre to negotiate a settlement of the line of the border with the Scottish wardens. Progress was very slow, and it was not until a French fleet landed supplies and troops in Scotland in February 1551 that negotiations began in earnest. Finally, in March 1552, it was agreed that the border would be restored to the line held before Henry VIII's Scottish campaigns.

Worsening relations with the Continental powers

During 1551 Northumberland maintained his policy of neutrality towards the Continental powers. Charles V continued to disapprove of the increasing Protestantism of the Church of England, and considered that English foreign policy was unpredictable. It was not until March 1552, when war broke out again between Charles V and the French king, Henry II, that Anglo-Imperial relations began to improve. Northumberland resisted French pressure to join in the war against the Holy Roman Empire, and Charles V was more conciliatory over English trade with the Netherlands. Finally, by June 1552, diplomatic relations were restored between the two countries. Then, when the French invaded the Netherlands, Charles V reminded England that it was bound under treaty obligations to assist the Empire if the Netherlands were attacked.

The garrison at Calais was reinforced, but England still took no active part in the war. Even so, England's relations with France deteriorated. The second half of the ransom for Boulogne remained unpaid and French privateers had begun to attack English shipping. Although England was in no position to take any military action, the French feared an Anglo-Imperial alliance and were careful to avoid open confrontation. In January 1553 Northumberland proposed to act as mediator between France and the Empire. This action was prompted by fears over Edward VI's declining health and the illness of Charles V. The French were not interested in making peace, and in June 1553 the negotiations collapsed, leading to a resumption in hostilities.

Northumberland's fall from power

Intelligent and well educated, Northumberland, like Somerset, had risen to political prominence during the last years of Henry VIII's reign. He had fought and had enhanced his military reputation in the Scottish and French wars. He was a member of the Council named in Henry's will and was as able a politician as he was a soldier. Although he was prone to greed and ruthlessness he was probably one of the most gifted and ablest rulers of his day. However, other than self-preservation, he seems not to have been a man of strong convictions or principles, as may be seen from the way he used Lady Jane Grey for his own political purpose and by his apparently hasty decision to renounce Protestantism in favour of Catholicism in order to save his life when Mary swept to power in 1553.

Although Northumberland's ambition for power contributed to his fall, it was the death of Edward VI that sealed his fate. Edward's illness presented Northumberland with a serious dilemma. He had no doubt that Mary's succession would result in his dismissal from office and possible arrest. A plan was hatched to omit Mary and Elizabeth from the succession and name their cousin, the seventeen-year-old Jane Grey, as heir to the throne. A document known as the *Devise* (see page 134) was drawn up that named Jane and her male heirs as the main beneficiaries of the change in succession. The original idea for the *Devise* may have come from Edward himself, but it was Northumberland who arranged the marriage between his son, Guildford Dudley, and the future Queen Jane.

Although many on the Privy Council were reluctant to accept the *Devise* they gave their assent. Edward died on 6 July, Jane was proclaimed queen three days later. Her rule lasted nine days. Northumberland had miscalculated; his fellow councillors deserted him and declared for Mary, who was proclaimed queen. Northumberland had failed to appreciate the depth of his unpopularity and the scale of the support for Mary; he was arrested and imprisoned before being executed.

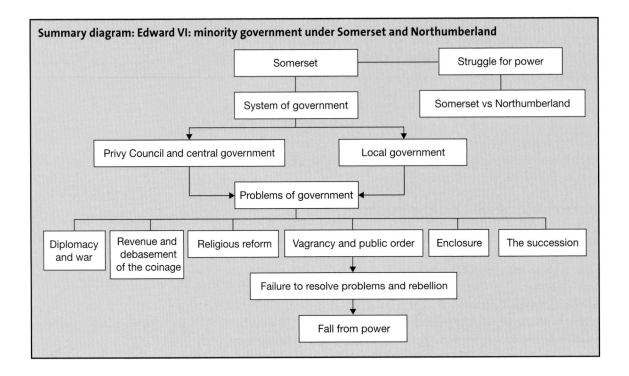

Summary diagram: Edward VI: minority government under Somerset and Northumberland

3 Cranmer and the Protestant revolution

▶ *How significant was Cranmer's role in promoting the Reformation?*

The accession of Edward VI, who had been educated as a Protestant, convinced English reformers that there would be a swing towards more Lutheran, and possibly Calvinist, doctrines. Somerset's appointment as Lord Protector in 1547 established the reform party firmly in power, and the man to whom the reformers turned to guide the Church towards the Protestant faith was Archbishop Thomas Cranmer.

Thomas Cranmer

Thomas Cranmer was the first Protestant Archbishop of Canterbury. He was consecrated on 30 March 1533 and had been in this post for nearly fourteen years when Edward VI succeeded to the throne. During the time Cranmer served Henry VIII he was widely believed to be either a Lutheran or a Lutheran sympathiser. Although his views fluctuated over the period as the influences on him changed, it is clear that he was always more of a Protestant than the king would have liked. Nevertheless, he served Henry with utmost loyalty which was reciprocated by the king, who trusted him implicitly. It is said that when he was appointed Henry's chaplain in 1531 he took a private oath not to let any other oath come between him and his duty to his king.

Cranmer distinguished between his personal faith (which he openly declared to the king) and the policies he was helping to implement. Thus, he was prepared to pass judgements of heresy (leading to death by burning) on individuals whose beliefs were no different from his own when the king instructed him so to do. This apparent inconsistency in his behaviour led to his being charged with hypocrisy. Indeed, history has not been kind to the founder of the Protestant revolution since he has been variously described as a timid time-server and a coward. However, recent research by Diarmaid MacCulloch has served to revise our opinion of a man whom he describes as a 'hesitant hero with a tangled life story' who deserves to be remembered as the 'architect of the Anglican Book of Common Prayer'. Indeed, it may be argued that whereas Cranmer's influence on the Henrician Reformation was minimal in comparison to that of Cromwell and Henry, his impact on the Edwardian Reformation was considerable.

Shaping future Reformation 1540–53

After Cromwell's execution, Cranmer emerged as one of the leading reform-minded councillors. With the king's support, Cranmer survived plots to oust him and was allowed to promote his own **English Litany** and *King's Prymer*. The death of Henry VIII and the succession of Edward VI and elevation to power of Somerset had a profound effect on Cranmer. He was by inclination a reformer but only within the parameters which the king laid down. Freed from the restraints put on him by the late king, Cranmer was able to explore, review and revise his personal religious convictions. According to his own testimony it was not until 1548 that he finally completed his conversion to Protestantism by abandoning the traditional doctrine of transubstantiation.

Infused with the spirit of reform, Cranmer issued his *Book of Homilies*, a set of official model sermons, followed by his English prayer book. Issued in March 1549, Cranmer's *Book of Common Prayer* has been described as his greatest achievement, but it was too conservative for the progressives and too radical for the conservatives – it even provoked the Western Rebellion. This was a rebellion of commoners and some landowners in Cornwall and Devon who were protesting about the religious changes. Undaunted, Cranmer set to work on a more radical edition of his prayer book which he issued in 1552. The second *Book of Common Prayer* was explicitly anti-Catholic and was adapted and adopted by the Elizabethan regime to become the standard work available to an increasingly Protestant clergy.

Swing towards Protestantism

Somerset was a moderate Protestant, but although he was devout, he had no real interest in theology. He was religiously tolerant and favoured a cautious

> ### 🔑 KEY TERMS
>
> **English Litany** A selection of prayers in English designed for use in a designated church service in which the parishioners respond to lines spoken by the priest leading the service.
>
> *King's Prymer* A devotional collection of prayers, psalms and religious lessons approved for use in church by the king.

approach towards reform. Although he is reputed to have had Calvinist leanings, and, certainly, exchanged letters with John Calvin (see page 137), there is little evidence of such influences when he was in power. The progressives, Cranmer prominent among them, were in the majority in the Privy Council. However, among the bishops, there was no agreement. Although the majority of them fully supported the royal supremacy and the separation from Rome, they remained hopelessly divided on the issue of religious reform. For example, of the 27 leading clerics in the Church:

- Nine bishops, led by Archbishop Thomas Cranmer and Nicholas Ridley, Bishop of Rochester, supported reform (the progressives).
- Ten bishops, led by Stephen Gardiner, Bishop of Winchester, and Edmund Bonner, Bishop of London, opposed reform (the conservatives).
- Eight bishops were undecided on doctrinal issues.

With such an even balance of opinion among the bishops, Somerset and the Privy Council moved very cautiously on matters of religious reform. In these circumstances the Privy Council decided to review the state of the Church of England, and to introduce some moderate Protestant reforms. Such a policy was opposed by the conservatives, prompted by Gardiner, who maintained that under the terms of Henry VIII's will, no religious changes could be made until Edward VI came of age. In spite of Gardiner's vigorous opposition, royal commissioners were sent to visit all the bishoprics. They were instructed to compile a report on the state of the clergy and the doctrines and practices to be found in every diocese. To help the spread of Protestant ideas, every parish was ordered to obtain a copy of Cranmer's **Book of Homilies** and **Paraphrases** by Erasmus.

An injunction was issued to the bishops ordering them to instruct their clergy to conduct services in English, provide an English Bible for each parish and preach a sermon every Sunday. Finally, the bishops were told to remove all superstitious statues and images from their churches.

Pressure from Protestant radicals

These modest moves towards religious reform did not satisfy the more vocal Protestant activists. The amount of anti-Catholic protest was increased by the presence of Protestant exiles who had returned from the Continent after the death of Henry VIII. The problem for the Privy Council was that, while it did not wish to introduce reforms too quickly for fear of provoking a Catholic reaction, it was anxious not to prevent religious debate by taking repressive measures. As a result, the Henrician treason, heresy and censorship laws were not enforced and a vigorous debate over religion developed.

The more radical reformers launched a strong attack through a pamphlet campaign on both the Catholic Church and the bishops, who were accused of being self-seeking royal servants and not true pastors. Other pamphlets attacked the wealth of the Church, superstitious rituals and, in particular, the **Eucharist**.

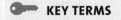 **KEY TERMS**

Book of Homilies A book of sermons written by Cranmer for use in church services.

Paraphrases A literary work by Erasmus that retells all or part of the Bible in a manner that can be more easily understood by worshippers.

Eucharist Also known as holy communion, this is a Catholic sacrament in which the bread and wine are taken in the belief that the body and blood of Christ are contained within.

However, there was no agreement among the protesters about the form of Protestant doctrine that should be adopted. With the government refusing to take any firm lead there was growing frustration.

In London, East Anglia, Essex and Lincolnshire, where large numbers of Protestant refugees from the Continent were settling, riots broke out. These frequently included outbreaks of iconoclasm, in which stained glass windows, statues and other superstitious images were destroyed. In some cases gold and silver candlesticks and other church plate were seized and sold, with the money being donated to the poor. Although the Privy Council was alarmed by the violence, it refused to take any action against the demonstrators. This inaction enraged the more conservative bishops such as Bishop Bonner, who was so strong in his opposition to the government that he was imprisoned for two months.

SOURCE E

The following extracts relate to the news and the events of 1547–52. Adapted from J.G. Nichols, editor, *Chronicle of the Grey Friars of London*, Camden Society, 1852.

5 September 1547: The king's visitation of St. Paul's where all the images were pulled down. At this same time was pulled up all the tombs, great stones, all the altars, with the stalls and walls of the choir and altars in the church that was the Grey Friars.

1548: In this year all the chantries were put down.

25 October 1552: saw the plucking down of all the altars and chapels in St. Paul's church with all the tombs, at the commandment of the Bishop, Nicholas Ridley, and all the goodly stonework that stood behind the high altar and so it was all made plain as it appears.

> Study Source E. What impact might this destruction have had on the religious experience of the people?

First steps towards reform and introducing Protestant doctrine

When Parliament and Convocation were summoned in November 1547, both assemblies were broadly in favour of reform. Yet the Privy Council was still reluctant to make any decisive move towards religious reform. The reason for this was that the new regime still felt insecure, fearing that any major changes to doctrine might provoke even more unrest and possibly lead to the fall of the government.

The two major pieces of legislation, the Chantries Act and the Treason Act, did little to resolve the doctrinal uncertainties:

- The Chantries Act (see pages 137–8). By closing the chantries, this Act not only confirmed legislation already passed in 1545 but went further in its confiscation of wealth and property. Although, as in 1545, the main purpose of the Act was to raise money to continue the war with France and Scotland, the reason given was that the chantries were centres of superstition.

- The Treason Act. This Act effectively repealed the Henrician treason, heresy and censorship laws. This measure served to increase the freedom with which the Protestant activists could discuss and demand radical doctrinal reforms. The immediate result was a renewed spate of pamphlets demanding that the Bible should be recognised as the only true authority for religious belief. At the same time English translations of the writings of Luther and Calvin were being widely circulated.

In January 1548 the Privy Council issued a series of proclamations to try to calm the situation. However, the proclamations indicated no clear policy, and so only added to the confusion. Justices of the Peace and churchwardens were ordered to enforce the existing doctrines of the Church of England, including transubstantiation. On the other hand, instructions were issued to speed up the removal of Catholic images from churches. Such indecision infuriated both reformers and conservatives alike. Finally, in September, the Council forbade all public preaching in the hope of stifling debate.

Act of Uniformity and the first *Book of Common Prayer*

When Parliament reassembled in November 1548, Somerset and the Council felt secure enough to take a more positive approach to religious reform. Their objective was to end the uncertainty over religious doctrine. It was hoped that the new law, known as the First Edwardian Act of Uniformity, passed in January 1549, would achieve this.

The Act officially ordered all the clergy of England and Wales to adopt Protestant practices in their daily worship:

- Holy communion (the mass), matins and evensong were to be conducted in English.
- The sacraments were now defined as communion, baptism, confirmation, marriage and burial.
- New prayers were added to the old communion service so that the clergy and the laity could take both the sacramental bread and the wine. Clerical marriage was made lawful.
- The worship of saints, although not banned, was to be discouraged, while the removal of statues, paintings and other images was encouraged.
- The practice of singing masses for the souls of the dead was no longer approved.

Many of the traditional Catholic rituals, which the Protestant reformers considered to be superstitious, disappeared. However, no change was made to the doctrine of the Eucharist, which was still defined in the Catholic terms of transubstantiation. This was a fundamental point that angered many of the more radical reformers, who continued to urge the government to adopt a more Protestant definition of the sacrament of communion.

The Privy Council hoped that these cautious measures would satisfy the majority of moderate reformers, without outraging the Catholic conservatives. Bishops were instructed to carry out visitations to encourage the adoption of the new services, and to test whether parishioners could recite the Lord's Prayer and the Ten Commandments in English. The effectiveness of the reform legislation depended on whether the bishops and ruling elites would enforce them. There was opposition in Cornwall, Devon, Dorset and Yorkshire. However, most of the country seems to have followed the lead of the aristocracy and gentry in accepting moderate Protestantism.

A further swing of the pendulum towards radical Protestantism

When Northumberland gained power in 1549–50 religious reform became more radical. The conservatives were driven out of office and Gardiner, the most able of the pro-Catholics, along with Bishop Bonner of London, was imprisoned in the Tower of London. At the same time active reformers were appointed as bishops of Rochester, Chichester, Norwich, Exeter and Durham. These changes cleared the way for more sweeping religious reforms.

It is perhaps ironic that in view of Northumberland's reconversion to Catholicism before his execution in 1553, many historians do not think it likely that Northumberland was a genuine religious reformer. Other historians feel that his support for such a Protestant enthusiast as **John Hooper** against Cranmer and Nicholas Ridley, the newly appointed Bishop of London, in the doctrinal dispute during the autumn of 1550 does show that he was interested in religious reform. Whatever the truth of the matter, there is no doubt that under Northumberland there was a move to introduce more radical Protestantism.

The first signs of this radical shift in thinking came in London, where Bishop Ridley ordered all altars to be removed and replaced by communion tables in line with the teachings of the Calvinists. In other dioceses the destruction of altars proceeded unevenly, and depended on the attitudes of the local ruling elites and clergy. At the same time, the parliamentary commission's proposals to change the form of the ordination of priests were introduced, and instructions were issued to enforce the first Act of Uniformity.

The new form of ordination, which was basically Lutheran, soon caused controversy. It removed the supposedly superstitious references to sacrifice, purgatory and prayers for the souls of the dead. However, it did not please some of the more extreme reformers, because it made no attempt to remove from usage any of the ceremonial vestments normally worn by bishops and priests while conducting services. These were regarded as superstitious by those clergy who wore plain surplices.

Hooper's dispute with Ridley

John Hooper, who had been invited to become Bishop of Gloucester, complained that the form of ordination was still too Catholic and started a fierce dispute

KEY FIGURE

John Hooper (1495–1555)

A radical Protestant priest. His radicalism made him enemies at the court of Henry VIII so he fled to the Continent. During the reign of Edward VI he returned to England and was promoted to the bishopric of Gloucester. He served as chaplain to both Somerset and Northumberland, whose patronage enabled him to promote his radical religious policies. Executed during the reign of Mary.

with Ridley over the question of vestments. As a result he refused the offered bishopric, and in July began a campaign of preaching against the new proposals. At first it appeared that Northumberland was sympathetic and supported Hooper, but in October he was ordered to stop preaching, and in January 1551 he was imprisoned for failing to comply. Finally, he was persuaded to compromise and was made Bishop of Gloucester, where he introduced a vigorous policy of education and reform. But he complained that both laity and clergy were slow to respond.

Doctrinal changes and the second *Book of Common Prayer*

Parliament was assembled in January 1552 and the government embarked on a comprehensive programme of reform. In order to strengthen the power of the Church of England to enforce doctrinal uniformity, a new Treason Act was passed. This made it an offence to question the royal supremacy or any of the articles of faith of the English Church.

In March the second Act of Uniformity was passed. Under the new Act it became an offence for both clergy and laity not to attend Church of England services, and offenders were to be fined and imprisoned. Cranmer's new *Book of Common Prayer* became the official basis for church services, and had to be used by both clergy and laity. All traces of Catholicism and the mass had been removed, and the Eucharist was clearly defined in terms of consubstantiation.

While these measures were being introduced, the government began a further attack on Church wealth. In 1552 a survey of the temporal wealth of the bishops and all senior clergy was undertaken. The resultant report estimated that these lands had a capital value of £1,087,000, and steps were taken to transfer some of this property to the Crown.

At the same time, commissioners had been sent out to draw up inventories and to begin the removal of all the gold and silver plate still held by parish churches, and to list any items illegally removed since 1547. The commissioners had only just begun their work of confiscation when the king died and the operation was brought to an end, but not before some churches had lost their medieval plate.

Assessment of the Edwardian Church

The death of Edward VI and the fall of Northumberland brought this phase of the English Reformation to an abrupt end. The Forty-two Articles which had been drawn up to list the doctrines of the new Protestant Church of England never became law. It is generally agreed that by 1553 the Edwardian Reformation had resulted in a Church of England that was thoroughly Protestant. There is less agreement over whether its doctrines were basically Lutheran, or to what extent they were influenced by **Zwinglian** or Calvinist ideas.

It is clear that although the doctrines of the Church of England had been revolutionised, the political and administrative structure of the Church had remained unchanged. There is equal agreement that there is insufficient

KEY TERM

Zwinglian Followers of Huldrych Zwingli, a radical religious reformer from Switzerland. He was a Protestant who believed in religious autonomy for local communities.

evidence at present to decide whether the people of England had wholeheartedly embraced the Protestant religion. Although a majority of the landed elites and those in government circles seemed to favour moderate Protestantism, only a few of them found it impossible to conform under the rule of Mary I.

Many of the lower clergy and a majority of the population seem to have been largely indifferent to the religious debate. Only in London, and the counties encircling London and East Anglia, does there appear to have been any widespread enthusiasm for the Protestant religion. Even there, a study of the county of Essex indicates more enthusiasm among the authorities in enforcing Protestantism than among the general public in accepting it. Earlier interpretations which indicated wild enthusiasm for either Protestantism or Catholicism are now treated with caution. It is considered that Protestantism, if not widely opposed, received only lukewarm acceptance.

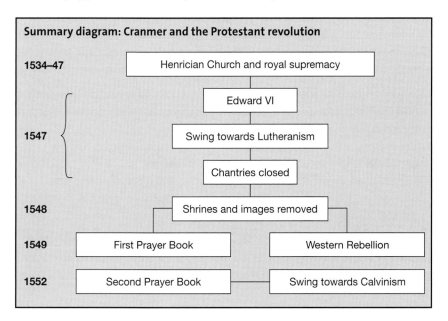

Summary diagram: Cranmer and the Protestant revolution

1534–47	Henrician Church and royal supremacy
1547	Edward VI Swing towards Lutheranism Chantries closed
1548	Shrines and images removed
1549	First Prayer Book — Western Rebellion
1552	Second Prayer Book — Swing towards Calvinism

④ The impact of social, economic and religious change

▶ *Was England a nation in crisis during Edward VI's reign?*

Economic and social problems

Aside from religious problems, the government was faced by equally pressing economic and social problems. The steadily rising population was matched by a rise in inflation, which meant that the living standards of the masses continued to decline, and work was more difficult to find. This was made worse by the growing instability of the Antwerp cloth market, which led to widespread unemployment among textile workers in East Anglia and the West Country. Government intervention tended to exacerbate the economic problems when the debasement of the coinage in 1551 raised inflation still further. Grain prices, too, rose rapidly; a situation worsened by below-average harvests.

In 1550 the country was still simmering after the recent popular uprisings and was further unsettled by the political power struggle among the privy councillors. Consequently, the administration had to act carefully if further serious disorder was to be avoided. The unpopular 1547 Vagrancy Act and the sheep tax of 1548 were repealed in 1550, and this helped to reduce unrest. In the same year a new Treason Act was passed, which restored censorship and gave the authorities more power to enforce law and order.

Initially, these measures helped to prevent the widespread popular discontent from turning into actual revolt. Northumberland benefited from the fact that the 1549 rebellions had badly frightened the government, aristocracy and gentry, who drew closer together to avoid further disorder among the masses.

- In 1552 a new poor law was passed which did nothing to help the able-bodied find work but did make it easier for the parish and town authorities to support the aged, infirm and crippled.
- The existing anti-enclosure legislation was rigorously enforced, and the unpopular enclosure commissions were withdrawn.
- The revaluation of the coinage halted inflation and reduced prices. Acts were passed to protect arable farming, and to stop the charging of excessive interest on debts.

Northumberland's administration showed a more positive approach than that adopted by Somerset. Although he did little to resolve the underlying economic problems, he checked inflation and eased some of the worst of the social distress.

The Vagrancy Act and public order

Governments tend to get nervous when there is a change of monarch, the more so when the new head of state is but a child. Consequently, the maintenance of public order was very much in the mind of Somerset's administration when it passed the Vagrancy Act of 1547. The harshness of this legislation showed little concern for the poor and needy. The earlier Poor Law of 1536 did recognise that the able-bodied were having difficulty in finding work, and ordered parishes to support the helpless poor. The 1547 Act was a savage attack on vagrants looking for work, who were seen by the government as a cause of riots and sedition.

Under the new law, any able-bodied person out of work for more than three days was to be branded with a V and sold into slavery for two years. Further offences were to be punished with permanent slavery. The children of vagrants could be taken from their parents and set to work as apprentices in useful occupations. The new law was widely unpopular, and many of the county and urban authorities refused to enforce it. Although it also proposed housing and collections for the disabled, this measure did little to support Somerset's reputation for humanitarianism.

SOURCE F

Adapted from an edict issued by the Mayor and Common Council of London to raise a compulsory poor rate, 1547. Quoted in E.M. Leonard, *The Early History of English Poor Relief*, Cambridge University Press, 2013, p. 29.

The Lord Mayor, aldermen and commons in this present Common Council assembled, and by the authority of the same order that all the citizens and inhabitants of the said city shall forthwith contribute and pay towards the sustenance and maintenance of the poor personages. It is also enacted and agreed by the said authority that it shall be lawful for all petty collectors of the said payments to distrain [force] every person that shall refuse or deny to pay such sums of money he shall be assessed.

Study Source F. Why was it considered so important to force people to pay towards municipal poor relief and what might the consequences be of enforcing this edict?

The rise in popular discontent

It is clear that as a result of rising prices and local food shortages, the level of popular discontent was increasing. The Privy Council was forced to take measures to appease public agitation but it did not fully appreciate the cause of this discontent. The government blamed all the economic problems on enclosure. It was felt that the fencing-off of common land for sheep pasture and the consequent eviction of husbandmen and cottagers from their homes was the major cause of inflation and unemployment. Proclamations were issued against enclosures, and commissioners were sent out to investigate abuses. The main effect of these measures was to increase unrest. Further measures limiting the size of leaseholds and placing a tax on wool only made the situation worse. In any case, many of the elites evaded the legislation, which fell most heavily on the poorer sections of society it was supposed to protect.

It is reasonable to suggest that the government was more concerned with avoiding riot and rebellion than with helping the poor and solving economic problems. This suspicion is supported by three proclamations issued in 1548, aimed specifically at maintaining law and order. These proclamations seem like emergency measures passed by a government which realised that the economic position was getting out of hand, and which feared the consequences.

Disorder and rebellion

It is difficult to judge to what extent underlying opposition to the changes in religion contributed to the rebellions of 1549 and to the fall of Somerset. Certainly, only the Western Rebellion was directly linked with religion, and even there underlying economic and social discontent played an important part in causing the uprising. To a certain extent, the rebels in the west were complaining about the gentry, whom they accused of making use of the Reformation to seize Church land for their own enrichment. Such views were held in other areas during the popular uprisings of 1549, but only in the West Country was direct opposition to the new Act of Uniformity the central issue.

The Western or Prayer Book Rebellion

The popular discontent began in Cornwall in 1549 when the Cornish people, fearing that the Act of Uniformity was going to be imposed on them, rose in rebellion and set up an armed camp at Bodmin. Because of the hostility expressed by the rebels towards landlords, only six of the more Catholic local gentry joined the uprising. However, the West Country elites were very unwilling to take any action against the rebellion on behalf of the government. The main leaders of the rebels were local clergy, and it was they who began to draw up a series of articles listing demands to stop the religious changes.

In Devon there was an independent uprising at Sampford Courtenay. By 20 June the Devon and Cornish rebels had joined forces at Crediton, and three days later they set up an armed camp at Clyst St Mary. Local negotiations broke down, and the rebels began to blockade the nearby town of Exeter with an army of 6000 men. Lord Russell, who had been sent to crush the rebellion, was hampered by a shortage of troops and a lack of local gentry support. Crucially, the rebels were led by a prominent local gentleman, Humphrey Arundell, who was a skilled tactician and an able commander. As a result it was not until August that the rebels were finally defeated.

The demands of the rebels

Some of the demands put forward in the final set of articles drawn up by the rebels clearly illustrate their religious conservatism and other grievances felt in the West Country. For example, they wanted:

- to end the changes that they claimed were taking place in baptism and confirmation
- to restore the Act of Six Articles
- to restore the Latin mass and images
- to restore old traditions like holy bread and water
- to restore the concepts of transubstantiation and purgatory
- the return of Cardinal Pole from exile and for him to have a seat on the King's Council.

The government clearly saw these articles as ultra-conservative demands for a return to Catholicism. They were rejected by Cranmer, who was particularly enraged by such insubordination.

Assessing the Western Rebellion

Historians agree that the rebels showed little knowledge of either Protestant or Catholic doctrines, but suggest that such ignorance in the West Country probably reflected similar confusion among the great mass of the population. Whether this is true or not, these demands do show that, in the West Country at least, many of the laity were still strongly attached to the familiar traditions of the old Church.

Although religion is acknowledged to be a key cause of the rebellion, some historians have drawn attention to the social and economic causes. For example, A.F. Pollard suggested that social tension lay at the heart of the rebellion and there is evidence to suggest that the rebels considered the gentry to be their enemies. Even the leader of the royal army, Lord Russell, referred to the unfair exploitation of the commons by the local landowners who, he claimed, were taxing and raising rents excessively. The rebels were particularly angry at the new sheep tax, which they wanted withdrawn. Nicholas Fellows (writing in 2002) has suggested that it is possible to make a link 'between the rebels' religious grievances and their attack on the gentry: it was, after all, the gentry who had gained from the Reformation'.

The Kett Rebellion 1549

East Anglia was the most densely populated and highly industrialised part of the country. Norwich was the second largest town after London, and was a major textile centre. The causes of the rebellion are symptomatic of the confused nature of lower order discontent against the economic changes. The rising was triggered by unrest over enclosures, high rents and unsympathetic local landlords like Sir John Flowerdew, a lawyer who had bought up Church property in the area.

Flowerdew was also in dispute with a local yeoman, Robert Kett, over land. Kett was a tanner and small landowner who had enclosed much common land. Flowerdew tried to turn the rioters against him but Kett retaliated by offering to act as spokesman for the rioters. Kett showed more organisational skill and decisive leadership than is usually found in the leaders of peasant risings. He quickly gathered an army of 16,000 men, set up camp for six weeks on Mousehold Heath and, in July, was able to capture Norwich. The rebellion is notable for the discipline which Kett imposed, electing a governing council and maintaining law and order. Every gentleman that the rebels could arrest was tried before Kett and his council at the Tree of Reformation.

Like the other popular uprising in the West Country, the rebellion was eventually crushed when John Dudley, Earl of Warwick (later the Duke of Northumberland), was sent to take command of the Marquis of Northampton's army of 14,000 men. Northampton had succeeded in taking Norwich but had been forced to abandon it after only a day. Unlike Northampton, Warwick was able to bring the rebels to battle at Dussindale, just outside the city, where nearly 4000 rebels and royal troops were killed. Kett was captured and hanged.

The demands of the rebels

The rebels drew up a list of 29 articles covering a range of topics. For example, they wanted:

- landowners to stop enclosing common land
- rents to be reduced to the levels they were under Henry VII
- rivers to be open to all for fishing and that fishermen be allowed to keep a greater share of the profits from sea fishing
- all **bondmen** to be given their freedom, 'for God made everyone free with his precious blood shedding'
- corrupt local officials 'who have offended the commons' to be punished 'where it has been proved by the complaints of the poor'
- incompetent priests to be removed from their churches, particularly those who were 'unable to preach and set forth the word of God to their parishioners'.

Assessing the Kett Rebellion

Unlike the West Country rebels, who seemed to wish for religion to be returned to the good old days of Henry VIII, the Norfolk insurgents supported the Protestant religious changes. Kett encouraged Protestant ministers to preach to the rebels on Mousehold Heath and to use the new Prayer Book.

Although enclosure has, in the past, been cited as the primary cause of the rebellion, in truth its abolition was just one among many agricultural demands made by the rebels. Indeed, apart from local incidents such as at Wymondham and Attleborough, there had been relatively few enclosures in Norfolk during the previous 50 years. Similarly, the requests that bondmen or serfs should be made free seems to be going back to past struggles, because there is no evidence that there were many unfree tenants in sixteenth-century Norfolk.

The major demands were for commons to be kept open and free for husbandmen to graze their livestock, and that rents should not be increased excessively. The Norfolk rebels appeared to yearn for the favourable economic conditions that existed under Henry VII. This does seem to support the notion that the major cause of the popular unrest in 1549 was the harsh economic conditions that prevailed in that year.

A nation in crisis?

If the nation was in crisis then it passed almost unnoticed by contemporary writers. None wrote specifically of crisis and no one suggested that the social and economic problems in Edward's reign, although serious, were any worse than they had been during Henry VIII's. The crisis, if that is what it was, was not so much social and economic and nor was it overtly religious; it was mainly to do with the succession. Contemporaries, particularly the landowning political

---

KEY TERM

Bondmen Medieval peasants who lived and worked on the lord's manor.

nation, were concerned at the accession of a child king and they were genuinely fearful of the succession of a female monarch. Add to this the failed *coup d'état* of Lady Jane Grey and the notion of a nation in crisis gains currency.

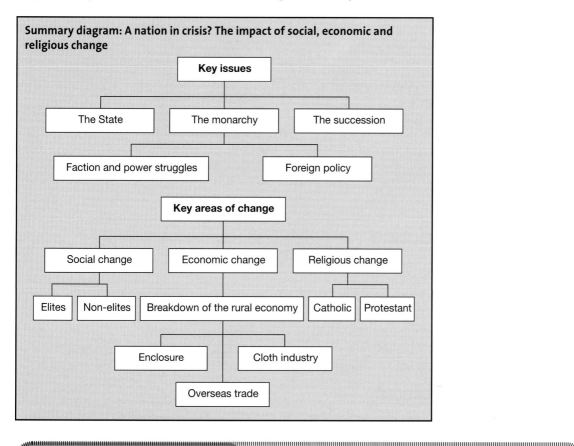

Summary diagram: A nation in crisis? The impact of social, economic and religious change

Chapter summary

In the view of some historians, Henry VIII left a toxic legacy to his son and heir, who inherited a kingdom in turmoil. The reign of Edward VI was dominated by the personalities and power of the Dukes of Somerset and Northumberland, who ruled the kingdom on behalf of the boy-king. It was a period of minority government in which the nobility took a leading role in governing the kingdom. Socially and economically, the period witnessed considerable change marked by price inflation, rising population, increasing unemployment, enclosures and the debasement of the coinage. When these are added to the changes in religion they generate a sense of national crisis made worse by an expensive foreign policy. This has caused some historians to suggest that Edward's reign (along with that of Mary) witnessed a mid-Tudor crisis. Archbishop Cranmer emerged as a man with the vision and authority to establish Protestantism as the State religion. Patronised and protected by both Somerset and Northumberland, Cranmer was able to fulfil his evangelical mission to convert the people to the Protestant faith. Cranmer's Protestant revolution is arguably the defining characteristic of Edward's short reign.

Refresher questions

Use these questions to remind yourself of the key material covered in this chapter.

1 How effective was Somerset's government of England?

2 Why did Somerset follow Henry VIII's foreign policy and what problems did he face?

3 Why was Somerset cautious about introducing religious reform?

4 Why did Somerset face disorder and rebellion?

5 Why did Somerset fall from power?

6 How did Northumberland seize power?

7 How effective was Northumberland's government of England?

8 What part did Cranmer play in shaping the Protestant Reformation?

9 Did Northumberland succeed in turning England into a Protestant country?

10 Why was there such widespread disorder and rebellion?

11 Why is this period often described as a mid-Tudor crisis?

Question practice

ESSAY QUESTIONS

1 'The Protestant faith was so firmly established by 1553 that England may fairly be described as a Protestant nation.' Assess the validity of this view.

2 To what extent did Henry VIII bequeath a Church in crisis to Edward VI?

3 How accurate is it to say that England experienced a social and economic crisis between 1533 and 1558?

4 How accurate is it to say that England was misgoverned in the period between 1525 and 1550?

SOURCE ANALYSIS QUESTIONS

1 Use your knowledge of the reign of Edward VI to assess how useful Source 1 is as evidence for the failure of the Crown's religious policies.

2 Using Sources 1–3 in their historical context, assess how far they support the view that Lord Protector Somerset had lost control of the kingdom.

3 Using Sources 1–4 in their historical context, assess how far they support the view that the king was in serious danger of being removed from power.

SOURCE 1

From Lord Protector Somerset's letter of 27 July 1549 to Lord Russell. Russell was commander-in-chief of the royal army sent to deal with the Western rebels.

You have declared that it has been difficult to recruit men to serve in the king's army in Somerset due to the evil inclination of the people and that there are among them many who speak openly using traitorous words against the king and in favour of the rebels. You shall hang two to three of them and cause them to be publicly executed as traitors. Sharpe justice must be used against those traitors so that others may learn the consequences of their actions in opposing the king.

SOURCE 2

From Matteo Dandolo's letter to the Senate of Venice of 20 July 1549. Dandolo, the Venetian ambassador, was writing to his government to report on the rebellions and the English government's response.

There is news of major risings against the government of his grace the duke of Somerset in England, and that the King has retreated to a strong castle outside London. The cause of this unrest is the common land, as the great landowners occupy the pastures of the poor people. The rebels also require the return of the Mass, together with the religion as it stood on the death of Henry VIII. The government, wishing to apply a swift and ruthless remedy, put upwards of five hundred persons to the sword, sparing neither women nor children.

SOURCE 3

From diary entries written by the twelve-year-old King Edward for May and June 1549. Edward kept a diary in which he described the events of the day.

The people began to rise in Wiltshire, where Sir William Herbert did put them down, overrun and slay them.

Then they rose in Sussex, Hampshire, Kent, Gloucestershire, Worcestershire and Rutlandshire, where by fair persuasions, partly of honest men among themselves and partly by gentle men they were often appeased.

And in the mean season the Council sat every day in the Tower.

SOURCE 4

From William Paget's letter of 7 July 1549 to Lord Protector Somerset. Paget was a senior member of the King's Council who advised the Lord Protector and the young King Edward.

I told your grace the truth and was not believed. The king's subjects are out of all discipline, out of obedience, caring neither for protector nor king. And what is the cause? Your own softness, your intention to be good to the poor. Consider, I beseech you most humbly, that society in a realm is maintained by means of religion and law. The use of the old religion is forbidden by a law, and the use of the new is not yet embraced by eleven out of twelve parts of the realm. Every man of the Council has not liked the way in which you have dealt with the rebellious commons and they had wished you had acted otherwise.

CHAPTER 6

Mary I: gender, government and Catholic restoration 1553–8

This chapter is intended to help you to understand the key features of the reign of Mary I. The chapter examines the political, religious and economic problems that faced the Marian regime. The fact that she was the first female monarch to rule England is noted and its political impact discussed. Foreign policy and the question of the queen's marriage will also be features for focus. These issues are examined as four themes:

★ Mary I: gender, politics and government

★ The reintroduction of Roman Catholicism

★ Marriage, Philip and foreign relations

★ Support or opposition? Rebellion and unrest

Key dates

1553	Succession of Mary I	**1554**	Cardinal Pole returned to England as papal legate; England and Rome reconciled
	Execution of the Duke of Northumberland		
	Catholic mass reintroduced		Reintroduction of the heresy laws
	Stephen Gardiner appointed Lord Chancellor	**1555**	Bishops Hooper, Ridley and Latimer burned at the stake
1554	Wyatt Rebellion	**1556**	Archbishop Cranmer burned at the stake
	Execution of Lady Jane Grey and Guildford Dudley		Cardinal Pole appointed Archbishop of Canterbury
	Marriage of Mary I and Philip of Spain	**1558**	Deaths of Mary and Cardinal Pole

1 Mary I: gender, politics and government

▶ *What problems did Mary face when she became queen?*

Mary I: character, personality and problems

Mary, the daughter of Catherine of Aragon, was 37 years of age when she came to the throne. During Edward VI's reign she had resisted Protestant reform just as strongly as she had under her father. While Somerset was in power she had been allowed to follow her Catholic religion in private, and she had remained on good terms with the Protector and Edward. With the swing towards Calvinism under Northumberland, increasing pressure had been put on Mary to abandon Catholicism and to conform to the doctrines of the Church of England.

During this difficult period Mary had received constant support and advice from her Habsburg cousin, Emperor Charles V. It was fear of the Habsburgs that may have prevented the reformers taking extreme measures against her. Mary was a proud woman, who resented the pressures put on her and was embittered by the treatment of her mother. Consequently, she mistrusted her English councillors when she became queen, and so leant heavily on advice from the imperial ambassador, **Simon Renard**.

When Mary proclaimed herself queen on 11 July 1553, Renard and Charles V had thought it a futile gesture. Yet when she entered London at the end of the month, she was greeted with enormous enthusiasm. Political prisoners such as the Duke of Norfolk and Stephen Gardiner were released. Following the advice of Charles V, she showed leniency towards her opponents. Only Northumberland and two of his closest confederates were executed. Although some members of Northumberland's Council, like Cecil, were imprisoned, others, such as Paget, were allowed to join the new Privy Council.

As a devout Catholic, Mary was insistent that England should return to the Church of Rome. At the same time, she was convinced that national safety depended on a close alliance with the Habsburgs. Until 1555 this strategy appeared to be prospering, but thereafter Mary's popularity among the landowning elite steadily declined until her death in 1558.

Growing unpopularity

The cause of this unpopularity has generally been attributed to Mary's character. Simon Renard's assessment that she was 'good, easily influenced, inexpert in worldly matters and a novice all round' was scarcely a flattering tribute. Elizabethan propagandists were eager to depict Mary as a weak and unsuccessful pro-Spanish monarch in order to highlight the achievements of their own queen. Protestant reformers reviled her as a cruel tyrant trying to enforce Catholicism through torture and burnings. This has produced a popular picture of 'Bloody Mary' – a stubborn, arrogant, Catholic bigot, who burned Protestants and lost Calais to the French (see page 175) because of her infatuation for Philip of Spain.

In a modified form, this has been the view of many historians, but recently there have been attempts to revise this critical appraisal. It has been pointed out that she showed skill and resolution in defeating Northumberland's attempted *coup d'état*. Mary has been criticised for indecision in the negotiations over the restoration of Catholicism to England and her marriage to Philip of Spain. This, it has been suggested, was in fact masterly political inactivity and pretended weakness, designed to win greater concessions from the papacy and the Habsburgs, similar tactics to those that her sister Elizabeth was to use so successfully.

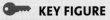

KEY FIGURE

Simon Renard (1513–73)

As Spanish ambassador to England he exercised considerable influence over Mary I, to the point where some believe he was virtually directing English affairs. He arranged Mary's marriage to Philip of Spain.

SOURCE A

Study Source A. How is Mary portrayed in this painting commissioned by Henry VIII?

ANNO DNI   1544

LADI MARI   DOVGHTER TO
THE MOST   VERTVOVS PRINCE
KINGE HENRI   THE EIGHT

THE AGE OF   XXVIII YERES

A portrait of Mary Tudor painted in 1544 when she was 28 years old by Master John.

Indeed, it is suggested that Mary had the broad support of the majority of the people until 1555. The problem was, it is suggested, not the weakness of Mary's character and policies, but her failure to produce an heir to consolidate her position. This, combined with the outbreak of war with France and the declining economic position, was the real cause of Mary's growing unpopularity.

Gender

In the opinion of Anna Whitelock (writing in 2014), gender is an issue that deserves to be highlighted and debated by historians: 'Mary was the Tudor trailblazer. Never before had a queen worn the crown of England. She won the throne against the odds, preserving the Tudor line of succession and establishing precedents for female rule.' Mary's father, Henry, had gone to extraordinary lengths to exclude Mary from the succession and to ensure the accession of a son and heir. To him, a woman could simply not rule England because she would be too emotional and not pragmatic or tough enough to make hard-headed political decisions, let alone handle her male advisers. Henry feared a return to the chaos of the Wars of the Roses, when weak monarchy had enabled ambitious 'overmighty subjects' to indulge in personal vendettas that led to civil war.

As Whitelock pointed out, 'The language, image, and expectations of English monarchy and royal majesty were unequivocally male.' On a practical level there was no guidance available to the clergy regarding the coronation of a woman as a ruler in her own right. In a male-dominated society there was a genuine fear and uncertainty about Mary's and Elizabeth's positions in the line of succession. Although Henry was sure his young son would succeed and rule without the need for either of his daughters to take up the reins of power, he, nevertheless, put in place a statute that he hoped would calm the fears of the people. In 1544 Henry VIII consented to Parliament passing 'An Acte declaring that the Regall power of thys realme is in the Queenes Maiestie as fully and absolutely as ever it was in anye her mooste noble progenytours kynges of thys Realme'. In effect, Mary's queenship would, in law, be equal to that of a king.

SOURCE B

Adapted from John Knox, *First Blast of the Trumpet Against the Monstrous Regiment of Women*, 1558. Knox was a Scottish religious reformer.

For who can deny that it [a woman ruler] is repugnant to nature, that the blind shall be appointed to lead and conduct such as do see? That the weak, the sick, and impotent persons shall nourish and keep the whole and strong, and that the foolish, mad and frenetic shall govern and give counsel to such as be sober of mind? And such are all women, compared unto man in bearing of authority. For their sight in civil regiment, is but blindness: their strength, weakness: their counsel, foolishness: and their judgement, frenzy, if it be rightly considered.

Study Source B. What is the meaning of Knox's message?

Mary's marriage

The passing of Henry's 1544 Act might change the law but it would not necessarily change minds. In an age of male domination Mary's marriage was a case in point, since she would be subject to the authority of her husband whomsoever he happened to be. That Mary must marry was taken for granted if the dynasty was to survive. The key question, of course, was that, once married, would Mary rule or would her husband rule through her? To marry a member of the English nobility was considered unacceptable because his elevation to power would cause jealousy and rivalry that might lead to conflict. On the other hand, to the increasingly nationalist English, marriage with a foreign prince was equally unacceptable. A foreign husband might drag England into Continental conflicts.

That Mary chose her husband and limited his constitutional power within the kingdom showed that she ruled with the full measure of royal authority. Mary did not let her gender limit the exercise of her God-given power. By making it possible for queens to rule as kings, Mary provided her successor Elizabeth with a template by establishing the gender-free authority of a queen.

Government

The system of central and local government remained fundamentally unchanged during Mary's reign. The Privy Council continued to be the centre of the administration. One of the main criticisms of Mary's Privy Council has been that it was too large to conduct business effectively. In addition, it has been claimed that the Council contained too many members who had no real political ability and who lacked administrative experience. The reason for this was that in the first few weeks of her reign Mary necessarily chose councillors from her own household, and from among leading Catholic noblemen who had supported her. By October, several moderate members of Northumberland's Council had been sworn in as councillors, although they were never fully in the queen's confidence. However, they supplied a nucleus of political ability and administrative experience previously lacking. Apart from this making the Council too large, it has been suggested that it caused strong rivalry between the Catholics, led by the Chancellor, Gardiner, and the moderates, led by Sir William Paget.

It is now thought that, although there was disagreement, these two very able politicians co-operated closely to restore effective government. In any case, affairs of State were soon largely handled by an 'inner council' consisting of those experienced councillors who had reformed the Privy Council under Northumberland. Much of the original criticism of the Privy Council came from Renard (see page 163), who was jealous of the queen's English advisers and wished to maintain his own influence with Mary. The main problem was that Mary did not appear to exert any leadership, or show any real confidence in her Council. Frequently, she did not consult the Privy Council until she had already decided matters of policy in consultation with Renard.

Parliament

It was once thought that Parliament was strongly opposed to Mary's policies but this view is no longer held. There seems to be little evidence that Mary controlled the House of Commons by packing it with Catholic supporters through rigged elections. She had strong support from the higher clergy in the House of Lords, especially after the imprisonment and execution of Cranmer, Ridley and Latimer. Apart from the dislike of the Spanish marriage, both houses seem to have co-operated with the administration throughout Mary's reign. As was the case in the Privy Council, there were lively debates and criticism of policy, but these were generally constructive. Like previous Parliaments, the main interest of the members centred on local affairs and the protection of property rights.

Financial reforms

The Marian administration was still faced by the financial problems that Northumberland had been trying to solve. To make matters worse, Mary had given away more Crown lands in order to re-establish some monastic foundations. Consequently, it was important both to find new sources of government revenue and to increase the income from existing ones. To achieve this, the Privy Council largely adopted the proposals put forward by the commissions in 1552.

In 1554 drastic changes were made to the revenue courts:

- The Exchequer was restored as the main financial department. It took over the work of the Court of First Fruits and Tenths, which had dealt with taxes paid by the senior clergy, and the Court of Augmentations, which had administered income from monastic and chantry lands.
- The Court of Wards, which collected a tax levied on the heirs to great estates, and the Duchy of Lancaster, administering lands belonging to the monarch as Duke of Lancaster, retained their independence.
- It was planned to remove the large number of debased coins (coinage in which the gold and silver content had been reduced) in circulation and to restore the full silver content of the coinage, but Mary's death meant that the scheme was not put into effect until 1560.
- The 1552 proposal to revise the custom rates, which had remained unchanged since 1507, was implemented. In 1558 a new Book of Rates was issued, which increased custom revenue from £29,000 to £85,000 a year.
- In 1555 a full survey of all Crown lands was carried out. As a result, rents and entry fines (a payment made by new tenants before they could take over a property) were raised in 1557.

Mary died before these measures had any real effect, and it was Elizabeth I who benefited from the increased revenue brought about by these reforms.

The economy

During Mary's reign the general economic situation grew even worse, with a series of bad harvests and epidemics of **sweating sickness**, **plague** and influenza. Towns were particularly badly hit, with high mortality rates and severe food shortages. The government's reaction was to continue the policy, started under Henry VIII, of restricting the movement of textile and other industries from the towns to the countryside. This, it was hoped, would prevent an increase in urban unemployment and reduce the number of vagrants seeking work. This, however, was short-sighted because what was really needed was an increase in the amount and variety of industries in both town and country, which would provide jobs for the growing number of unemployed.

KEY TERMS

Sweating sickness
A mysterious and highly virulent disease that struck England in a series of epidemics between 1485 and 1551.

Plague A deadly infectious disease that is spread by the fleas carried by rats.

To achieve this, the government needed to encourage the search for new overseas markets to replace the trade lost with the decline of the Antwerp market. In 1551 English ships had begun to trade along the North African coast, and between 1553 and 1554 Sir Hugh Willoughby was trying to find a north-east passage to the Far East. However, until after 1558 successive English governments were too anxious to avoid offending Spain and Portugal to encourage overseas enterprise. It was not until the reign of Elizabeth I that any real progress was made in this direction.

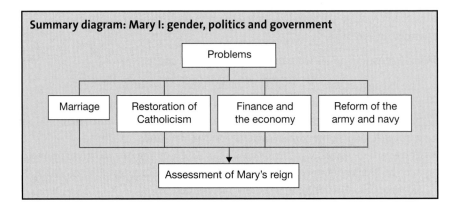

Summary diagram: Mary I: gender, politics and government

2 The reintroduction of Roman Catholicism

▶ *How successful was the restoration of the Pope and reintroduction of Roman Catholicism?*

The religious situation in 1553

In 1553 no one in England doubted that Mary, after her twenty years of resistance to the royal supremacy, would restore Roman Catholicism. There is good evidence to suggest that it was just as much Edward VI's wish to preserve Protestantism as Northumberland's personal ambition that led to the attempt to exclude Mary from the throne. Mary and her Catholic supporters saw the failure of the scheme as a miracle, and she was determined to restore England to the authority of Rome as quickly as possible. What Mary failed to realise was that her initial popularity sprang not from a desire for a return to the Roman Catholic Church, but from a dislike of Northumberland, and respect for the legitimate succession.

Mary's supporters in England and abroad urged caution. Both Charles V and Pope Julius III warned her not to risk her throne by acting too rashly. Cardinal Reginald Pole, appointed as papal legate to restore England to the authority of

Rome, stayed in the Netherlands for a year before coming to England. Whether this was because Charles V refused to allow the cardinal to leave until the planned marriage between Philip and Mary had come to fruition, or whether it reflected Pole's natural caution about returning to his native land and a possibly hostile reception, is difficult to decide. Even Gardiner, Mary's most trusted adviser, who had consistently resisted reform, was unenthusiastic about restoring papal authority.

Mary singularly failed to realise the political implications of restoring Roman Catholicism to England. A return to papal authority would mean an end to the royal supremacy, which was strongly supported by the ruling and landed elites. Even the most ardent of the leading conservatives had been firm in their allegiance to the Crown and the Tudor State. It is agreed by the majority of historians that the major causes of Mary's widespread unpopularity by the end of her reign, apart from the religious persecution, were the return to papal authority and the Spanish marriage. Most of the population regarded these as interference by foreigners and an affront to English nationalism.

The restoration of Anglo-Catholicism

In 1553 there was no doubt about Mary's popularity, and the elites rallied to her support. The aristocracy and gentry were initially prepared to conform to Mary's religious views, and the bulk of the population followed their example. But some 800 strongly committed Protestant gentry, clergy and members of the middle orders left the country and spent the remainder of the reign on the Continent. Such an escape was less easy for the common people and most of the 274 Protestants executed during Mary's reign came from this group. At the beginning of the reign even the most zealous religious radicals were not prepared to go against public opinion, and waited to see what would happen. Certainly, when Mary, using the royal prerogative, suspended the second Act of Uniformity and restored the mass, there was no public outcry.

This lack of religious opposition was apparent when Parliament met in October 1553. Admittedly, the arrest and imprisonment of Cranmer, Hooper and Ridley, along with other leading Protestant bishops, removed the major source of opposition in the House of Lords. After a lively, but not hostile debate, the first step towards removing all traces of Protestantism from the Church of England was achieved with the passing of the first Statute of Repeal. This Act swept away all the religious legislation approved by Parliament during the reign of Edward VI, and the doctrine of the Church of England was restored to what it had been in 1547 under the Act of the Six Articles.

Although Mary had succeeded in re-establishing the Anglo-Catholicism of her father, her advisers had managed to persuade her into some caution. There had been no attempt to question the royal supremacy, or to discuss the issue of the Church lands which had been sold to the laity. Both these issues were likely to provoke a more heated debate.

Gardiner's policies

Opposition to Mary's proposed marriage to Philip II of Spain and the consequent rebellion meant that further religious legislation was postponed until the spring of 1554. Gardiner, anxious to regain royal favour after his opposition to Mary's marriage, tried to quicken the pace at which Protestantism was removed by persuading Parliament to pass a bill to reintroduce the heresy laws. He was successfully opposed by Sir William Paget, who feared that such a measure might provoke further disorder.

Thwarted in this direction, Gardiner proceeded to turn his attention to Protestant clergy. The Bishops of Gloucester, Hereford, Lincoln and Rochester, and the Archbishop of York were deprived of their bishoprics, and were replaced by committed Catholics. In March 1554 the bishops were instructed to enforce all the religious legislation of the last year of Henry VIII's reign. Apart from ensuring a return to 'the old order of the Church, in the Latin tongue', these injunctions demanded that all married clergy should give up their wives and families, or lose their parishes. The authorities largely complied with these instructions, and some 800 parish clergy were so deprived. Although some fled abroad, the majority were found employment elsewhere in the country.

From Anglo-Catholicism to Roman Catholicism

Cardinal Pole finally arrived in England in November 1554, and this marked the next decisive stage in the restoration of Roman Catholicism. Parliament met in the same month and passed the second Statute of Repeal. This Act ended the royal supremacy, and returned England to papal authority by repealing all the religious legislation of the reign of Henry VIII back to the time of the break with Rome. The restoration of the Pope as head of the Church came at a price. To achieve this Mary had to come to a compromise with the landowners. Careful provision was made in the Act to protect the property rights of all those who had bought Church land since 1536. This demonstrates that Mary had to recognise the authority of Parliament over matters of religion. It meant that she had to forgo her plans for a full-scale restoration of the monasteries. Instead, she had to be content with merely returning to the Church the monastic lands, worth £60,000 a year, still held by the Crown.

Attempted measures to consolidate the Marian Church

Although Pole actively tried to eradicate Protestantism, his first priority appears to have been to restore stability after twenty years of religious turmoil. It is widely considered that, in view of his lack of administrative experience and ability, such a formal and legalistic approach was a mistake. Ecclesiastical revenues had been so denuded that there were insufficient resources available to reorganise the Marian Church effectively. Indeed, a great part of Pole's three years in office was spent in the virtually hopeless task of trying to restore the Church of England's financial position.

Pole's attempts to reorganise and reconcile the Church of England to Rome were not helped by the death of Pope Julius III in 1555. The new Pope, Paul IV, disliked Pole and hated the Spanish Habsburgs. He stripped Pole of his title of legate and ordered him to return to Rome. Pole refused to comply, and continued his work in England as Archbishop of Canterbury, but the papacy would not recognise his authority. This further hindered his work because he could not appoint bishops, and by 1558 seven sees were vacant. Such quarrels, and papal intervention in English affairs, did little to convince anyone except the most zealous Catholics of the wisdom of returning to the authority of Rome.

Winning hearts and minds

Certainly, such events, along with the persecution and burnings of Protestants, did not help the government in its task of winning the hearts and minds of English men and women back to the Roman Catholic faith. Pole's hopes that, while he struggled with his administrative tasks, the re-establishment of the old religion would lead to wholehearted acceptance of Roman Catholicism were not realised. Pole was fully in favour of the educational programme which was being adopted on the Continent. He appointed capable and active bishops, all of whom subsequently refused to serve in the Elizabethan Protestant Church of England.

In 1555 the Westminster **synod** approved the passing of the Twelve Decrees that included the establishment of seminaries in every diocese for the training of priests, but shortage of money limited the programme to a single creation at York. This meant that the majority of the parish clergy remained too uneducated for the new laws to have any immediate impact on the laity. Mary's death in November 1558 came too soon for Catholic reform to have had any lasting effect. That is not to say that if Mary had lived longer, Catholicism would not have gained wider support than the significant minority, who clung to their faith after the establishment of the Elizabethan Church.

> **KEY TERM**
>
> **Synod** A council of senior members of the Church convened to decide on issues of doctrine.

SOURCE C

Adapted from Cardinal Pole's decrees drawn up at the 1555 Westminster synod.

First Decree: On the thanks that should be given to God for the return of this kingdom to the unity of the Church by the daily celebration of mass. …

Fourth Decree: That bishops and others who have a cure of souls should preach to the people and parish priests should teach children the basic elements of the faith. …

Eleventh Decree: That in the cathedrals a certain number of boys should be educated from which, as if from a seed-bed, it will be possible to raise up those who are worthy of a career in the Church.

> Study Source C. Why might these decrees suggest that the Roman Catholic faith is not as strong as it once was prior to the Reformation?

Stephen Gardiner

c.1483	Born in Bury St Edmunds to John Gardiner, a prosperous cloth merchant
1530–4	Principal secretary to Henry VIII
1532	Appointed Bishop of Winchester
1535–8	Ambassador to France
1539	Promoted Act of Six Articles
1548	Forced out of government and imprisoned in the Tower of London for opposing Somerset
1553	Appointed Lord Chancellor
1555	Died

Educated at Cambridge University, Gardiner became a doctor of civil and canon law. His legal expertise in both common and ecclesiastical law contributed to his promotion. His appointment in 1521 as tutor to the Duke of Norfolk's son began a close relationship with one of the most powerful ducal families in the kingdom. His first significant appointment to public office came in 1524 when he became secretary to Lord Chancellor Wolsey, Henry VIII's chief minister.

Gardiner supported the king over the annulment and approved of the royal supremacy, but he disagreed with the religious changes proposed by Cromwell. His opposition to Cromwell caused him to fall out of favour with the king. He contributed to the destruction of Cromwell. Together with the Duke of Norfolk, he led the conservative faction at court. He became one of Henry VIII's leading ministers between 1542 and 1547. In Edward's reign he fell foul of the new Protestant regime; he was imprisoned and stripped of his bishopric of Winchester. In 1553 he was restored to all his offices and titles by Mary, who appointed him Lord Chancellor. He married Philip and Mary.

Gardiner was a talented government minister and respected thinker and theologian. His opposition to Somerset in the last years of Henry VIII's reign ensured his downfall after the king's death. Although Somerset was prepared to work with Gardiner, the two could not agree on the religious direction the Edwardian government should take. In spite of his strong Catholic beliefs, he tried to save the leaders of the reformist party, Cranmer and Northumberland, from execution. The accession of Mary rescued his career and although he had supported the break with Rome in 1534 he was willing to restore the Pope as head of the Church in 1554. He led the Catholic Counter-Reformation and promoted conservative legislation in Parliament. He served out the remainder of his life as a trusted adviser to the Crown.

Assessment of the Church of England in 1558

To assess the state of religion in England in 1558 is just as difficult as it is to measure the advance of Protestantism by 1553. It is difficult to decide to what extent the bulk of the population had any particular leanings towards either the Protestant or the Catholic faith. While it is easy to trace the changing pattern of official doctrine in the Church of England through the Acts and statutes passed in Parliament, it is a much greater problem to determine what the general public thought about religion. At present, the consensus among historians is that the ruling classes accepted the principle of the royal supremacy, and were prepared to conform to whichever form of religion was favoured by the monarch.

Although the lower orders are generally considered to have had a conservative affection for the traditional forms of worship, it is thought they were prepared to follow the lead of the local elites. Whether the religious legislation passed in parliament was put into effect very much depended on the attitudes of the local elites, and to a lesser extent those of the parish authorities.

In general, it appears that by 1558 the majority of people in England were still undecided about religion. Among the elites there was strong support for the royal supremacy, but the landowners were willing to follow the religion of the legitimate monarch. The mass of the population do not appear to have had strong formalised convictions, and in most cases they were prepared to follow the lead of their social superiors. Although there were small minorities of committed Protestants and Catholics, neither religion seems to have had a strong hold in England when Mary I died. When Elizabeth I came to the throne the country was willing to return to a form of moderate Protestantism. However, during her reign deeper religious divisions began to appear, and the unity of the Church of England ended.

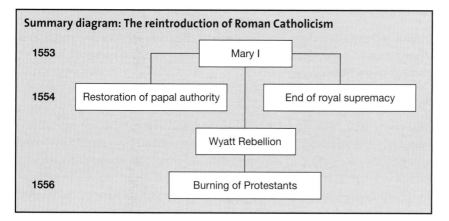

Summary diagram: The reintroduction of Roman Catholicism

3 Marriage, Philip and foreign relations

▶ *Why was the Spanish marriage so controversial and what impact did it have on English foreign policy?*

The Spanish marriage

Mary's political inexperience and stubbornness is shown in the first major issue of the reign: the royal marriage. The Privy Council was divided on the matter. There were two realistic candidates for Mary's hand:

- Edward Courtenay, Earl of Devon, who was favoured by Gardiner
- Philip of Spain, who was supported by Paget.

Courtenay was a descendant of the Plantagenet kings and such a marriage would have strengthened the Tudor dynasty, but Mary favoured a closer link with the Habsburgs through Philip. It was not until 27 October that Mary raised the matter in Council, and then only to announce that she was going to marry Philip. This disconcerted Gardiner, who was blamed by Mary for the petition from the House of Commons in November, asking her to marry within the realm. Mary disregarded all opposition to her plans.

On 7 December a marriage treaty, drafted by Mary, Paget, Gardiner and Renard, was presented to the Council. It was ratified at the beginning of January 1554. Mary had achieved her objective of forming a closer alliance with the Habsburgs. The terms of the treaty were very favourable to England. Philip was to have no regal power in England, no foreign appointments were to be made to the Privy Council, and England was not to be involved in, or pay towards, the cost of any of Philip's wars. If the marriage was childless, the succession was to pass to Elizabeth.

In spite of these safeguards, Mary's popularity began to ebb as many people still thought that England would be drawn into Philip's wars and become a mere province of the Habsburg Empire.

Philip's arrival in England

After many delays Philip finally arrived in England in July 1554. In a carefully staged reception, Prince Philip met Queen Mary at Winchester on 23 July. Two days later they were married in Winchester Cathedral. Nationalist distrust of foreigners apart, Mary's subjects feared the reputation of the Spanish Inquisition and the influence Philip's hard-line religious advisers might have on the English Church. Of the half dozen or so of Philip's religious advisers, Friar Alfonso de Castro was especially feared because he was an authority on the theory and practice of persecuting heretics. Although far from impartial in his judgement, the Protestant Bishop John Jewel believed that de Castro and his fellow Spanish clerics had exerted considerable influence in Mary's court. In 1559, less than a year after Mary's death, he wrote that 'one could scarce believe that so much mischief could have been done in so short a time'. Philip did not long remain in England and the following year, 1555, he returned to Spain.

Foreign policy

There is no evidence to suggest that the persecution and burning of heretics in England was planned and led by Philip's advisers although their influence and advice cannot be entirely discounted. What is certain is that Philip's political advisers had more success in persuading Mary to involve herself in Spain's conflict with France. Initially, Mary was reluctant to commit English resources in war and she did her best to remain at peace with France. She even tried to mediate between the two sides, but with limited success. Nevertheless, after some hard bargaining Spain and France agreed to sign the Treaty of Vaucelles in February 1556. To Mary's relief, both sides agreed to a five-year peace.

Unfortunately, the peace did not last and in 1557, after nearly two years away, Philip returned to England seeking the support of his wife in war with the French. Although Mary was not obliged to lead England into a Spanish war, she succumbed to pressure brought to bear on her by Philip and his advisers. Added to the effects of the persecution and burning of heretics, Philip's success in drawing the country into his war against France contributed to Mary's growing unpopularity.

A war on two fronts

England was faced with a war on two fronts. As expected, Scotland renewed its alliance with France and attacked northern England. The English were well prepared but bad weather contributed to a Scottish defeat. Meanwhile in France, an English army, 5000 strong, joined a Spanish army of nearly 70,000 in the siege of St Quentin. The capture of St Quentin and defeat of the French in August 1557 was greeted with delight and celebration in England. However, the inexperienced Philip did not press home his advantage and he retired to build up his forces. This allowed the French to do the same and in a surprise attack in January 1558 a force of nearly 30,000 Frenchmen determined to defeat the English garrison at Calais. The Calais garrison, some 2000 Englishman and several hundred Spanish troops, held out for three weeks, but with no reinforcements coming from either England or Spain had no choice but to surrender.

The loss of Calais was seen as a national disaster. The last Continental possession had been lost and although plans were made to recapture it, they were never put into action. It may be argued that the loss of Calais was the crucial moment when England turned its attention away from fruitless and expensive Continental conquest towards opportunities in the New World. Some historians would go as far as to claim that Mary's greatest failure was not the loss of Calais or the re-establishment of Roman Catholicism but her childlessness. It was reported that, on her death bed, Mary said 'When I am dead they will find Calais inscribed on my heart.'

SOURCE D

Adapted from a report on Mary sent by the Venetian ambassador, Giovanni Michiel, to his government in Venice, 1557.

Not only is she brave and valiant, unlike other timid and spiritless women, but so courageous and resolute that neither in adversity nor peril did she even display or commit any act of cowardice, maintaining always a wonderful grandeur and dignity. It may be said of her, as Cardinal Pole says with truth, that in the darkness and obscurity of that kingdom she … kept burning and defended by her lively faith that it might shine in the world as it now does shine.

Study Source D. Why might the reliability of this report be questioned?

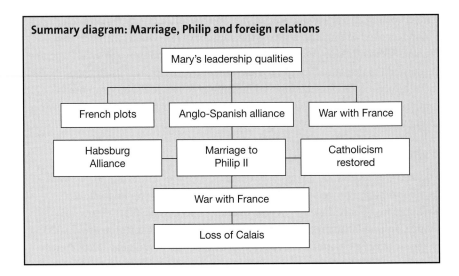

Summary diagram: Marriage, Philip and foreign relations

Mary's leadership qualities

French plots — Anglo-Spanish alliance — War with France

Habsburg Alliance — Marriage to Philip II — Catholicism restored

War with France

Loss of Calais

4 Support or opposition? Rebellion and unrest

▶ *Why was there unrest and rebellion in Mary's reign?*

The succession crisis

Mary's reign began in crisis. Although she was, by right of inheritance, the next in line to the throne, Northumberland made every effort to prevent her succession. Mary had to fight for her throne.

Earlier, to retain power, Northumberland, with the full support of the king, had attempted to change the succession. As the Succession Acts of 1534 and 1536 making Mary and Elizabeth illegitimate had not been repealed, it was decided to disinherit them in favour of the Suffolk branch of the family. Frances, Duchess of Suffolk, was excluded as her age made it unlikely that she would have male heirs, and her eldest daughter, Lady Jane Grey, was chosen to succeed. To secure his own position, Northumberland married his eldest son, Guildford Dudley, to Jane in May 1553.

Unfortunately for Northumberland, Edward VI died in July before the plans for the seizure of power could be completed. Jane Grey was proclaimed queen by Northumberland and the Council in London, while Mary proclaimed herself queen at Framlingham Castle in Suffolk. However, Northumberland's plot was doomed from the start because he made two basic errors:

- He failed to arrest Mary and keep her in custody.
- He underestimated the amount of support for Mary in the country.

Mary takes power

On 14 July Northumberland marched into Suffolk with an army of 2000 men, but his troops deserted him. The Privy Council in London hastily changed sides and proclaimed Mary as queen. Northumberland was arrested in Cambridge, tried, and executed on 22 August in spite of his renunciation of Protestantism. The ease with which Mary upheld her right to the throne shows the growing stability of the State and the nation. Potential political crisis had been avoided because the majority of the nation supported the rule of law and rightful succession. The direct line of descent was still considered legitimate in spite of Acts of Parliament to the contrary. A period of dynastic weakness and minority rule had passed without the country dissolving into civil war.

Two Acts were passed, one in 1553 and another in 1554, to resolve the constitutional position. This legislation was designed to confirm Mary Tudor's legitimacy, and to establish the right of female monarchs to rule in England. However, no attempt was made to make Elizabeth legitimate, although she was recognised as Mary's heir in the event of her dying childless.

Sir Thomas Wyatt

Wyatt was a member of a wealthy and well-connected gentry family from Kent. He succeeded to the family estates on the death of his father, also called Sir Thomas, in 1542. Sir Thomas Wyatt senior had been a courtier and diplomat, and his son was expected to follow suit. He became friendly with the influential Henry Howard, Earl of Surrey, who acted as his patron. Wyatt fought in France under Surrey in 1543–4 and in 1545 he was promoted to the English council governing English-controlled Boulogne. As a committed Protestant, Wyatt found favour with the Edwardian regime, which he defended in 1549 when riots broke out in Kent. He was trusted by Northumberland, who appointed him to represent the English government in negotiations with the French in 1550.

Wyatt served the Edwardian regime loyally but he declared his support for Mary when Jane Grey was proclaimed queen. Wyatt's initial support for Mary soon evaporated when he heard of the Spanish marriage. As a Member of Parliament he became involved in the opposition to the proposed marriage in Parliament but his hopes of persuading the queen to reject the marriage failed. The public outcry against the proposed marriage was such that the Crown was compelled to issue a proclamation banning 'unlawful and rebellious assemblies'. In spite of this, reports of 'lewd words' and 'seditious tumults' poured into the court.

Wyatt's Rebellion

By the end of January 1554 anti-Spanish feelings led to rebellion. Unlike the rebellions of 1549, this was a political conspiracy among the elites with little popular support. The rebellion was led by Sir James Croft, Sir Peter Carew and Wyatt. They feared that the growing Spanish influence at court would endanger their own careers. The conspirators planned to marry Elizabeth to Edward Courtenay, Earl of Devon, who had been rejected by Mary as an unsuitable match.

Simultaneous rebellions in the West Country (Carew), the Welsh borderland (Croft), the Midlands (Suffolk, father of Lady Jane Grey) and Kent (Wyatt) were to be supported by a French fleet. The plan failed because Carew, Croft and the Duke of Suffolk bungled the uprisings. Wyatt succeeded in raising 3000 men in Kent, and this caused real fear in the government because the rebels were so close to London. The situation was made worse because a number of royal troops sent to crush the revolt deserted to the rebels. Realising the danger, the Privy Council desperately tried to raise fresh forces to protect London.

An overly cautious Wyatt failed to press home his advantage and his delay in marching on London gave Mary the time she needed to see to the capital's defence. In refusing to flee her capital, Mary's courage impressed those whom she called on to support her regime. By the time Wyatt arrived at the gates of the city the revolt was doomed to fail. Repulsed at London Bridge and the Tower, Wyatt found Ludgate closed and his troops began deserting.

Wyatt surrendered and the revolt was crushed. The rebels were treated leniently for fear of provoking further revolts. Most of the rebels among the commons were pardoned, and fewer than a hundred executions took place. As for the rebel elite, apart from Wyatt and Suffolk, only Jane Grey and her husband Guildford Dudley were executed. Croft was tried and imprisoned, but he was pardoned and released after nine months in the Tower. Both Elizabeth and Courtenay were interrogated and imprisoned but were later released.

The failure of the Wyatt Rebellion

The Wyatt Rebellion came as close as any to overthrowing the monarchy. Frustrated and increasingly desperate, men like Wyatt felt compelled to act in a way that had only two possible outcomes: failure would result in his own death while success would almost inevitably lead to the death of the monarch.

The failure of the Wyatt Rebellion owed as much to Mary's resolute courage in the face of adversity as it did to the rebels' mistakes. It was the high point of Mary's reign insofar as her popularity peaked during this crisis. The Spanish marriage went ahead and, although there were no further outbreaks of rebellion, the period from 1555 witnessed a rise in anti-Spanish feelings, mounting opposition to religious persecution, and discontent with the adverse economic conditions. The war with France and the loss of Calais, England's last Continental possession, united the country against the ailing queen, who was dying of cancer. The enthusiasm which marked her death in November 1558 and the succession of Elizabeth to the throne was even greater than that which had greeted Mary's overthrow of Northumberland five years earlier.

Religious persecution

In December 1554 Parliament approved the restoration of the old heresy laws. This marked the beginning of religious persecution. The first Protestant was burned at the stake for heresy on 4 February 1555, and Hooper suffered a similar fate five days later in his own city of Gloucester. In October, Ridley and Hugh Latimer, the former Bishop of Worcester, were likewise executed at Oxford, where they were followed by Cranmer in March 1556. The death of Gardiner in November 1555 had removed a trusted and restraining influence, and thereafter the regime became more repressive. Although Gardiner had started the persecution on the grounds that some executions would frighten the Protestant extremists into submission, he was too astute a politician not to see that the policy was not working. Far from cowing the Protestants, he realised that the executions were hardening the opposition to Mary and encouraging the colonies of English exiles on the Continent. He counselled caution, but his advice was ignored.

After Gardiner's death, Mary, and Pole, who had been made Archbishop of Canterbury in December 1555, felt that it was their sacred duty to stamp out heresy, and stepped up the level of persecution. It is now estimated that the 274 religious executions carried out during the last three years of Mary's reign exceeded the number recorded in any Catholic country on the Continent over the same period, even though it was much lower than in some other periods. This modifies the claim by some historians that the Marian regime was more moderate than those on the Continent.

SOURCE E

Adapted from a report by Simon Renard to King Philip of Spain, February 1555.

Sire, The people of London are murmuring about the cruel enforcement of the recent acts of parliament on heresy which has now begun, as shown publicly when a certain Rogers was burnt yesterday. Some of the onlookers wept; others prayed to God to give them strength … others gathered the ashes and bones … yet others did threaten the bishops. The haste in which the bishops have proceeded in this matter may well cause a revolt. I do not think it well that your Majesty should allow further executions to take place unless the reasons are strong. Tell the bishops that they are not to proceed without having first consulted you and the Queen. Your Majesty will also consider that the Lady Elizabeth has her supporters and that there are Englishmen who do not love foreigners.

> Study Source E. What does the source reveal about the dangers of the Marian persecution?

Popular reactions against religious persecution

Gardiner's unheeded warnings were soon justified, and Mary's popularity waned rapidly. There was widespread revulsion in the south-east of England at the persecution, and to many people Catholicism became firmly linked with hatred of Rome and Spain. Many local authorities either ignored, or tried to avoid enforcing, the unpopular legislation. The number of people fleeing abroad increased, reinforcing the groups of English exiles living in centres of Lutheranism and Calvinism on the Continent. They became the nucleus of an active and well-informed opposition, which began to flood England with anti-Catholic books and pamphlets. The effectiveness of this campaign is shown in the proclamations issued by the Privy Council in 1558, ordering the death penalty for anyone found with heretical or seditious literature. If before 1555 the English people were generally undecided about religion, the Marian repression succeeded in creating a core of highly committed English Protestants.

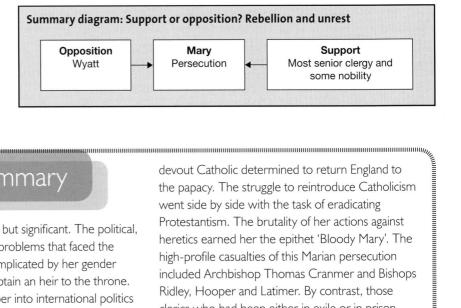

Summary diagram: Support or opposition? Rebellion and unrest

| **Opposition** Wyatt | → | **Mary** Persecution | ← | **Support** Most senior clergy and some nobility |

Chapter summary

Mary I's reign was short but significant. The political, religious and economic problems that faced the Marian regime were complicated by her gender and need to marry to obtain an heir to the throne. This drew England deeper into international politics because her husband, Philip of Spain, would inevitably exert some influence over English foreign policy. Critics feared that he might also have a say in setting the political agenda in England. Perhaps the greatest challenge facing Mary and her government was religion. She had inherited a Protestant Church and State from her half-brother but Mary was a devout Catholic determined to return England to the papacy. The struggle to reintroduce Catholicism went side by side with the task of eradicating Protestantism. The brutality of her actions against heretics earned her the epithet 'Bloody Mary'. The high-profile casualties of this Marian persecution included Archbishop Thomas Cranmer and Bishops Ridley, Hooper and Latimer. By contrast, those clerics who had been either in exile or in prison during Edward VI's reign, most notably Cardinal Pole and Bishop Gardiner, were promoted to Archbishop and Lord Chancellor, respectively. In the final analysis, Mary failed to establish Roman Catholicism firmly.

Refresher questions

Use these questions to remind yourself of the key material covered in this chapter.

1 How effective was the system of government under Mary?

2 What financial problems faced Mary and how did she deal with them?

3 Why was the economy in crisis during Mary's reign?

4 Who exerted the greater influence on the queen, Simon Renard or Stephen Gardiner?

5 Why did Mary restore Catholicism and what problems did this cause?

6 How influential was Philip of Spain in English affairs?

7 To what extent did England become involved in Spain's quarrel with France?

8 Why did Mary follow a policy of religious persecution?

9 What was the state of the English Church at the end of Mary's reign?

10 To what extent did Mary's actions or policies provoke the Wyatt Rebellion?

11 Why was the Wyatt Rebellion so dangerous to Mary and her government?

Question practice

ESSAY QUESTIONS

1 'The Marian Counter-Reformation was a failure and the persecutions and burnings prove it.' Assess the validity of this view.

2 To what extent was Mary's foreign policy a complete disaster?

3 'Mary's reign was a complete failure.' Assess the validity of this view.

4 To what extent did England's religious policy change between 1533 and 1558?

INTERPRETATION QUESTION

1 Using your understanding of the historical context, assess how convincing the arguments in Extracts 1–3 are in relation to Mary's historical reputation.

EXTRACT 1

From P. Williams, *The Later Tudors: England 1547–1603*, Oxford University Press, 1995, p. 113.

For centuries Mary's reputation has suffered from a bombardment of hostile propaganda, its intensity determined from the beginning by John Foxe. In Protestant and Elizabethan tradition she is displayed as the arch opponent of true religion and as the friend of England's enemy, Spain. Her contribution to English history has been scorned as a legacy of hatred both for her faith and for the country of her husband. 'Sterility', in Pollard's cruel judgement, 'was the conclusive note of Mary's reign.' However, within the last decade several historians have modified, even in some respects reversed that verdict.

The restoration of the Catholic Church was Mary's supreme purpose and her rule must primarily be assessed in the light of that policy. Although there was much more to it than the destruction of Protestants, the persecution has loomed largest in the case against her.

EXTRACT 2

From G.R. Elton, *England Under the Tudors*, Methuen, 1974, pp. 214–15.

The reign of Mary Tudor lasted only five years, but it left an indelible impression. Positive achievements there were none: Pollard declared that sterility was its conclusive note, and this is a verdict with which the dispassionate observer must agree. All her good qualities went for nought because she lacked the essentials. Two things dominated her mind – her religion and her Spanish descent. In the place of the Tudor secular temper, cool political sense, and firm identification with England and the English, she put a passionate devotion to the Catholic religion and to Rome, absence of political guile, and pride in being Spanish. The result cannot surprise. She died only five years later execrated by nearly all. Her life was one of almost unrelieved tragedy, but the pity which this naturally excites must not obscure the obstinate wrong-headedness of her rule.

EXTRACT 3

From C. Erickson, *Bloody Mary*, St. Martin's Press, 1978, pp. vii–viii.

Mary Tudor has no monument in England. In her will she asked that a memorial be raised to herself and her mother, 'for a decent memory of us', but her request was ignored. The day of her death, November 17 – the day of Elizabeth's accession – was a national holiday for two hundred years. Succeeding generations called her Bloody Mary, and saw her reign through the pictures in Foxe's Book of Martyrs – pictures of Protestant prisoners fettered with leg irons, being beaten by their Catholic tormentors, praying as they awaited execution, their faces already touched with the ecstatic vision of heaven. Mary Tudor bore an extraordinary burden, yet she ruled with a full measure of the Tudor majesty, and met the challenges of severe economic crises, rebellion and religious upheaval capably and with courage.

SOURCE ANALYSIS QUESTIONS

1 Use your knowledge of Mary and Pole's religious policies to assess how useful Source 2 is as evidence for the effectiveness of religious changes.

2 Using Sources 1–3 in their historical context, assess how far they support the view that Mary's religious policies were popular.

3 Using Sources 1–4 in their historical context, assess how far they support the view that Mary and Pole's religious policies were a failure.

SOURCE I

From Henry Machyn's diary, February 1555. Machyn was a London merchant. He welcomed Mary Tudor's accession and her intention to return the people to the Catholic faith.

The fourth day of February the Bishop of London went into Newgate prison with other doctors to degrade Hooper and Rogers, sometime vicar of St Paul's. The same day was Rogers carried, between 10 and 11 o'clock into Smithfield and burned for his critical opinions, with great company of the Queen's guard. The fifth day of February between 5 and 6 in the morning, departed master Hooper to Gloucester and Saunders to Coventry, both to be burned.

SOURCE 2

From Simon Renard's confidential report to his master, King Philip of Spain, 1555. Renard, the Spanish ambassador, was a significant figure at Mary's court. He acted as one of her closest advisers and he regularly sent detailed reports to King Philip of Spain.

The people of London are murmuring about the cruel enforcement of the recent acts of parliament against heresy now begun, as shown publicly when a certain Rogers was burnt yesterday. Some of the onlookers wept. Others prayed to God to give them strength, and patience to bear the pain and not to convert back to Catholicism. Others gathered the ashes and bones and wrapped them up to preserve them. Yet others threatened the bishops. The haste with which the bishops have proceeded in this matter may well cause a revolt. If the people got the upper hand, not only would the cause of religion be again menaced, but the persons of your Majesty and the Queen might be in peril.

SOURCE 3

From John Foxe, *Acts and Monuments*, 1563. Foxe was a Protestant writer who proved highly skilled in turning reports of Catholic brutality and persecution into effective propaganda during Elizabeth's reign. Here he describes the execution of Agnes Potter and Joan Trunchfield.

These two advocates and sufferers for the pure gospel of Jesus Christ, lived in the town of Ipswich. Being apprehended on information of heresy, they were brought before the Bishop of Norwich, who examined them concerning their religion in general and their faith in the real presence of Christ in the sacrament of the altar in particular. With respect to the latter they both delivered their opinion, that in the sacrament of the Lord's supper there was represented the memorial only of Christ's death and passion, saying that according to the scriptures he was ascended up into heaven and sat on the right hand of God the Father, and therefore his body could not really be in the sacrament.

SOURCE 4

From a proclamation issued by Mary I and her Council in August 1553, which set out the government's religious policy.

Her Majesty will observe the Catholic religion she has professed all her life, and desires that all her subjects would quietly follow suit. However she will not compel any to this until further decisions are made. She commands her subjects to live together in Christian charity, avoiding the new and devilish terms of papist and heretic, and trying to live peaceful Christian lives. Any man who stirs up the people to disorder will be severely punished. Printers have published books and ballads written in English which discuss controversial religious teachings. Let nobody do so in future without the Queen's permission.

AQA AS level History

Interpretations guidance

Section A of the examination for AQA Component 1: Breadth Study: The Tudors 1485–1603 contains extracts from the work of historians. This section tests your ability to analyse different historical interpretations. Therefore, you must focus on the interpretations outlined in the extracts. The advice given here is just for the AS exam as this book is only suitable for the AS unit.

- For the AS exam, there are two extracts and you are asked which is the more convincing interpretation (25 marks).

An interpretation is a particular view on a topic of history held by a particular author or authors. Interpretations of an event can vary, for example, depending on how much weight a historian gives to a particular factor and largely ignores another one.

Interpretations can also be heavily conditioned by events and situations that influence the writer. For example, judging the merits or otherwise of the dissolution of the monasteries will tend to produce different responses. A Protestant writer might be less critical of the dissolution than a Catholic writer. Whereas the Protestant might regard the dissolution as a necessary step in the reform of clerical abuse and corruption, the Catholic would be likely to see it as an unjustified attack on the Church resulting in the wholesale destruction of English monasticism.

The interpretations that you will be given will be largely from recent or fairly recent historians, and they may, of course, have been influenced by events in the period in which they were writing.

Interpretations and evidence

The extracts will contain a mixture of interpretations and evidence. The mark scheme rewards answers that focus on the *interpretations* offered by the

extracts much more highly than answers that focus on the *information or evidence* mentioned in the extracts. Therefore, it is important to identify the interpretations:

- *Interpretations* are a specific kind of argument. They tend to make claims such as 'Henry VII's success in establishing the Tudor dynasty was almost entirely due to that fact that he was a brutal tyrant.'
- *Information or evidence* tends to consist of specific details. For example, 'Henry VII's ruthlessness was important in establishing royal authority.'
- *Arguments and counter-arguments*: sometimes in an extract you will find an interpretation which is then balanced in the same paragraph with a counter-argument. You will need to decide with which one your knowledge is most in sympathy.

The importance of planning

Remember that in the examination you are allowed an hour for this question. It is the planning stage that is vital in order to write a good answer. You should allow at least one-quarter of that time to read the extracts and plan an answer. If you start writing too soon, it is likely that you will waste time trying to summarise the *content* of each extract. Do this in your planning stage – and then think how you will *use* the content to answer the question.

Analysing interpretations: AS (two extracts)

The same skills are needed for AS and A level for this question, although only AS is covered here as only the AS unit is covered in this book.

> With reference to these extracts, and your understanding of the historical context, which of these two extracts provides the more convincing interpretation of a revolution in government during the reign of Henry VIII? (25 marks)

Extracts A and B are used for the AS question.

EXTRACT A

A view of the changes in government in the 1530s. (From G.R. Elton, *The Tudor Revolution in Government*, Cambridge University Press, 1953, pp. 424–5.)

When an administration relying on the household was replaced by one based exclusively on bureaucratic departments and officers of state, a revolution took place in government. The principle then adopted was not in turn discarded until the much greater administrative revolution of the nineteenth century, which not only destroyed survivors of the medieval system allowed to continue a meaningless existence for some

300 years, but also created an administration based on departments responsible to parliament – an administration in which the crown for the first time ceased to hold the ultimate control. Medieval government was government by the king in person and through his immediate entourage. Early modern government was independent of the household, bureaucratically organised in national departments, but responsible to the crown.

EXTRACT B

An alternative view of the changes in government in the 1530s. (From John Guy, *Tudor England*, 1988, Oxford University Press, p. 156.)

It has been argued over the last thirty years that Cromwell achieved a 'revolution in government' during the 1530s, though this interpretation has been attacked. The 'revolution' thesis maintains that Cromwell consciously – that is, as a matter of principle – reduced the role of the royal household in government and substituted instead 'national' bureaucratic administration within departments of state under the control of a fundamentally

reorganised Privy Council. Such argument is, however, too schematic. The thesis that a Tudor 'revolution in government' took place is comprehensible when the periodization of change is extended to Elizabeth's death, though whether the word 'revolution' is appropriate – as opposed to 'readjustment' or straightforward 'change' – is a matter of judgement. If 'revolution' is supposed to designate permanent change, it will not do.

Analysing Extract A

From the extract:

- The administration had changed from a household system to a bureaucratic one.
- This 'revolution' in the system of government lasted nearly 400 years.
- Government was bureaucratically organised in national departments.

Assessing the extent to which the arguments are convincing:

- Deploying knowledge to corroborate that the system of government in the sixteenth century differed from that in the fifteenth.

- Deploying knowledge to highlight the limitations of the changes in that the Crown remained the principal feature of government.
- Suggesting that the reform of government was so thorough and that its operation was so efficient that it lasted for a few centuries after its implementation.
- The extract comes from a specialised study of Tudor government, written by an expert to show how the system of government underwent a revolution in the 1530s.
- The extract omits any reference to the politician credited with planning and implementing that revolution – Thomas Cromwell.

Analysing Extract B

From the extract:

- The government had been transformed but not to the extent that the author of Extract A claims.
- The word revolution is rejected in favour of less controversial words such as 'change' or 'readjustment'.
- However, the word 'revolution' may apply if the period of governmental reform is extended beyond the 1530s to include the reign of Elizabeth.

Assessing the extent to which the arguments are convincing:

- Deploying knowledge to agree with the assessment of the nature and extent of change in Tudor government (and agreeing with Extract A).
- Deploying knowledge to highlight the phrase 'too schematic', for example, the changes that did take place did so over a longer period, with more than one person responsible for them.
- The extract comes from a respected British historian, published in 1988 – some 35 years after the original revolution in government thesis was first published.

Comparing the analysis of each extract should give the direction of an overall conclusion and judgement about which of the extracts is more convincing. In this case it may be that Extract B is more convincing because it does try to present a balanced view.

The mark scheme for AS

The mark scheme builds up from Level 1 to Level 5, in the same way as it does for essays:

- Do not waste time simply describing or paraphrasing the content of each source.
- Make sure that when you include your knowledge it is being used to advance the analysis of the extracts – not as knowledge in its own right.

- The top two levels of the mark scheme refer to 'supported conclusion' (Level 4) and 'well-substantiated conclusion' (Level 5).
- For Level 4, 'Supported conclusion' means finishing your answer with a judgement that is backed up with some accurate evidence drawn from the source(s) and your knowledge.
- For Level 5, 'well-substantiated conclusion' means finishing your answer with a judgement that is very well supported with evidence, and, where relevant, reaches a complex conclusion that reflects a wide variety of evidence.

Writing the answer for AS

There is no one correct way! However, the principles are clear. In particular, contextual knowledge should be used *only* to back up an argument. None of your knowledge should be standalone – all your knowledge should be used in context.

For each extract in turn:

- Explain the evidence in the extract, backed up with your own contextual knowledge, for a revolution in government during the reign of Henry VIII.
- Explain the points in the extract where you have evidence that contradicts this view.

Then write a conclusion that reaches a judgement on which is more convincing as an interpretation. You might build in some element of comparison during the answer, or it might be developed in the last paragraph only.

Edexcel A level History

Essay guidance

Edexcel's Paper 1, Option 1B: England, 1509–1603: Authority, Nation and Religion is assessed by an exam comprising three sections:

- Sections A and B require you to write essays that test the breadth of your historical knowledge.
- Section C tests your ability to analyse and evaluate interpretations about the past, and focuses on two extracts from the work of historians. This book does not cover Section C.

Questions in Sections A and B test your knowledge of four themes, covering the period 1509–88:

- monarchy and government
- religious changes
- state control and popular resistance
- economic, social and cultural change.

Paper 1: Sections A and B

The following advice relates to Paper 1, Sections A and B. It is relevant to A level and AS level questions. Generally, the AS exam is similar to the A level exam. Both examine the same content and require similar skills; nonetheless, there are differences, which are discussed below.

The questions in Paper 1, Section A and B, are structured differently in the A level and AS exams.

AS exam	Full A level exam
Section A requires you to answer one question from a choice of two. Each question is worth 20 marks: • The question tests the breadth of your knowledge and therefore will normally focus on a period of at least ten years. • Questions can take a variety of different forms, but will only focus on cause and consequence.	Section A requires you to answer one question from a choice of two. Each question is worth 20 marks: • The question tests the breadth of your knowledge and therefore will normally focus on a period of at least ten years. • Questions can take a variety of different forms, and can focus on cause, consequence, change, continuity, similarity, difference and significance.
Section B is largely similar to Section A, but questions are likely to cover longer periods, usually at least one-third of the period you have studied. Unlike Section A questions, Section B questions can focus on cause, consequence, change, continuity, similarity, difference and significance.	Section B is largely similar to Section A, but questions are likely to cover longer periods, usually at least one-third of the period you have studied.
Questions can start with the following: • Were … Explain your answer. • To what extent … • How significant …	Questions can start with the following: • How far … • How successful … • How significant … • How accurate is it to say … • To what extent …

Essay skills

To get a high grade in Sections A and B of Paper 1 your essays must contain four essential qualities:

- focused analysis
- relevant detail
- supported judgement
- organisation, coherence and clarity.

This section focuses on the following aspects of exam technique:

- Understanding the nature of the question.
- Planning an answer to the question set.
- Writing a focused introduction.
- Deploying relevant detail.
- Writing analytically.
- Reaching a supported judgement.

The nature of the question

Questions in Sections A and B are designed to test the breadth of your historical knowledge. Therefore, they can focus on periods that are usually more than a decade. Questions will not focus on single events or single years, unless the question concerns the causes or consequences which take place over a longer period.

As noted above, questions can focus on a variety of different historical processes or 'concepts'. These different question focuses require slightly different approaches (see table).

Some questions include a 'stated factor'. The most common type of stated factor question would ask how far one factor caused something. For example, for the first question in the table:

> **How far was Henry VIII's desire to ensure a secure succession responsible for religious reforms in the years 1529–40?**

In this type of question you would be expected to evaluate the importance of 'Henry VIII's desire to ensure a secure succession' – the 'stated factor' – compared to other factors.

All questions can focus on these concepts (but you will not find questions on continuity and change, similarities and differences, and significance in Section A of the AS paper)	Cause	**1** How far was Henry VIII's desire to ensure a secure succession responsible for religious reforms in the years 1529–40?
	Consequence	**2** To what extent was discontent with Tudor rule the main consequence of English economic problems in the years 1536–69?
	Continuity and change	**3** How accurate is it to say that there were major changes in English culture in the years 1547–88?
	Similarities and differences	**4** How accurate is it to say that there was a revolution in English religion in the period 1529–63?
	Significance	**5** How significant was the role of Parliament in English government in the years 1529–58?

AS and A level questions

AS level questions are generally similar to A level questions. However, the wording of AS questions will be slightly less complex than the wording of A level questions.

A level question	AS level question	Differences
How accurate is it to say that royal power grew continually in the period 1514–40?	How far did Henry VIII's power grow in the years 1514–40?	The AS level question focuses on Henry VIII's power, whereas the A level question focuses on the more abstract notion of 'royal power.' Additionally, the A level question is more complex as it requires focus on the extent to which power grew 'continually' across the period.
How accurate is it to say that Catholicism remained the dominant religion in England between 1536 and 1562?	To what extent was Catholicism the main religion in England between 1536 and 1562?	Both questions focus on the influence of Catholicism. However, the A level question is harder because the notion of a 'dominant religion' is more complex than the notion of a 'main religion'. Additionally, the A level question is more complex because it also requires students to focus on how far Catholicism remained dominant.

To achieve the highest grade at A level, you will have to deal with the full complexity of the question. For example, if you were dealing with the second question, you would have to deal with the question of the dominance of Catholicism, not merely how far it was the main religion.

Planning your answer

It is crucial that you understand the focus of the question. Therefore, read the question carefully before you start planning. Check:

- The chronological focus: which years should your essay deal with?
- The topic focus: what aspect of your course does the question deal with?
- The conceptual focus: is this a causes, consequences, change/continuity, similarity/difference or significance question?

For example, for question 1 (on page 188) you could point these out as follows:

> How far was Henry VIII's desire to ensure a secure succession[1] responsible for[2] religious reforms[3] in the years 1529–40[4]?

1 Stated factor: Henry VIII's desire to ensure a secure succession.
2 Conceptual focus: causation.
3 Topic focus: religion.
4 Chronological focus: 1529–40.

Your plan should reflect the task that you have been set. Sections A and B ask you to write an analytical, coherent and well-structured essay from your own knowledge, which reaches a supported conclusion in around 40 minutes:

- To ensure that your essay is coherent and well structured, it should comprise a series of paragraphs, each focusing on a different point.
- Your paragraphs should come in a logical order. For example, you could write your paragraphs in order of importance, so you begin with the most important issues and end with the least important.
- In essays where there is a 'stated factor', it is a good idea to start with the stated factor before moving on to the other points.
- To make sure you keep to time, you should aim to write three or four paragraphs plus an introduction and a conclusion.

The opening paragraph should do four main things:

- answer the question directly
- set out your essential argument
- outline the factors or issues that you will discuss
- define key terms used in the question – where necessary.

Different questions require you to define different terms, for example:

A level question	Key terms
1 How accurate is it to say that Catholicism remained the dominant religion in England between 1536 and 1562?	Here it is worth defining 'dominant religion'.
2 How accurate is it to say that there was a revolution in English religion in the period 1529–63?	In this example, it is worth defining 'revolution in English religion'.

Here is an example introduction in answer to question 1 in the table above:

How accurate is it to say that Catholicism remained the dominant religion in England between 1536 and 1562?

While Catholicism retained some influence on the hearts and minds of English people it is hard to argue that it remained the dominant religion in England between 1536 and 1562[1]. Catholicism came under legal attack from Henry VIII, Edward VI and Elizabeth I. However, on its own this does not prove that Catholicism lost its dominant position. Indeed, religious dominance is not simply a matter of which religious faith is approved by the government. A dominant religion must also have a widespread influence over the lives of the people[2]. Nonetheless, by 1562 Catholicism had lost its place as the official religion of England, and therefore, although it still had considerable popular appeal, particularly in the North and the West, Catholicism was no longer legally dominant[3].

1. The essay starts with a clear answer to the question.
2. This sentence sets out some evidence that Catholicism lost its dominant position, and also considers the meaning of 'dominance' in this context.

3. Finally, the introduction considers the sense in which Catholicism was and was not dominant by 1562.

The opening paragraph: advice

- Don't write more than a couple of sentences on general background knowledge. This is unlikely to focus explicitly on the question.
- After defining key terms, refer back to these definitions when justifying your conclusion.
- The introduction should reflect the rest of the essay. Do not make one argument in your introduction, then make a different argument in the essay.

Deploying relevant detail

Paper 1 tests the breadth of your historical knowledge. Therefore, you will need to deploy historical detail. In the main body of your essay your paragraphs should begin with a clear point, be full of relevant detail and end with an explanation or evaluation. A detailed answer might include statistics, proper names, dates and technical terms. For example, if you are writing a paragraph about the extent to which Catholicism remained dominant in the hearts and minds of English people, you might include: regional differences, anti-Protestant rebellions and how far there was popular support for the Catholic restoration under Mary.

Writing analytically

The quality of your analysis is one of the key factors that determines the mark you achieve. Writing analytically means clearly showing the relationships between the ideas in your essay. Analysis includes two key skills: explanation and evaluation.

Explanation

Explanation means giving reasons. An explanatory sentence has three parts:

- a claim: a statement that something is true or false
- a reason: a statement that justifies the claim
- a relationship: a word or phrase that shows the relationship between the claim and the reason.

Imagine you are answering the question:

> How accurate is it to say that Catholicism remained the dominant religion in England between 1536 and 1562?

Your paragraph on popular support for Catholicism should start with a clear point, which would be supported by a series of examples. Finally, you would round off the paragraph with some explanation:

Clearly, the resurgence of support for Catholicism under Mary indicates that, at least until 1553, Catholicism remained popular[1] because[2] of the speed with which Catholic religious practices were re-established across the country[3].

1 Claim.   **2** Relationship.   **3** Reason.

Make sure of the following:

- The reason you give genuinely justifies the claim you have made.
- Your explanation is focused on the question.

Reaching a supported judgement

Finally, your essay should reach a supported judgement. The obvious place to do this is in the conclusion of your essay. Even so, the judgement should reflect the findings of your essay. The conclusion should present:

- a clear judgement that answers the question
- an evaluation of the evidence that supports the judgement
- finally, the evaluation should reflect valid criteria.

Evaluation and criteria

Evaluation means weighing up to reach a judgement. Therefore, evaluation requires you to:

- summarise both sides of the issue
- reach a conclusion that reflects the proper weight of both sides.

So, for question 2 in the table on page 190:

> How accurate is it to say that Catholicism remained the dominant religion in England between 1536 and 1562?

The conclusion might look like this:

In conclusion, the extent of religious change in the period 1536–62 makes it difficult to argue that Catholicism remained dominant[1]. Certainly, Catholicism was England's official religion for the first part of Henry's rule and under Mary. However, dominance is a broad concept, and therefore Catholicism's official status during this period does not necessarily mean that it was the dominant religion. The apparent popularity of Catholicism during Mary's relatively short reign, the Prayer Book Rebellions and the reluctance of Elizabeth's first Parliament to reinstate the Royal Supremacy and Second Prayer Book all indicate that Catholicism still had a widespread appeal even after the introduction of Protestant policies under Edward VI[2]. Nonetheless, with the exception of Mary's rule, Catholicism came under sustained attack from successive governments. Indeed, by the end of the period Elizabeth had once again passed laws guaranteeing royal supremacy, as well as the Act of Uniformity[3]. Therefore, while it is true that Catholicism's influence over the hearts and minds of English people never died, constant legal attacks on the religion meant that by 1562 it was no longer England's dominant religion[4].

1 The conclusion starts with a clear judgement that answers the question.
2 This section considers evidence that Catholicism remained an important part of English life during the period. Indeed, it links it to a discussion of the meaning of the term 'dominant'.
3 This section considers the counter-argument.
4 The essay ends with a final judgement that is supported by the evidence of the essay, which clearly considers the ongoing dominance of Catholicism in England.

The judgement is supported in part by evaluating the evidence, and in part by linking it to valid criteria. In this case, the criterion is the definition of modernisation set out in the introduction. Significantly, this criterion is specific to this essay, and different essays will require you to think of different criteria to help you make your judgement.

OCR A level History

Essay guidance

The assessment of **U**nit Y106: England 1485–1558: The Early Tudors depends on whether you are studying it for AS or A level:

- for the AS exam, you will answer one essay and one two-part source question
- for the A level exam, you will answer one essay question and one source question.

The guidance below is for answering both AS and A level essay questions.

For both OCR AS and A level History, the types of essay questions set and the skills required to achieve a high grade for Unit Group 1 are the same. The skills are made very clear by both mark schemes, which emphasise that the answer must:

- focus on the demands of the question
- be supported by accurate and relevant factual knowledge
- be analytical and logical
- reach a supported judgement about the issue in the question.

There are a number of skills that you will need to develop to reach the higher levels in the marking bands:

- understand the wording of the question
- plan an answer to the question set
- write a focused opening paragraph
- avoid irrelevance and description
- write analytically
- write a conclusion which reaches a supported judgement based on the argument in the main body of the essay.

These skills will be developed in the section below, but are further developed in the 'Period Study' chapters of the *OCR A level History* series (British Period Studies and Enquiries).

Understanding the wording of the question

To stay focused on the question set, it is important to read the question carefully and focus on the key words and phrases. Unless you directly address the demands of the question you will not score highly. Remember that in questions where there is a named factor you must write a good analytical paragraph about the given factor, even if you argue that it was not the most important.

Types of AS and A level questions you might find in the exams	The factors and issues you would need to consider in answering them
1 Assess the reasons why Cardinal Wolsey fell from power.	Weigh up the relative importance of a range of factors as to why Cardinal Wolsey fell from power.
2 To what extent was Wolsey's failure to secure the annulment the most important cause of his downfall?	Weigh up the relative importance of a range of factors, including comparing the importance of Wolsey's failure to secure the annulment with other factors.
3 'The influence of Anne Boleyn was the most important reason for the fall of Wolsey from power.' How far do you agree?	Weigh up the relative importance of a range of factors, including comparing the importance of Anne Boleyn's influence with other issues to reach a balanced judgement.

Planning an answer

Many plans simply list dates and events – this should be avoided as it encourages a descriptive or narrative answer, rather than an analytical answer. The plan should be an outline of your argument; this means you need to think carefully about the issues you intend to discuss and their relative importance before you start writing your answer. It should therefore be a list of the factors or issues you are going to discuss and a comment on their relative importance.

For question 1 in the table, your plan might look something like this:

- The significance of the annulment – Wolsey's promise to secure it.
- Diplomatic campaign – link to Charles V and the impact of the sacking of Rome.
- Leadership failure – Wolsey's overconfidence.
- Opposition – political machinations of the Boleyn and Aragonese factions.
- Diminishing confidence in and support for Wolsey by the king.
- Papal failure to assist or support Wolsey's campaign to secure the annulment.
- Hatred of Wolsey by the aristocratic political elite at court.

The opening paragraph

Many students spend time 'setting the scene'; the opening paragraph becomes little more than an introduction to the topic – this should be avoided. Instead, make it clear what your argument is going to be. Offer your view about the issue in the question – what was the most important reason for the fall of Cardinal Wolsey – and then introduce the other issues you intend to discuss. In the plan it is suggested that Wolsey's failure to secure the annulment was the most important factor. This should be made clear in the opening paragraph, with a brief comment as to why – perhaps that the failure to secure the annulment enabled Wolsey's opponents at court to undermine his authority and discredit him in the eyes of the king. This will give the examiner a clear overview of your essay, rather than it being a 'mystery tour' where the argument becomes clear only at the end. You should also refer to any important issues that the question raises. For example:

There are a number of reasons why Cardinal Wolsey fell from power, including the complex diplomatic situation, leadership failure, strength

of the opposition, and Henry VIII's growing dissatisfaction with Wolsey because of the king's infatuation with Anne Boleyn and desire to marry her**[1]**. However, the most important reason was Wolsey's failure to secure the annulment, both in terms of the promises he made to the king and the Pope's reluctance to support the process**[2]**. This was particularly important once it became clear that Wolsey could not secure the annulment as quickly as he had promised**[3]**.

1 The student is aware that there were a number of important reasons.
2 The answer offers a clear view as to what the student considers to be the most important reason – a thesis is offered.
3 There is a brief justification to support the thesis.

Avoid irrelevance and description

Hopefully, the plan will stop you from simply writing all you know about why Cardinal Wolsey fell from power and force you to weigh up the role of a range of factors. Similarly, it should also help prevent you from simply writing about the events connected with Wolsey's fall from power. You will not lose marks if you do that, but neither will you gain any credit, and you will waste valuable time.

Write analytically

This is perhaps the hardest, but most important skill you need to develop. An analytical approach can be helped by ensuring that the opening sentence of each paragraph introduces an idea, which directly answers the question and is not just a piece of factual information. In a very strong answer it should be possible to simply read the opening sentences of all the paragraphs and know what argument is being put forward.

If we look at the second question, on the importance of Wolsey's failure to secure the annulment of Henry's marriage to Catherine of Aragon (see page 192), the following are possible sentences with which to start paragraphs:

- Failure to secure the annulment became an important factor once it became clear that Wolsey could not deliver on his promise to do so quickly, and this undermined his authority.

- The strength of the opposition, particularly that by the Boleyn faction, ensured that in a long drawn-out campaign to secure the annulment, Wolsey's position at court would get weaker.
- Henry VIII's diminishing confidence in and support for Wolsey was important because the king alone could guarantee the safety and survival of his chief minister.
- Anne Boleyn and Catherine of Aragon may have been enemies but their shared antipathy towards Wolsey (latterly in the case of Boleyn) added to the pressure on the king to remove him from power.

You would then go on to discuss both sides of the argument raised by the opening sentence, using relevant knowledge about the issue to support each side of the argument. The final sentence of the paragraph would reach a judgement on the role played by the factor you are discussing in the downfall of Wolsey. This approach would ensure that the final sentence of each paragraph links back to the actual question you are answering. If you can do this for each paragraph you will have a series of mini-essays, which discuss a factor and reach a conclusion or judgement about the importance of that factor or issue. For example:

Henry VIII's diminishing confidence in Wolsey was an important factor in causing the latter's downfall, but this was only in the latter stages of the annulment process when it became clear that the chief minister's promise to bring a swift end to the marriage was unlikely to happen[1]. It was only with the growing influence of Anne Boleyn over the king that Wolsey's position began to crumble. Initially she had supported Wolsey because they shared a mutual interest in securing the annulment, but this changed once it became clear he could not deliver. Boleyn then turned on Wolsey. Similarly, the diplomatic pressure Catherine of Aragon was able to bring to bear

on the king added to Wolsey's problems. He was fighting a war on more than one front[2].

1 The sentence puts forward a clear view that Henry VIII's faltering support for Wolsey only became important in the later stages of the campaign to secure the annulment.
2 The claim that it was the growing influence of Anne Boleyn that contributed to Wolsey's downfall is developed and some evidence is provided to support the argument.

The conclusion

The conclusion provides the opportunity to bring together all the interim judgements to reach an overall judgement about the question. Using the interim judgements will ensure that your conclusion is based on the argument in the main body of the essay and does not offer a different view. For the essay answering question 1 (see page 192), you can decide what was the most important factor in Wolsey's downfall, but for questions 2 and 3 you will need to comment on the importance of the named factor – the failure to secure the annulment or the influence of Anne Boleyn – as well as explain why you think a different factor is more important, if that has been your line of argument. Or, if you think the named factor is the most important, you would need to explain why that was more important than the other factors or issues you have discussed.

Consider the following conclusion to question 2 (see page 192): To what extent was Wolsey's failure to secure the annulment the most important cause of his downfall?

Although Wolsey had failed to deliver on his promise to the king that he would secure the annulment it was not the most important factor in his downfall[1]. After all, in the early stages of the annulment process success seemed assured. Wolsey had been the king's chief minister for over a decade, during which time he had given the Crown excellent service. It was therefore Wolsey's ability to maintain the king's trust and support that was crucial; as long as that held, and Anne Boleyn's influence was important in that respect, the ever shifting political and diplomatic events of time might have changed in Wolsey's favour**[2]**.

1 This is a strong conclusion because it considers the importance of the named factor – failure to secure the annulment – but weighs that up against a range of other factors to reach an overall judgement.
2 The answer is also able to show links between the other factors to reach a balanced judgement, which brings in a range of issues, showing the interplay between them.

Glossary of terms

Almoner   A priest in charge of distributing assistance or alms to the poor on behalf of the king.

Annates   Money equivalent to about one-third of the annual income paid to the Pope by all new holders of senior posts within the Church in England and Wales.

Attainted   Accused and declared guilty of treason by a vote in Parliament.

Bondmen   Medieval peasants who lived and worked on the lord's manor.

Book of Homilies   A book of sermons written by Cranmer for use in church services.

Book of Rates   An account book recording the rates of tax paid by foreign merchants on goods imported and sold in England.

Calvinist   Follower of the radical religious reformer John Calvin of Geneva who attacked Catholicism and promoted the Protestant faith.

Cardinal protector   A cardinal appointed to speak for and defend the rights of the Church in a particular country at the papal Curia in Rome.

Catholic Inquisition   Institution set up in 1478 by the Catholic Church to search for and destroy heretics or non-conformists. There were a number of different inquisitions and the operation was often in the hands of the secular authorities assisting the Church.

Chantries   Religious foundations or chapels (often located in churches or cathedrals), sometimes with land attached, established by wealthy patrons and endowed with money to employ a priest to sing masses for the souls of the dead.

Commonwealth   A term derived from 'commonweal', meaning the wealth, health and good of the community.

Comperta Monastica   'Monastic discovery'. A book compiled by Cromwell's agents which contained lists of transgressions and abuses admitted by monks and nuns.

Confession   Where parishioners confess their sins to a priest in order to receive absolution.

Consubstantiation   The belief that the wine and bread taken at communion were symbolic and merely represented the blood and body of Christ.

Convocation   Church equivalent of Parliament where clerics meet in two houses – upper house of senior clerics and lower house representing parish priests – to discuss and transact Church affairs.

Coup d'état   French term to describe a sudden and illegal seizure of a government.

Court of Chancery   Dealt with disputes over inheritance and wills, lands, trusts, debts, marriage settlements and apprenticeships.

Court of Requests   Known as the 'poor man's court', it was intended to provide easy access for poor men and women to royal justice. Types of cases heard included title to property, forgery, perjury, forfeitures to the king and marriage contracts.

Court of Star Chamber   Dealt with crimes such as disorder, riot, assault, fraud, corruption, municipal and trade disputes, and disputes over the enclosure of land.

Cure of souls   An ancient practice of nourishing and defending the souls of parishioners by sermons, rituals and confession.

Dei gratia   By the will of God.

Dowry   Money or property paid by the bride's father to the groom's family on his daughter's marriage.

Eltham Ordinances   A set of instructions drawn up to reform the king's court and Privy Chamber, including its financial system.

Embargo   The prohibition of commerce and trade with a particular country.

English Litany   A selection of prayers in English designed for use in a designated church service in which the parishioners respond to lines spoken by the priest leading the service.

Escheat   When a landholder died without heirs, his lands passed by right to the king.

Eucharist   Also known as holy communion, this is a Catholic sacrament in which the bread and wine are taken in the belief that the body and blood of Christ are contained within.

Expeditionary force   An army sent to fight in another country.

Feudal   The medieval social and political system.

Great Chain of Being   Belief in the divine order of things extending from God down through the angels, humans, animals, vegetables and minerals. It was used by the Church to justify the hierarchy of life from the king down through the nobility, gentry and peasantry.

Humanists   Scholars who question the belief systems of the Church and who embrace free thinking, culture and education.

Hundred   An administrative subdivision in a county.

Indicted   Legal term used to describe those charged with a crime.

Intercursus Magnus   Used to describe the protection of commercial contacts between England and the Netherlands in an agreement of 1496.

Justices of the peace (JPs)   Chief magistrates in quarter sessions and responsible for general administration in a county.

King's Prymer   A devotional collection of prayers, psalms and religious lessons approved for use in church by the king.

League of Venice   Diplomatic and military organisation formed by the Italian states to resist the French conquest of Italy.

Legatine powers   The authority to represent and act on behalf of the Pope in England.

***Legatus a latere* or papal legate**   A position normally awarded for a specific purpose so that a representative with full papal powers could be present at a decision-making occasion far distant from Rome.

Machiavellian   Cleverly deceitful and unscrupulous. Named after an Italian political writer and thinker, Niccolo Machiavelli (1469–1527) of Florence.

Magnate   A powerful nobleman.

Nepotism   The promotion or employment of family members and friends to important offices.

Non-residence   When priests did not live in their parish.

Order of the Garter   Founded in 1348, this honour was bestowed on the most important knights who then attained the senior rank of knighthood.

Papal dispensation   When the Pope exempted a person from a certain punitive clause in law.

Paraphrases   A literary work by Erasmus that retells all or part of the Bible in a manner that can be more easily understood by worshippers.

Patronage   The award and distribution of royal favours.

Petty constable   Assistant law enforcement officer serving under the high constable.

Plague   A deadly infectious disease that is spread by the fleas carried by rats.

Pluralism   When priests served more than one parish.

Praemunire   A legal provision, arising from three fourteenth-century laws, which forbade clerics to take any action that cut across the powers of the Crown – especially recognising any external authority without the monarch's explicit permission.

Proclamations   Official or public announcements issued by the Crown that included the right to make laws.

Quartermaster-general   The person responsible for feeding, arming and generally supplying the army.

Regent   A member of the royal family who governs on behalf of the reigning monarch.

Renaissance   An intellectual and cultural movement dedicated to the rediscovery and promotion of art, architecture and letters. It promoted education and critical thinking and ranged across subjects such as politics, government, religion and classical literature. Its spread was encouraged by humanist scholars such as Erasmus.

Retaining   Employing and maintaining servants.

Royal prerogative   Certain rights and privileges enjoyed by the monarch such as making war, negotiating peace treaties and calling and closing Parliament.

Sanctuary   A place of safety within a church or monastery guaranteed by the authority of the Church.

Schism   Literally meaning 'break', but used by historians to describe England's break with the Pope in Rome.

Sheriff   Chief law enforcement officer in a county.

Simony   The selling of Church appointments and offices.

Subsidy   A grant of money made by Parliament to the king, usually for a specific purpose.

Sweating sickness   A mysterious and highly virulent disease that struck England in a series of epidemics between 1485 and 1551.

Synod   A council of senior members of the Church convened to decide on issues of doctrine.

Transubstantiation   The belief that the wine and bread taken at communion were actually the blood and body of Christ when they were blessed.

Treason   The act of betraying one's monarch and country.

Treasurer of the Chamber   Chief financial official responsible for the king's money.

Valois–Habsburg   Names of the French (Valois) and Austrian (Habsburg) royal families.

Vicegerent   King's deputy in Church affairs.

Zwinglian   Followers of Huldrych Zwingli, a radical religious reformer from Switzerland. He was a Protestant who believed in religious autonomy for local communities.

Further reading

General texts

A.G. Dickens, *The English Reformation* (Batsford, 1989)
A ground-breaking work on the causes and course of the Reformation

S. Ellsmore, D. Rogerson and D. Hudson, *The Early Tudors: England 1484–1558* (John Murray, 2001)
Accessible text designed for sixth formers covering the key issues with clarity

G.R. Elton, *England Under the Tudors* (Routledge, 1991)
General but thorough coverage of the main aspects of the Tudor period

N. Fellows, *Disorder and Rebellion in Tudor England* (Hodder & Stoughton, 2002)
A brief but very informative and up-to-date analysis

A. Goodman, *The New Monarchy: England 1471–1534* (Blackwell, 1989)
A survey and discussion of the New Monarchy theory

J. Guy, *Tudor England* (Oxford University Press, 1988)
Accessible and useful general analysis of the history of Tudor England

C. Haig, *English Reformation: Religion, Politics and Society Under the Tudors* (Oxford University Press, 1993)
An in-depth analysis of the nature, scale and impact of the Reformation

J. Loach, *Parliament Under the Tudors* (Oxford University Press, 1991)
Excellent study of the role and development of Parliament in Tudor government

D.M. Loades, *The Mid-Tudor Crisis, 1545–65* (Macmillan, 1992)
A focused account of the so-called mid-Tudor crisis

W.J. Sheils, *The English Reformation 1530–1570* (Routledge, 1989)
Excellent synopsis with documents on the cause, course and impact of the Reformation

A.G.R. Smith, *The Emergence of a Nation State 1529–1660* (Longman, 1984)
Thorough survey of power politics in Tudor England with a useful survey of the development of government

D. Starkey, *The Reign of Henry VIII: Personalities & Politics* (Vintage, 2002)
Thorough survey of the key characters, together with their role and influence in government and court

J.A.F. Thompson, *The Transformation of Medieval England 1370–1529* (Routledge, 1983)
Excellent survey of political developments up to and including Henry VII and the first part of the reign of Henry VIII

Chapter 1

S.B. Chrimes, *Henry VII* (Yale University Press, 1999)
Excellent biography of Henry Tudor and history of his reign

S. Cunningham, *Henry VII* (Routledge, 2007)
Accessible discussion of Henry's claim to and retention of the throne

R. Lockyer and A. Thrush, *Henry VII* (Longman, 1997)
Accessible account with selected sources on key aspects of the reign

Chapter 2

I. Arturson, *Documents of the Reign of Henry VII* (Cambridge University Local Examination Syndicate, 1984)
A wide and useful range of sources to help guide readers through the key aspects of Henry's reign

J. Hunt and C. Towle, *Henry VII* (Longman, 1998)
Short but very useful general survey of Henry's reign

C. Pendrill, *The Wars of the Roses and Henry VII: England 1459–c.1513* (Heinemann, 2004)
Wide coverage including the period before and immediately after Henry's reign

Chapter 3

P. Gwyn, *The King's Cardinal: The Rise and Fall of Thomas Wolsey* (Barrie & Jenkins, 1990)
Large and comprehensive biography of Wolsey with some useful comments on politics and government in general

D. MacCulloch, editor, *The Reign of Henry VIII: Politics, Policy and Party* (Macmillan, 1995)
A set of informed essays dealing with politics and government in Henry VIII's reign

J.J. Scarisbrick, *The Reformation and the English People* (Blackwell, 1984)
Analysis of the reaction to and impact on the people of England of religious change

Chapter 4

G.R. Elton, *The Tudor Revolution in Government* (Methuen, 1953)
A thought-provoking and controversial work on the nature and scale of the changes in Tudor government

G.R. Elton, *Thomas Cromwell* (Headstart History, 1990)
Short but incisive discussion of Cromwell bringing all of Elton's research up to date

R. Rosemary O'Day, *The Debate on the English Reformation* (Methuen, 1986)
Excellent debate on key aspects of the Reformation

J.J. Scarisbrick, *Henry VIII* (Methuen, 1968)
Full coverage of Henry's life and career together with an analysis of the king's impact on religion and politics

J. Youings, *The Dissolution of the Monasteries* (Allen & Unwin, 1972)
Solid revision of the causes, course and impact of the dissolution

Chapter 5

C. Davies, *A Religion of the Word: The Defence of the Reformation in the Reign of Edward VI* (Manchester University Press, 2002)
Focused study of the nature and impact of religious change during the reign of Edward VI

J. Loach, *Edward VI* (Yale University Press, 1999)
Full coverage of Edward's life together with an analysis of his influence on political and religious affairs

D. Loades, *John Dudley, Duke of Northumberland 1504–1553* (Clarendon, 1996)
In-depth analysis of Northumberland's role and impact as governor of England under Edward VI

D. MacCulloch, *Thomas Cranmer* (Yale University Press, 1996)
Large-scale biography of a man credited with establishing the Protestant faith

Chapter 6

E. Duffy and D.M. Loades, editors, *The Church of Mary Tudor* (Ashgate, 2006)
A set of informed essays dealing with religious change but with useful references to wider issues in politics and government in Mary's reign

T.S. Freeman and Susan Doran, editors, *Mary Tudor: Old and New Perspectives* (Palgrave Macmillan, 2011)
A set of informed revisionist essays with useful references to issues in politics, religion and government in Mary's reign.

R. Tittler, *Mary I* (Routledge, 2013)
Short but very useful biography of Mary with valuable selection of source material

Index

Acknowledgements: Cambridge University Press, *The Early History of English Poor Relief* by E.M. Leonard, 2013; *The English Reformation Revised* by C. Haigh, 1987; *The Tudor Revolution in Government* by G.R. Elton, 1953. Camden Society, *Chronicle of the Grey Friars of London*, by J.G. Nichols, editor, 1852. Collins, *Wolsey* by A.F. Pollard, 1965. Eyre Methuen, *Henry VIII* by J.J. Scarisbrick, 1968. Harvard University Press, *Reform and Reformation: England 1509–1558* by G.R. Elton, 1977. Headstart History Publishing, *The Reformation in Wales* by Glanmor Williams, 1991. Her Majesty's Stationery Office, *Acts of the Privy Council of England*, J.R. Dasent, editor, 1890; *Calendar of State Papers Relating To English Affairs in the Archives of Venice, Volume 2, 1509–1519*, 1867; *Calendar of State Papers, Foreign*, 1861; *Calendar of State Papers, Spain, Volume 1, 1485–1509*, 1862; *Letters and Papers, Foreign and Domestic, Henry VIII, Volume 18, Part 1, January–July 1543*, 1901. Longman, Green & Co., *History of England from the Fall of Wolsey to the Defeat of the Spanish Armada* by J.A. Froude, 1893. Methuen, *England Under the Tudors* by G.R. Elton, 1974. Oxford University Press, *Revolution Reassessed: Revisions in the History of Tudor Government and Administration* by C. Coleman and David Starkey, editors, 1986; *The Later Tudors: England 1547–1603* by P. Williams, 1995; *Tudor England* by John Guy, 1988. Pimlico, *The King's Cardinal: The Rise and Fall of Thomas Wolsey* by P. Gwyn, 1990. Routledge, *The English Reformation 1530–1570* by W.J. Sheils, 1989; *The Transformation of Medieval England 1370–1529* by J.A.F. Thompson, 1983. St. Martin's Press, *Bloody Mary* by C. Erickson, 1978. Williams & Norgate, *The History of England: A Study in Political Evolution* by A.F. Pollard, 1912.